Industry Recipes

Industry Recipes

An Enquiry into the Nature and Sources of Managerial Judgement

J.-C. Spender

Basil Blackwell

Copyright © J.-C. Spender 1989

First published 1989

Basil Blackwell Ltd
108 Cowley Road, Oxford, OX4 1JF, UK

Basil Blackwell, Inc.
3 Cambridge Center
Cambridge, Massachusetts 02142, USA

British Library Cataloguing in Publication Data

A CIP catalogue record for this book is available from the British Library.

Library of Congress Cataloging in Publication Data

Spender, J.-C.
    Industry recipes: an enquiry into the nature and sources of
managerial judgement / J.-C. Spender.
        p.   cm.
    Revision of thesis (Ph. D.)—Manchester Business School, 1980.
    Bibliography: p.
    Includes index.
    ISBN 0–631–16993–8
    1. Creative ability in business. 2. Entrepreneurship.
3. Uncertainty. I. Title
HD53.S72 1989
658.4'09—dc19   89–31377
                                                                    CIP

Typeset in 10½ on 12 pt Baskerville
by Photo·graphics, Honiton, Devon
Printed in Great Britain by
Billing & Sons Ltd, Worcester

Contents

1

Introduction

This monograph is an extensive revision of my Ph.D. thesis, submitted at the Manchester Business School in 1980. The original work, and its reworking for publication here, consists of reflections on a set of personal and intellectual experiences which cannot be separated from those who shared them. Hence this chapter is both a preface, relating some of the history of this work, and an introduction to its principal themes. Since the thesis's completion, I have had many opportunities to learn from others and many second thoughts about the material. I have also had some new ideas about strategic management. Rather than rewrite and enlarge, I have tried to sift the original's main and more interesting points and present them more clearly.

Inevitably, working with these ideas for several years has produced a change in emphasis. Hindsight enables me to see more clearly what I was trying to achieve. Implicit in the thesis, but more explicit in this book, are five principal themes:

1 A critical analysis of classical management theory focused on its inability to deal with uncertainty and, in consequence, with managerial creativity.
2 A methodology for investigating how managers deal with uncertainty; by implication a method of measuring the entrepreneur's creative contribution.
3 A redefinition of the organization as a body of limited and contextually specific knowledge.
4 A redefinition of management as the task of creating and manipulating this knowledge-base.
5 The notion that competitive advantage generally lies in this

knowledge-base rather than in a tangible resource, no matter how idiosyncratic.

It seems obvious that organizations persist only because, somewhere within them, there are people who know what needs to be done. Until recently it has been common to focus on what needs to be known about, and to leave the processes of knowing unexamined. Thus we stress, for example, the need to keep accounts and do market surveys because these have to do with what effective managements 'know about'. We have assumed that once these facts have been gathered, we can make the necessary decisions. Ever since Simon's well-known critique of 'rational economic man' (1957), much greater attention has been focused on the processes of managerial and organizational thinking. This book follows this more recent tradition. Thus, I suggest a theory more comprehensive than Simon's. At the concept of 'bounded rationality' is replaced with a more detailed system. Secondly, I propose an empirically researchable model.

It is useful, at this preliminary stage of the argument, to distinguish between a manager's knowledge and his skills. Management education tends to focus on knowledge – what managers should know about. We see the conventional MBA syllabus covering finance, production, marketing, human relations and so forth. These are the kinds of knowledge with which we judge competent managers must be familiar. If the proficient manager does not know the answers himself at least he knows how to get answers and how to judge their correctness. Management educators are also concerned with helping students acquire managerial skills. Foremost among these are skills with people. Role playing, small group laboratories, team projects and a multitude of other techniques are used to help students to an awareness of the difficulties facing those who interact with and directly manage others. But this book is about another kind of skill, that of dealing with the normally uncertain state of a manager's knowledge. As Simon points out, it is extremely unlikely that organizational decisions are ever taken with full information. However, the manager's awareness of uncertainty in no way diminishes his or her responsibility to decide and act. On the contrary, this defines his or her special purview. It may be argued that managers are involved in a two-step process; rational decision, yes, but prior to decision, a process of dealing with uncertainty through the application of their judgement. There is something here of William James's distinction between a rather academic 'knowledge about' and a more pragmatic 'knowledge of acquaintance', where the second implies knowing how to apply knowledge in the real context of human activity.

Scientists, pilots, engineers, surgeons and all such others who bring their considerable and sophisticated professional knowledge into contact with the world know from their experience that knowledge alone is not enough. The situations they confront are seldom as neat or as readily understood as their textbooks imply. They must learn to temper their perfectly appropriate faith in knowledge with skill in its application, learning how and when to compromise and manipulate their theories to fit their experience of the situation. Likewise we can help students see that finance theory needs to be balanced by skills in dealing with the uncertainties of market behaviour, that production systems theory needs skills in judging the uncertainties of the results of product development, that market research must be tempered by a 'nose' for customers' changing tastes, and so forth.

In this book I argue that these skills become progressively more important as we approach the governance of the firm as a whole. Senior managers obviously require knowledge. They must have skills with people, bureaucracies, markets, products, technology, money and all the other components of the managerial condition. They must also have the emotional and psychological capacity to be effective leaders. I explore the idea that they need, in addition to the daunting list above, some special cognitive skills which, following Locke, I call judgement.

The thesis was written as a critical response to my experience of teaching Business Policy and Strategy. I had come to the Manchester Business School as a 'mature student' with experience as an engineer, salesman, manager, banker and entrepreneur. My teaching in the UK began long before I completed my thesis, and was augmented by a semester at Kent State University in Ohio, in the company of Professor Child of Aston University. John Child and I both began our working lives at Rolls-Royce, only to become fascinated by organizations and their management. Our time together at Kent State was germane to my intellectual development. Together we visited other US business schools and shared many hours of discussion about management theory and teaching.

As my teaching experience grew, I became convinced that our theories were not taking management's creative contribution into adequate account, especially when it came to the obviously poorly defined area of corporate strategy. Indeed, our theories seemed to push managers out of the analysis and so completely contradict my experience. I still thought management's inputs were crucial. I began to look for a new approach to entrepreneurship, by which I meant more than the simple psychological disposition or get-up-and-go which causes individuals to make risky decisions or set up in business. I wanted to investigate the successful entrepreneur's intellectual talents for spotting a business opportunity and knowing how to exploit it. My experience was of entrepreneurs who were successful, seemingly because they had created a sense of certainty about what they were doing. I wanted to tell students about business the way I had experienced it myself, as an activity that many people engaged in but few really mastered, an art form through which a small number of creative people shape many others' lives. Missing this aspect of management's activity, I believed, we were bound to produce sterile theory and alienate ourselves from our most important audiences, practising and aspiring managers.

The literature on entrepreneurship and leadership seemed to offer little insight so I turned to organization and information theory. Eventually I began to argue that the idea of management means nothing without its corresponding theory of the organization. Every concept of organization defines the activities of the managers within. The firm and its management are complementary images. In due course I saw that the technical problem of defining managerial creativity is to develop a testable theory of the business that has a place for this kind of entrepreneurial input.

Our concept of theory derives largely from the physical sciences. This is what gives theory its empirical nature, shifting the emphasis from the abstraction of what is said to the tangible experience that is predicted. A theory is strong when it successfully predicts future observations. Much recent theorizing about governing a business focuses on predicting the results of management's choices of strategy and structure. Structure, the corporation's internal resource dispositions and controls, and strategy, the corporation's chosen external market relationships, become the principal causes whose effects need to be forecast. The manager's place in this kind of theory is to analyse the firm's resources and environment, discover the structural and strategic options available and choose appropriately. This is widely known as a SWOT analysis (Strengths, Weaknesses, Opportunities, Threats). The manager is treated as a decision-making 'black box' automaton rather than as the lively entrepreneurial creator of the business. Indeed, the better the theory of how strategy and structure should be matched, the more firmly it proscribes management's choices. The manager is no longer part of the decision; he is simply the theory's instrument. His only options are to follow the theory's dictates or to make an error.

Others have protested this picture of the manager 'grinding out the custom-fitted organisation' (Lawrence & Lorsch 1969). My protest is similar to that of the astronauts in Tom Wolfe's *Right Stuff*. I believe real businesses need constant creative input just as Wolfe's astronauts argued that space-research vehicles need human pilots/ scientists rather than electronic or dumb cargoes. Paradoxically, a business actually operates in an even more uncertain environment than a spacecraft, so the need for human pilots/CEOs (Chief Executive Officers) is in fact far greater.

There is a sense in which all theory is prescriptive, for it predicts. Unpredictive and unprescriptive theory is probably non-theory. If we have difficulty it is likely that it is because we theorize about the wrong things. Thus I believe the prescriptive kind of thinking noted and criticized above is not a fault of theory, but an unintended result of the way we interpret classical management theory. Defining managers as rational decision-makers is a misinterpretation which leads, inter alia, to a lack of respect for managers as well as to a misunderstanding of their real contribution to the firm. As a corollary, there is also the ever vital issue of managerial responsibility. Managers make enabling and disabling choices about other people's lives for which they must be held responsible. If managers seem to make no personal or creative input, they can defend their actions, however objectionable or damaging, by pointing to 'objective facts' and bureaucratic rules.

Theorists, writers, researchers and teachers of management know perfectly well that managers make an impact. The problem is to find an appropriate way of capturing that impact and relating it to the 'straw man' of the black box model. Rather than attempt to develop a completely new theory, we can grow new theoretical variants in the crevices created when we effectively critique old theory. The black box 'rational' model is the target of much criticism. In fact these criticisms have inspired most of the important developments in managerial theorizing since the classicists laid our discipline's foundations at the turn of the century. Thus one now obvious weakness with classical thinking is the unreality of the assumption that the necessary data is, in fact, available. Managers find that the data has not been collected, is stored in an inaccessible place, is temporarily unavailable or is simply incorrect. Murphy's Law is at work, corrupting management's database.

Trite as this kind of informational defect is, it provides the clue to an alternative line of thought. If our theory acknowledges information defects, and deals with them explicitly, it creates a new theory with a different place for the entrepreneur. Instead of being the person disposed to irrationality or to taking decisions which can be rationally shown to be risky, the entrepreneur is redefined as the person having a particular talent for making good decisions in the absence of the necessary data.

These are dangerous intellectual waters, so I was fortunate that the doctoral programme at Manchester had a strong methodological coursework component. This went far beyond statistics to cover sociology, psychology, field research methods and, most important to me, philosophy. As my interest grew, I began to see how epistemology, by providing ways of analysing the structure of knowledge, could be harnessed to analysing the task of overcoming defects in the managers' data.

The first step of my research was into information defects and into grasping how these relate to uncertainties. Then the processes by which managers overcome these uncertainties were categorized. I began to argue for a cognitive model of entrepreneurship whose essence is uncertainty resolution. This definition of managerial creativity became the core of the thesis. It has an honourable history in the older managerial literature. But it does not sit too well with modern writing on entrepreneurship because it forces a distinction between 'real' entrepreneurs who create a business concept and then, maybe, a successful business, and those 'second-raters' who merely copy and start a business by implementing someone else's business concept.

This problem can be turned into an opportunity. Clearly we cannot hope to develop a predictive theory by 'explaining' creativity as a response to uncertainty. But the notion of the entrepreneur copying and thereby sharing the burden of having to overcome data defects leads to a testable hypothesis. Having worked in several different industries before I began my research work, I already suspected that managers often deal with the problems that uncertainty creates in ways that are characteristic of that industry – part of what experienced managers take uncritically as professional common sense. I now focused on this body of knowledge – what everyone who knows this industry understands – and gave it the name 'industry recipe'. This has not suited everybody. No better alternative has yet appeared, though 'frame', 'paradigm', 'organizational culture' and 'business idea' have been variously used by others since. I wanted a term that was loose and ambiguous, open to some re-interpretation, able to adapt itself to the specifics of situations much as a creative chef adapts to missing ingredients. Later I discovered others, principally the interpretive sociologist Alfred Schutz, had used the term in similar ways.

Part of the problem is of analytic level. I needed a clear distinction between the firm and its industry. The industry recipe is not the knowledge that is both necessary and sufficient for the firm. For the manager responsible for thinking out what to do about the firm's problems, the industry recipe deals with uncertainties of many types in addition to suggesting appropriate corporate structures and strategies. My hypothesis was that managers drew on this body of knowledge to cope with defective data about their company's situation. But this gave them only part of the answer. There were still sufficient specifics to make their personal contribution important. In the sense of my previous definition of entrepreneurship, I imply managers are often being unenterprising in copying others' solutions rather than creating new answers for themselves. Inasmuch as the recipe is like a comprehensive theory, those managers adopting it would seem to approach the decision-making automata I criticize above. In fact, I hypothesized that this would be found to be an over-simplification which I could only explore once I had identified a recipe. I hoped that I could elicit several recipes, and that I would see that they were significantly different from theories. Ultimately, as will be seen, recipes are merely suggestive about the consequences of following them, though they also imply cautions against ignoring them. But they say nothing about the consequences of following different lines of action. They are more like road maps which show only the correct route; once off that route they offer the traveller no guidance. In this respect theory is much more powerful and comprehensive.

Despite Popper's protests to the contrary, a well formed theory is logically complete, with this very completeness rendering entrepreneurial input or 'subjective' interpretation unnecessary. A recipe, by contrast, is open, incomplete, ambiguous and in need of interpretation before it can be used as a guide to the firm's action even within its own rationality. It is much more like a local culture. Indeed the industry recipe is the business-specific world-view of a definable 'tribe' of industry experts, and is often visibly articulated into its rituals, rites of professional passage, local jargon and dress.

Cultural anthropology has helped us understand that other peoples often behave differently for reasons that are perfectly understandable once they are explained. People we may think of as primitive are often living out cultures as richly complex and sophisticated as our own, and so deserve our respect. Indeed, they often display a greater understanding of their society than we do of our own. Similarly, industry recipes are perfectly comprehensible from their adoptees' viewpoint. Yet they deal with only part of the perceived uncertainties. The managerial task of dealing with those remaining is clear. The methodological position is one of respect for management and for its creative contribution. But once we, as uninvolved observers who need not accept the local culture, analyse the recipe's structure and content, we are able to consider it against the wider socio-economic background.

Towards the end of this book I argue that, irrespective of the theoretical implications, the recipe should prove to be a useful analytic device for both practising managers and industry analysts. They could use it, for instance, to diagnose corporate performance, measure the fitness of the firm for its industry, guide strategic thinking and evaluate the appropriateness of mergers, etc. It suggests a different type of corporate history which focuses on the recipes senior management adopt to guide their decision-making (Grinyer & Spender 1979). It is also a training tool for raising the level of managements' awareness above what they uncritically take to be the self-evident truths of the situation (Spender 1983).

But observing the power that the relevant industry recipe had over the managers in my research sample gave me a sense of closure on this line of research. I could not see that it led anywhere else. It had little value for that substantial majority of business academics who search for those predictive theories that ignore managerial creativity. Although the industry recipe provided an interesting context for longitudinal methods, research was hobbled by the difficulty of operationalizing the recipe as a body of knowledge. In the absence of a strong theory of managerial cognition, how could one know the recipe was adequately complete except by observing its use? How could one validate a proposed recipe? How could one relate events unconsidered within the recipe to its subsequent development?

I see the industry recipe as part of a particular firm's response to the varying competitive conditions, work practices, technologies, public policies, legislation, and so forth prevailing at the time. With the considerable benefit of hindsight, academic research may well reveal which of the many obvious changes occurring at any particular time lead to responses which eventually find their way into the recipe. My research was not directed towards this objective. I was interested in the practicality of my new analytical concept, the industry recipe. I also believe managers differ from academic researchers, for they must respond to their present. For this reason, I have not provided data about what has happened since the 1970s in the industries I examined. I see such data as irrelevant to an understanding of the recipes used at the time of my research.

Sometime after this research was complete I began to hear about expert systems. I saw that I had made a crude attempt to codify what might now be called the industry's strategic knowledge-base. This book's methodology section is about doing what is now called 'knowledge engineering'. The recipe is not a theory; it is actually a primitive knowledge-base for an as yet unspecified expert system. Like most practical expert systems, the recipe is advisory rather than prescriptive. It offers managers support without relieving them of their responsibilities. In the same way that expert systems demand interaction with those they support, the recipe leaves a place for the manager's creative contribution.

There is an exploding interest in all types of expert systems, from those that relieve us of mind-dulling repetitive work to those that act as tentative but portable encapsulations of extremely scarce expert knowledge. Senior managers are clearly experts, and senior management decision support is clearly one of the most exciting areas for expert system development. I have hopes that the research covered here can make a contribution in this new field.

Several other people, who knew as little as I did of uncertainty or of expert systems, have to answer for the fact that they encouraged me to press ahead, both with the original research and with this re-write. I am moved by their faith in me. John Child became a demanding external examiner yet remains a friend. He was largely responsible for getting me going again after our time at Kent State. He also brought my ideas to the attention of his research students, especially Gerry Johnson and Homa Bahrami. Both have since encouraged me most persistently. Peter Grinyer showed great generosity as we worked together at the City University Business School. We were able to use earlier versions of these ideas in a study of change in a 200-year-old engineering company (Grinyer & Spender 1979). David Weir was my internal thesis supervisor, a severe critic and a fast friend. He was also instrumental in getting me to rework this material after a difficult period at UCLA. John Grant and unknown others shepherded the original thesis to the 1980 A. T. Kearney Award. Dan Schendel and Chuck Hofer, who have earned an important place in our discipline's history with their determination to codify the strategy and policy area, were persistently supportive. All these, and others, set me a fine example of academic collegiality which I want to acknowledge here and hope to repay to future students of our subject. My thanks to them all.

J.-C. Spender
University of Glasgow

╫   ╫   ╫

Note to the Reader

Throughout this book I have used the masculine pronouns, 'he', 'him', 'his', wherever the alternatives 'he or she' etc. would be clumsy and would interfere with readability. However, the masculine pronouns should always be understood in their generic, not in their gender-specific, senses.

2

Classical Management Theory

2.1 Introduction

In this chapter I begin assembling the hypothesis that I eventually
test in the field research. Uncertainty resolution is theory construction.
So my ultimate objective is to build and test a theory of strategic
management as a process of theory construction. I argue that theory
is required to make sense of the world, and that managers are often
without appropriate theory. But managements' problems are also
highly varied. Some of the activities for which they are responsible
may be readily modelled. Many of the classic operational research
applications fall into this category. But this monograph focuses on
determining the firm's strategy. I argue that the task of creating or
choosing strategy is at the other extreme, a 'wicked' problem that
can scarcely be framed, let alone modelled. In this area managers
are so short of theory, and their firms' circumstances are so
contextually specific, that to understand and control what is happening
managers must build the theories they use.

In Section 2.2 I begin the task of revealing the theories of
management implicit in classical management theory. This is defined
broadly to include the work of Adam Smith, Max Weber, Henri
Fayol, and Frederick Taylor as well as that of the post-war Human
Relations movement and the Contingency Theorists. My purpose is
to reveal these theorists' axiomatic presuppositions, their basic
building blocks, rather than their work's finer points, weaknesses and
implications.

If, as I assert, this book is about practical management it is
reasonable to ask why the reader must be dragged through this dusty

literature. The most important part of the answer is that these writers' thoughts live on in our everyday managerial practice. In this case at least, a knowledge of history is a floodlight on the present. In detail, this analysis will also reveal why classical theory still forms the backbone of managerial theory, and is still the basic substance of most management education programmes. We see first that many of the everyday ideas that managers bring to their sense of their function and to their theory-building are derived from these early writings, even though they may be unaware of it. Second, we see that classical theory is perfectly adequate for framing the theoretical problems with which most of today's researchers are struggling.

Classical management theory successfully spells out the issues with which a manager's constructed 'theory of the situation' must deal. In particular, classical theory spells out most of the terms and topics that must be brought together in any comprehensive theory of management. While job definition, co-ordination, direction, motivation and profit and so forth are familiar, the terms 'strategy' and 'policy' are vague and are used very wildly. Part of my purpose in analysing classical theory is to show that policy differs from strategy, and that both can be adequately defined.

Theories develop, and are replaced, because criticism shows them to be flawed. New theory starts out as an answer to particular previously noted defects. Classical theory has many weaknesses, yet it has survived decades of criticism. In Section 2.16 I look at these criticisms. My purpose is to identify and frame the particular weakness that my new theory will address. It is directed at classical theory's inability to handle the uncertainty in management's information about the firm. I then review the meaning of 'policy' and 'strategy' in the light of these criticisms. This sets the scene for Chapter 3.

2.2 The Background

One tradition of organizational theorizing, dating back beyond Adam Smith's *Wealth of Nations* and the beginnings of micro-economics, treats the firm as an independent entity operating in a social or economic market environment. Smith's theorizing separates two elements, firms (suppliers) and markets. The firm is an atom operating within a market-place made up of firms and, possibly, other types of atoms such as public institutions. The theory links the market at one level with the firm at another.

A second, quite different tradition of organizational theorizing, found in Weber (1969), Taylor (1967) and Fayol (1949), treats the firm itself as the larger context, the atoms being the individuals or work groups who make up the firm. While Smith deals with individuals, he does not obviously propose a theory of how they come together into a firm. This second kind of theory separates firms and their constituent individuals and deals with how team members with varying skills can be organized to produce a coherent response.

2.3 Markets

The first tradition, which conflates the organization with its members, focuses on the firm's external relationships, that is those between the firm, its customers, its competitors and its broader socio-economic environment. Management chooses, for instance, to market particular products at particular prices in particular locations. The firm is treated as a 'black box', a production function without differentiated work-roles or control mechanisms. Hence it is often equated with its entrepreneur or managing coalition. The more rigorous of these theories are known as Theories of the Firm.

The second tradition treats the organization an an interactive system. It is about structuring different kinds of work group and role, and is the domain of Organization Theory. The analysis focuses on the inter-group or inter-individual relations and the control mechanisms which make this system organized, stable and purposive rather than a disorganized rabble.

These two traditions address quite different aspects of organization, generate different types of analysis and suggest different kinds of managerial activity. They clearly diverge. Taken together they imply three analytic levels; the market-place, the firm and the individual. The modern firm, which must employ ordinary people and integrate their activities into a democratic capitalist economy, clearly requires decisions at all three levels, grounded in both traditions. Consequently much recent theorizing has been devoted to integrating the two traditions. Despite many assertions that convergence has occurred, or is imminent (Leibenstein 1960), the more substantial literature denies it (Coase 1937; Simon 1952b; Krupp 1961).

Identifying these three levels helps us see that theorists tend to focus their attention on particular parts of this general model. Both Smith and Weber are sociological theorists, concentrating on the upper level, with far broader concerns than most organization theorists. Sociology analyses the nature and persistence of social order. It is irrelevant to those who see society as wholly chaotic. Sociology's origins lie in conservative reactions to the implicitly individualistic anarchy of Enlightenment Philosophers (Bramson 1961: 13). Its first objective is to understand social order, and only in that context investigate change. Every theory of social order must posit a mechanism for achieving order between individuals. The theory must also have appropriate models of the individuals between whom such order is thought to exist. Theories are consistent to the extent that they deal with overlapping or convergent individual and ordering mechanism concepts.

All analysis begins with a categorization scheme, built upon distinctions. These help us see whether an instance belongs in one category or another. To analyse the consistency of theories, we must make their categorization schemes or axiomatic structures explicit and check whether they are convergent or discontinuous.

2.4 Social Order

The first axiom in contemporary sociology is that there is a distinction between a naturally occurring social order, typified by the innate sense of order in the family, and an order that is deliberately created, typified by an elected government. The world of Rousseau contrasts with that of Hobbes. In sociology, this distinction is due to Toennies who writes: 'for I claim this to be the fundamental sociological insight: that aside from the real units and relations between men (Gemeinschaft), there exist units and relationships posited by and depending on their own will, and therefore essentially of an ideally conceived character (Gesellschaft). They must be understood as created or made by men, even though, in fact, they may have attained an external objective power over the individual' (1971: 33).

Sociology's second basic distinction is implicit in the Enlightenment Philosophers' idea of the individual as a free agent with inalienable or 'natural' rights. The immediate widespread appeal of this idea, with the resulting political consequences around the world, brings sociology into existence to solve the problem of order among free men. The distinction separates the free, who have a consequent ethical responsibility for their actions, from those constrained by slavery, imprisonment and other forms of bondage. It proposes individuals able to choose, and so immediately demands examination of the reasons why individuals act in the way they do, choosing, for instance, democracy over anarchy.

Adam Smith produces enduring grand sociological theory because he effectively combines the two distinctions. He works out a theory of free individuals, self-interested entrepreneurs or 'undertakers', competing in a *Gemeinschaftlich* society, which is nevertheless stabilized by the 'invisible hand' or market forces. He shows how the single-minded pursuit of self-interest leads not to anarchy but to an efficient, technologically aggressive, politically acceptable, self-stabilizing system of social order.

2.5 Individual Rationality

While Smith founds micro-economics, a theory of society expressed in the language of economics, the two distinctions owe more of their present place in sociology to Max Weber. Weber's objective is an empirical science for analysing society and social relations. Like Smith, he begins with the behaviour of rational individuals. But he does not see the same individual freedom. He proposes, instead, people whose behaviour suggests various types of rationality. As Aron writes: 'Weber's point of departure is the distinction between four types of action:

(i)   Zweckrational, or rational action in relation to a goal
(ii) Wertrational, or rational action in relation to a value
(iii) Affective or emotional action
(iv) Traditional action, (1970, vol. 2: 186).

Like Smith, Weber grounds his theorizing in study of a vast body of empirical observations of many human societies. He concludes that societies are dominated either by 'zweckrational' behaviour (which Parsons translates as rational-legal), or by various behaviours implied by the last three types of action, grounded in that society's traditions and culture.

Weber also introduces the concept of charisma, associated with affective commitment to a particular person. This does not fit into his overall schema as simply as do the rational-legal or traditional categories. It is there because Weber wishes to incorporate mechanisms which allow society to be created and changed. Initially there is the charismatic group, where personal authority binds individuals together into a proto-society. This is followed by the process of 'routinizing charisma', as a society founded on rules legitimated by appeal to tradition emerges in the process of preparing for the founder's departure. As the memories of that source and, thus, the basis for the rules, recede into the past, a search for social efficiency begins. The arbitrary traditional rules are replaced by more scientific ones and rational-legal society emerges.

These suppositions and categories enable Weber to build a grand sociological scheme incorporating both social order and change. We can see, incidentally, that Weber's use of charisma is matched, at the lowest of our three levels of analysis, by Smith's use of the 'undertaker' or Defoe's earlier use of the 'projector' as the creative source of a business. Nowadays we expect organizational leaders to possess both charisma and entrepreneurial creativity.

2.6 Power

Weber's chosen mechanism for achieving social order is power. His definition of power, one person's ability to force another to specific actions in spite of that other person's wishes, is still commonly used. Weber is less clear with his model of the individual, who is simply rational according to the type of action forming the basis of that society.

While Smith's society is primarily *Gemeinschaftlich*, emerging unintended and unconceived by any one citizen, Weber's modern society is predominantly *Gesellschaftlich*, the result of conscious activity on the part of the few with power over the majority. The ordering hand is now wholly visible. But, Weber argues, societies differ according to whether the social power is 'legitimated' by the citizenry, who rationally and voluntarily choose to accept the 'authority' of others, or whether there is coercion, which denies individuals that choice.

Smith's agenda is similarly sociological and political. He appeals to a new kind of economic science to legitimate free enterprise intellectually at a time when the national economy is being conducted along highly interventionist lines (Skinner in Smith 1970: 77). His mechanism for achieving social order is also radically different from Weber's. It is presented in his *Theory of Moral Sentiments*, the necessary companion to his *Wealth of Nations*. In brief, this proposes a voluntarily shared morality and, of course, business ethic. The resulting individual sense of enlightened interdependence is the attractive social and moral force which balances the anarchic tendencies of enlightened self-interest, and so completes Smith's theory of a naturally emerging stable economic society.

It is clearly difficult to adopt Smith's theory at the organizational level. Entrepreneurs and organization theorists approach organizations as highly intended instruments, created for a purpose, be it for private profit or to execute a public programme. Even though we see much current interest in creating market-like conditions within established organizations, we can still usefully define organizations as purposive. As Coase notes, the essence of the firm is its use of authority rather than market forces as the means of co-ordination (1937).

2.7 Bureaucracy

Any of Weber's social types can exist at the organizational level. We can readily imagine, for instance, a firm organized on a purely charismatic basis. But Weber's sharpest organizational analysis focuses on the preconditions, processes and consequences of the purely *Zweckrational* goal-oriented 'bureaucratic' form. Here power is vested in organizational rules and individuals are appointed because of their fitness for the work, which is scientifically planned and directed towards defined organizational objectives.

Weber argues that bureaucracy is the purest rational-legal form of organization. In it well-informed and trained individuals voluntarily choose to let others, and the rules, have authority over them. It is the least arbitrary, most scientific and efficient consciously co-ordinated form. But given our democratic commitment to personal freedom, we must consider why anyone would voluntarily accept another's authority. I look at this later in this chapter. This question precisely determines the problems that Weberian classical organizational theory must solve.

Note also that bureaucracy cannot be a societal form, embracing an entire Kafkaesque society. That would deny all individuals – rather than some relatively disenfranchised ones – the choice of membership which is axiomatic to a bureaucracy's legitimacy in a politically free society. Although bureaucracy is nowhere society's dominant form, it becomes increasingly evident at the institutional and organizational level. While Weberian bureaucracy is a powerful theory of the consciously co-ordinated organization, it is not a theory of society.

Weber's purpose is also overtly political, to propose a science of social analysis immune to special interests and, as part of that endeavour, to sound a strong warning. Although we might favour bureaucracy because of its efficiency, we should understand its extreme political vulnerability. However apparently powerful over those enmeshed within them, bureaucracies are never more than instruments in the hands of those who consciously co-ordinate them. Weber's worry is that democracy, which swept away feudal tyranny, can, in turn, be swept away by bureaucratic tyranny (Aron 1970, vol.2: 188). He writes: 'the question is always who controls the existing bureaucratic machinery' (1969: 338). This machinery has no capacity for creative response or change. It is wholly dependent on controlling components external to the bureaucracy. Hence Weber concludes 'the capitalistic entrepreneur is, in our society, the only type who has been able to maintain at least relative immunity from subjection to the control of rational bureaucratic knowledge' (1969: 339).

2.8 The Relevance of Bureaucracy to Management Theory

Where does all this leave us? First, we must be concerned with the appropriateness of the analysis. If we are to apply either micro-economic or bureaucratic theories to organizations, we must ask whether their preconditions and presuppositions are realistic. Is Smith's imagined society adequately like our own? How realistic is it for management to expect enlightened interdependence? In practice, the call for greater co-operation between management and workers is probably more common now than at any previous time. In this respect, Smith is an early optimist telling us we have nothing to fear from market forces, or from those of our fellows who see the whole picture as he does. In contrast, Weber is dourly pessimistic, suggesting that we live in a power ridden world and that, with bureaucracy co-opted, even science's advances are double-edged. But note that he follows Smith in looking to market forces for an answer. As Rex remarks, Weber's real objective is to discover scientifically whether market behaviour is natural, as Smith presumes, or is the product of particular social interests, as he fears (in Raison 1969: 173).

Second, given the obvious clash of presuppositions, we must be concerned with the integrity of our analysis. We might, for instance, adopt micro-economic thinking about how the firm should control its external market relationships. We can also adopt ideas drawn from bureaucracy to help us allocate internal resources and control employees. But we cannot expect optimal conclusions within a coherent plan of action for the firm as a whole unless we can integrate these two analyses. We must limit the confusion caused by their divergent and mutually exclusive suppositions.

The first answer to this challenge is likely to be that the two sets of ideas apply to different domains; Smithian enlightenment to the firm's external relations, Weberian power structures to the employees. This seems feasible, though the use of two such radically different models of the individual might be dangerous. But our analysis breaks down completely when we think about those, such as long-term customers, who seem to belong to both categories. We become unsure whether such customer relations should be dominated by market forces, in that customers can take their business elsewhere, or by the power relations manifest in specially negotiated terms. In practice we know that both types of thinking apply. But theory cannot tell us which and so help us conclude the analysis.

This illustrates some of the problems we face when we apply classical theory to the management of real firms which are neither inanimate production functions nor bureaucratically organized groups isolated from their dynamic economic and legal environment.

2.9 The Apparent Coherence of Bureaucracy

The difficulties get worse once we look more deeply at Weber's detailing of bureaucratic theory, and at Taylor's and Fayol's contrasting treatments of the same organizational phenomena. Smith's theory is coherent because enlightened individualism meshes perfectly with the enlightened interdependence of the Theory of Moral Sentiments. Weber's theory has no such coherence, and both Taylor and Fayol see that fundamental problems remain to be solved.

Bureaucratic theory's achievement is to show how to combine the socio-politics of the democratic society outside the firm with the wholly artificial political context within it. The theory tells us that organizations are not societies writ small but, as Simon notes, 'among the most artificial and most contrived of human artefacts'. While democratic society implies open debate and the criss-cross of many power structures, power in a bureaucracy is always absolute. Why, then, do people accept and so legitimize this? Marx argues the working-class's sale of its labour is fundamental to capitalist society.

Weber's answer is more specific and relies on Adam Smith's division of labour, for in his socio-economy both the individual employee and the firm specialize. Bureaucratic organizations integrate into democratic society as a matter of social expediency. As problem solvers at the uppermost of our three level model, they deal with only a small part of society's needs. Were they to attempt to dominate society and to try to hold it to ransom, things might be different. By accepting the existence of a firm and equating it with the goods and services it brings to the market-place, society suspends its interest in the firm's internal power structure and in its chosen mechanisms for achieving order.

Similarly, at the lowest level of the model, a bureaucratic firm demands absolute power over only a small part of the individual's capabilities. The individual gives over control of one part of his life, unpooling their conner acting in particular precisely limited organizational demands will give him greater freedom in the other uncommitted parts over which he retains control. He makes a voluntary decision to participate in the bureaucracy.

Weber's model of the individual presupposes people's ability to segment their lives. Here he diverges from Smith's more integrated but less sophisticated model. Weber sees that people behave very differently in different contexts. They actually operate within bounded sub-worlds which may each entail sharply different rationalities. In this sense, modern people clearly adapt to many more different roles than their forebears. Indeed, it may be a measure of our society's sophistication that people now do this. One of Spencer's Darwinist contributions to sociology is the idea that: 'the development of every organism is a change from homogeneity to heterogeneity' (1904, vol. 2: 9).

Weber's theorizing separates the individual, as a citizen, from that same person as a role occupant. The work-role, an abstract depersonalized component of the organization as conceived by its extra-bureaucratic creator, is separated from the person occupying that role. Bureaucratic organizations cannot come into existence, or persist, unless citizens are willing and able to occupy these roles. Similarly, management theory must go beyond the scientific design of work-roles to include the individual's decision to participate. This decision must, of course, be grounded in the individual's extra-role context and rationality, that is he will have 'his own' reasons for accepting the role. Here Weber is showing that organizations can exist only when the individual postpones attending to his immediate interests, in the same way that economists argue wealth is a postponement of expenditure. Just as people's propensity to save is an empirical fact, beyond economic theory, so bureaucratic theory defines itself as insufficient to the managerial task of motivating people to participate. Bureaucratic theory cannot deal with both designing and staffing a real organization. Nor can it help us analyse the organization's creators or its external relations.

2.10 Scientific Management

These points can be illustrated by looking at Frederick Taylor's *Scientific Management*. Many write in treat Taylor as a founding father of organization theory, though, as Hoagland makes clear, he merely participates in a tradition of scientific, even mechanical, theorizing that goes back beyond Babbage (1955). There is common ground with Weber, but there may be greater convergence with Smith, and this can tell us something important about the subsequent development of *Scientific Management* and its critics.

Taylor is clearly concerned with the detail of how the organization's work is divided up into work-roles. Smith's focus is on the division of labour in pin-making, how a team of ten can make 48,000 pins a day, while one man on his own may make scarcely 20 (1970: 111). Taylor is interested in shovelling and in moving pig-iron. Both suggest that organizations are primarily mechanisms for exploiting the way specialization raises productivity. Both see technology as important because it facilitates the division of labour. Equally, the division of labour leads workers to build specialized tools to ease their task, and so invent new technology. Note the possibilities for creating organizations are also constrained by the market's ability to take up the massive increase in output so occasioned. Thus Smith's maxim that: 'the division of labour is limited by the extent of the market' (1970: 121).

2.11 The Technologies of Administration and Production

Technology is a vastly abused term, so some clarification is in order. My position is that technology is, as the Greeks would have it, knowledge. The contemporary usage with its implication of hardware and machinery diverts attention from the real technology which is the knowledge made manifest in the physical objects and systems. There are other types of knowledge, especially that made manifest in *Gesellschaftlich* groups. Much managerial knowledge is social, oriented towards understanding and controlling market behaviour and people's feelings. Not only are these two types of knowledge about different phenomena, they also have differing structures.

Notice that, after updating their technology, none of Smith's high productivity pin-makers actually makes pins any more. One man draws out the wire, another straightens it, another grinds it at the top for receiving the head. This is technology as we conventionally understand it. But who co-ordinates these very different activities, and on what basis? What we need here is not a technology for making pins; we need a technology for creating work groups. Smith does not deal with this obvious corollary of the much quoted division of labour. The gap shows us that one type of knowledge is about imaginatively disassembling the completed pin into its components and determining their corresponding production processes. The other type of knowledge is about bringing differing work-roles into a harmonious interaction, so producing a coherent group response.

As far as Smith's pin-makers go, we might suspect that he would rely on some intra-organizational market force. But that would require an effective market in straightened wire and part-finished unheaded pins. Smith actually supposes enlightened interdependence, that the individual's shared knowledge of the significance of each different task would make the group effectively self-organizing, a true worker co-operative.

This suggests that we need to distinguish the various technologies. In this example we see that those which enable large tasks to be divided up into a number of smaller tasks are different from the technologies used when creating a co-ordinated work group.

2.12 Separating the Work-role and its Occupant

Weber separates the worker from his work-role with the absoluteness of his democratic freedom to decide to participate. It is the work-role that is co-ordinated by the organization's design and the exercise of managerial power, not the individual. Each work-role carries with it the power and responsibility to co-ordinate its hierarchically subordinate work-roles. Thus, as both Gouldner and Parsons note, each role lies at the intersection of two structures, one based on the worker's position in the firm's production system, the other based on his position in the co-ordinating power structure (in Salaman 1979: 131).

Effective role-occupancy requires knowing how both of these structures work. This knowledge is the role-occupant's technical expertise, and it covers two distinct technologies. We can call one the 'horizontal' technology of production. This deals with the processes through which the organization transforms material inputs into product outputs. The second is the 'vertical' technology of administration which co ordinates the horizontally defined work-roles. The first is dependent on the firm's line of business, is responsive to technological progress, and reveals itself in the extension of the division of labour. Bureaucratic theory says the second in the technology of social power, its generation and administration. Weber leaves these two structures, which depend on completely different types of knowledge, quite unresolved. Yet managers must clearly become competent in both technologies if they are to design and co-ordinate the work group so efficiently that the firm appears to the market to be a black-box production function.

2.13 The Coherence of Scientific Management

Taylor deals specifically with the integration of these two structures. He resolves the incoherence in Weber's scheme by replacing the bureaucrat's arbitrary power with scientific knowledge. Taylor develops a new technology of administration. In the scientific search for efficiency, he subjects administration to the same intensive division of labour as Smith takes to pin production. Work group administration is split between eight 'functional specialists' who are appointed on the basis of their proficiency with the administrative technology.

With the productive and administrative structures both based on scientific knowledge, Taylor asserts, co-ordination is straightforward. Taylor assumes, in keeping with most scientific opinion at the turn of the century, that scientific understanding, like Nature herself, is homogeneous. Here Taylor proposes a profoundly Durkheimian scheme in which the role-occupant submits voluntarily to the scientifically revealed natural order in both structures.

This confidence that science can render the exercise of power unnecessary may now strike us as naive. But it is useful to understand the larger historical context of Taylor's theorizing (Wren 1979: 260).

The US labour pool was increasingly immigrant, uprooted, without manufacturing skills, and unprotected from all manner of national and local political abuse. Scientific Management was timely and could address several immediate needs. Increased division of labour made industrial work simpler (de-skilled) and therefore much more accessible to these willing but unskilled workers. It also promised owners and management something through increased productive efficiency in a time of exploding demand and stretched capacity. Second, and central to Taylor's social reform programme, obedience to science would cut through the widespread exploitation of workers by foremen, so enabling technically trained management to penetrate the work group and establish justice and scientific control over even the humblest task. Each task could be analysed, each worker's output measured and each trained in the most efficient procedures. The payoff would be shared: management would benefit from increased output and capacity utilization; workers would benefit from being able to make choices guided by effective economic incentives.

Taylor's mechanism for achieving organizational order is the individual's shared morality, specifically the universal respect for science and economic motivation. Here we see Taylor's ideological convergence with Smith. Both propose theories which integrate internally coherent models of individual, organization and society, but in idealized societies, rather than in the interventionist political-economics and power ridden organizations of our society.

Both propose purely economic worlds in which the decision to participate is economic, and productive efficiency alone ensures organizational and social survival. Kakar, Taylor's psycho-biographer, notes that Taylor was almost pathological in his rejection of the power-based socio-industrial reality that he experienced as a young man (1970). Kakar also notes that Scientific Management appealed to societies undergoing political change, especially France and Russia who used science as a politically neutral instrument for destroying existing power structures (1970: 3).

The uproar attending the introduction of Scientific Management in the US, which led to widespread union protest, industrial unrest and Senate hearings, was a reaction to its implicit political message. Generally the shop-floor's reaction was even more violently negative than the owner's. Far from accepting Taylor's science-oriented social vision, those with power on the shop-floor saw that their power-base would disappear. While management took many of the constituent parts into everyday use, Scientific Management became an ideology and a tool for radicals. Indeed, much to Taylor's eventual displeasure, Scientific Management became a central element in Populist-Progressive political thinking (Wren 1979: 283).

2.14 Fayol and other Critics of Scientific Management

There are many criticisms of Scientific Management In Section 2.10, I will discuss the Human Relations movement, which criticizes Scientific Management on the grounds that it turns workers into one-dimensional robots. But there are also critics within the more immediate circle of Taylor's contemporaries who seek to introduce science into management. Taylor seemingly denies the external reality that these others accept. Ignoring all types of social power, Taylor cannot then distinguish legitimate from non-legitimate power. Thus Church and Alford develop a scheme similar to Taylor's, but argue that Taylorism overlooks the possibilities of effective leadership, that is organizational power legitimated and harnessed to the enterprise's purpose (1912).

The French industrialist, Henri Fayol, offers more detailed criticism (1949), arguing that Scientific Management denies what most managers take to be their normal functions and responsibilities. He extends Weber's analysis, accepting the power hierarchy, but focusing on the principle of unity of command, that is one person must be in charge. He also deals explicitly with the information, decision, command and control activity within the hierarchy. He sees managers as part of an information gathering, processing and distributing mechanism, which partners the material gathering, processing and distributing mechanism Smith analyses. The familiar hierarchical shape of the bureaucratic organization is the necessary result of combining the technologies of administration and production whilst following Fayol's principles of the unity of command. Administration is the bridge between central direction and the final division of productive labour. Most importantly, as an experienced mining executive and government bureaucrat, Fayol accepts that the design principles for these two technologies are unrelated and make organizational design difficult.

2.15 Line/Staff Relations

Fayol is probably best known for his analysis of the line/staff relationship. Behind Smith's idea of the division of labour is the empirical generalization that organization enables people to do, through specialization and co-operation, things that they could not do alone. Barnard, a major theorist, puts it beautifully: 'co-operation justifies itself as a means of overcoming the limitations restricting what individuals can do' (1968: 23). Like Taylor, Fayol applies the divison of labour to the technology of administration. But unlike Taylor, whose 'functionalism' divides the administrative task among eight specialists, Fayol sees the need for centralized direction. He accuses Taylor, who had a large and profitable consultancy practice, of bending his principles to the evident needs of the market place. He writes: 'in practice Taylor was able to reconcile functionalism with the principle of unity of command' (1949: 69).

Fayol recognizes that centralizing direction must eventually lead to the responsible manager being overloaded beyond his limitations. The resulting design problem is to increase this manager's information gathering, processing and distributing capacity without corrupting or confusing the hierarchical power-structure. Based on the military model, he proposes 'staff', people who are technically trained to support management. They are neither decision-makers nor responsible for more than merely advising the manager they support. But this is no simple answer. He concedes that this 'local' power structure is inherently in conflict with the organization's. The manager is now at the intersection of three structures, the organization's horizontal and vertical ones, and this new one between himself and his staff support. Fayol notes that these will be the very devil to reconcile.

2.16 Classical Theory's Achievement

With this brief review we touch on a body of theory whose steady development encompasses many of the issues with which managers must deal. It goes beyond social theory, as advanced by Smith, and beyond organization theory, as advanced by Weber and Taylor. Fayol and his American contemporary Church understand the way the choice of production method constrains the organizational designer. They lay out the principles of a technology of administration without abandoning bureaucratic theory. They directly address the task of designing organizations with differentiated work-roles and realistically limited role-occupants. They also go beyond organizational structure to a theory of managing organizations as information systems. As these classicists define it, management now includes integration at the upper level, between the firm and its markets. It also includes forecasting and planning. The organization has external relations which must be both modelled out into the future and controlled in the present.

Fayol and Church management also includes lower level integration, between the firm and the individual, for it must deal with the training, organizing and motivating of individual workers. Finally, the organizational model can display problems in terms of the conflict between three different technologies; of production, of administration and of staff. This organizational model is richly realistic and perfectly recognizable. Its strength is such that it is basic to most contemporary managers' thinking after well over half a century of great social and technological change. Its weakness is that its prescriptive tone is not matched by its usefulness. It is a very tentative body of knowledge. We cannot expect too much of it. If we tried to design an organization using classical theory alone we would fail. We would see that classical theory is a loose set of ideas about how to define work-roles, fit people into them and co-ordinate the resulting organizational activity. Woodward's work illustrates that classical theory is unable to specify even the span of control (1965). It offers no substantial guidance on the building of work groups, or of how to divisionalize. It has little specific to say about how to control subordinates or staff.

2.17 The Classical Approach to Policy and Strategy

Notwithstanding its looseness, the Fayol and Church model succeeds in giving some meaning to the terms 'policy' and 'strategy'. Despite these terms' importance to most management writers, there is a noticeable lack of agreement about what they mean. As McNichols (1977: 8) and Steiner and Miner (1977: 24) note, they are seldom adequately distinguished.

Using our three level analysis of classical theory, we can define policy as the selection of organizational purpose, the upper level decison. Bureaucratic theory argues that purpose is determined logically prior to and therefore outside the organization. It is necessarily bound by the environment in which the organization is embedded. It is not constrained by the organization's intellectual or tangible resources. These can be changed, as a matter of policy, by raising funds, selling the business, etc. In capitalist society the right to select the private organization's purpose belongs to its owners. They may, of course, allow executive management to make policy decisions on the grounds that they know the situation better. As the environment changes, and as the organization changes, so policy needs to be re-made. Similarly, the lower level problem, the individual's decision to participate, is a matter of his personal policy and outside the organization's purview.

We can use this classical structure to define strategy as the task of building the plan that implements these upper and lower level policy decisions. The strategic plan is clearly constrained by the organization's tangible and intellectual resources. Indeed, the inventory of resources will include inter alia the organization's information flows, database, morality and esprit de corps. Clearly, the organization can be designed only within what its designers know and within the resources they have available. They can control only what they have information about and power over.

It can be seen that classical theory is adequate to frame the central topic of this enquiry, how managers make corporate strategy. It also lets us distinguish policy and strategy from administration and operations. Administration refers to the design and use of co-ordinating mechanisms, operations refers to the design and use of input/output transformations.

My intention here is to suggest a semantic and conceptual link between classical theory and the four terms which dominate much contemporary teaching and practice. But the price paid for this broad sense of relevance between theory and managerial practice is severe. What is covered is alarmingly fragmented and far from being a single coherent framework. Frequently criticized as overly prescriptive, we see that classical theory is actually insufficiently integrated to supply management with any complete answers.

As we move on from classical theory to its critiques, and to contemporary lines of managerial theorizing, we should recognize that the classical quality in this earlier work is its attempt to grasp the organizational problem in its entirety. It aspires to deal with both upper and lower level integration, as well as with the organizational design, role co-ordination, resource allocation and information flow issues. Until recently few writers have made such determined attempts to produce integrated theory for those responsible for the overall management of the enterprise.

2.18 The Human Relations Critique

Bureaucratic theory implies that, having made the decision to participate, the individual intends to fulfil the role's demands. History has it that the Hawthorne researchers were the first to reveal that even the most willing workers are unlikely to deliver against this contract. This is clearly nonsense. The early industrialists understood the problems of acculturating the labour force to systematic factory ways (Pollard 1968: 213). However, the Hawthorne studies, still the most extensive and richest body of research on factory work, successfully drew attention to the powerful but extremely mixed social consequences of organizational life. Their observations eventually led them to reject the classicists' assumption that people work for economic reasons alone. Workers, they found, are at the intersection of many potentially competing structures.

First, there is the individual's private place in the social system outside the factory. Bureaucratic theory argues this is irrelevant to the power holders within the organization. In practice we know that organizations can threaten our personal privacy, although there are limits to what an organization needs to know about us. Second, there is the social network that forms within the workplace, unknown to and uncontrolled by the organization. The individual's place within this internal or 'informal' society may be quite unrelated to his 'formal' place in the production system. Thus, even a non-supervisory role-occupant, without subordinates to control or staff to assist him, finds himself at the intersection of three power-structures; the horizontal production system, the vertical administrative system and the omnidirectional informal social system of the workplace. The senior manager is at the intersection of no less than five, these three plus the supervisory structures relating him to his subordinates and to his staff. Each structure responds to quite different design and control principles. Indeed, every organizational member must negotiate a place in each of these structures to survive the organizational experience.

The Human Relations school, which grew directly from the Hawthorne Studies, attempts to replace the classicists' 'economic man' with its own 'social man'. Several streams of thought develop.

One, in which the managerialist position is adopted, looks to motivate people towards organizational objectives by augmenting economic rewards with psychological and social rewards such as One Minute 'strokes', citations in the company magazine and 'beer busts'.

More radical theorists see an inherent conflict between the organizational power system and that within the work group. The Hawthorne Studies, and field work by authors such as Roy (1952), endorse Taylor's view that informal groups form to develop methods for challenging managerial power by, for instance, withholding information or by restricting output. The divergence revealed between the rationalities of the organizational designer and the employee's informal structure profoundly challenges bureaucratic theory's purely rational mechanisms for achieving social order. Bureaucratic theory implies the role-occupant is unable to perform without organizational direction and is likely to sit idle until told otherwise. The Hawthorne Studies suggest the organization must fight continuously to achieve and sustain its influence over the role-occupant who is always actively doing something even if only being mischievous. Life inside the organization is no longer so controlled, contrived and artificial. It becomes much more like the society in which it is embedded and management becomes a more overtly political activity.

Although the Human Relations critique extends management's concerns beyond those covered by classical theory, it further fragments the thinking. No coherent theory emerges, save a renewed interest in New Society worker co-operatives.

2.19 Contingency Theory

There is much academic debate about the nature and purpose of contingency theory. Some, such as Lupton (1971) and Hofer (1975), argue that its roots lie in opposing the supposedly classicist idea that there is one 'best way', one prescribed answer. Burns and Stalker's influential work can be read differently (1961). Their conclusion, that there are several possible organizational designs and that the one most appropriate depends on the rate of technical and market change, actually deals with only one of the three principal design determinants (1961: 102). It is more likely that contingency theorizing began as a methodological critique of the way management theory seemed to push the managers themselves out of the analysis. Burns and Stalker specifically research management's understanding of how upper level integration is dealt with.

Contingency theories attempt to link pairs of sub-theories with empirical generalizations. These sub-theories are seldom spelt out, more often left implicit in taxonomies whose relevance is accepted uncritically. The types of contingency theory relevant to management generally deal with (a) theories of the organization's environment and (b) theories of the organization's structure. These theories are then linked. Thus Child argues environments can be categorized according to five variables: complexity, variability, illiberality and, less directly, the results of management's choice of technology and organizational size (1972: 3). These influence the choice of organizational design. Similarly, Chandler defines manufacturing environments as single product and centralized, or multi-product and multi-location (1962). Lupton shows how different market behaviours affect organizational structure and work relations in the garment trade (1963). Woodward shows how different production technologies lead to different adminstrative forms in the engineering industry (1965). Trist and Bamforth look at the impact changing coal-mining technology has on the formal and informal structures (1951). Lockwood looks at the effect the social system outside the factory has on auto workers' attitudes (1966). Lawrence and Lorsch show how methods of integrating organizations differ in three different industries (1967).

Each of these is a partial integration of a theory of the firm's environment and a theory of the organization's structure. The objective is to make systematic comparisons and so generate a more encompassing theory. There are methodological problems. The environmental and organizational characteristics lack common definitions and may refer to quite different phenomena, both between theorists and within any one sample. Second, the theories underlying the characterizations are neither explicit nor tested. It is possible, for instance, that some of Burns and Stalker's organizations might be both mechanistic and organic at the same time. The method does not protect the manager's place. When the appropriate generalizations have been made, a prescriptive theory results. The manager is once again excluded as a significant mediating or input variable.

2.20 Control

Fayol distinguishes between management's organizing and controlling activities. By and large, the other classicists do not look too carefully at why control is necessary. Fayol's extensive managerial experience forces him to confront this issue.

Bureaucratic theory implies that power is used to achieve control over the role-occupant's behaviour. His behaviour is not only directed, it is directed towards the organization's planned objectives. His efficiency and achievement are measured only in terms of the organization's purpose, that is not with reference to his own objectives. Thus control means nothing unless the terms of reference are defined. Note that the need for control arises only because the organization's designers are unable to structure role behaviour completely   the occupant is left the option to mal perform.

Recognizing that control is necessary introduces a powerful criticism which will be enlarged in Chapter 3 until it becomes central to the analysis. It is that people make mistakes, misunderstand, forget and in many other ways fail to conform to all the various abstract models of the individual that the classical theorists adopt. Nor can people adequately match the perfect structure of the organization, as its designers envision it. The classical theorists tend to imply that the worker can be held responsible for his role-performance. The Human Relations school modifies this position so that we recognize management has some responsibility for confronting the workers' limited abilities. Both Taylor and Fayol are sympathetic, stressing that management needs to train and support all levels of employee, as well as deliberately creating and managing an organizational 'esprit de corps'.

Fayol also accepts that senior managers and staff have their failings and have difficulty understanding, or controlling, the firm's environment. Although Smith argues for free markets, he sees clearly that, on the one hand, a firm with power over a market can be abnormally profitable, while on the other, powerful agencies, such as government bodies, can destroy a firm. Thus the contingency theorists tend to divide the manager's world into parts according to management's degree of control. The organization is that which they can control, while the environment is defined as that which management cannot control, that is everything else. This is far from satisfactory, since every firm is likely to vary somewhat in this respect.

This use of differential controllability produces a further result. The environment now becomes the cause to which organizational design is the response. As Lawrence and Lorsch remark, management becomes the programmable task of 'reading the environment and grinding out a custom-fitted organisation' (1969: 98).

2.21 Conclusion

In this chapter I have reviewed classical theory. My purpose was to reveal the assumptions lying behind many of the ideas which today's managers take as natural ways of thinking about their functions and responsibilities. The literature examined is still the basis of current theorizing and teaching. Despite its relative age and its evocation of somewhat unfamiliar patterns of business activity, given our high-tech information society, it has successfully defied rejection in favour of more powerful theory. With it a large part of the management problem has become clear; the upper level policy problem, reflecting the options available to owners in a democratic market oriented society, the lower level problem reflecting the employee's options, and the management's strategic task of articulating all of this within the constraints of available resources and technology. A crucial distinction has been made between the technologies of administration and production.

It can be seen that classical theory is actually a large body of relatively fragmentary thought. Parts, such as Scientific Management, are well integrated but incorporate social or individual models which are unrealistic. Other parts, such as Fayol's work, are recognizable and pertinent, but are theoretically incoherent. It can be seen that bureaucratic theory continues to underpin thinking about organizational design and that it too lacks coherence. My primary purpose has been to demonstrate that classical theory ultimately fails because the relevant parts of it do not fit together well enough to provide management with more than the sketchiest indication of how to create, design, staff and control an integrated purposive organization. Nor does it deal adequately with introducing that organization into a dynamic competitive market-place for products, technologies, funds and people.

In Chapter 3 this lack of coherence is treated as the most serious information defect facing managers. A link is made between incoherence and uncertainty. Reviewing the work of Simon, Shubik and Barnard, we will see how classical theory has been criticized from this viewpoint. Some of the uncertainties with which managers have to cope will be categorized. My general position will be that information about the world is inherently uncertain, and that making rational decisions requires the decision-maker to close off all uncertainty in the course of building his theory of the situation. He thereby assumes a closed knowable situation to which his prescriptive theory applies.

As uncertainty is introduced, the entire focus of the discussion is changed. The emphasis is shifted from the facts of the situation, which the classicists assume are available, to the ideas that managers have about what is going on. This sets the stage for Chapter 4 in which I examine managers' sense making and closure processes and so complete my cognitive theory of the firm.

3

Uncertainty and Management's Response

3.1 Introduction

In Chapter 2 I argue that management theory is not well matched to managers' problems. Although some authors take classical theory to be overly rigid and prescriptive, it is actually a fragmented and incoherent body of thought incapable of securely or completely grasping the full range of managerial concerns. This is especially true when we consider analysing the firm as a whole, attempting to cover both the upper, market relationship, and lower, employee relationship, issues. The Human Relations and Contingency analyses reveal other weaknesses, but as critiques they miss their mark. Classical theory is neither debunked nor extended.

In Chapter 3 I move on to a new criticism. I argue that data is meaningless without a theory to frame the problem being analysed. We allude to this when we say theory makes data into information. Theory defects lead to information defects. Fragmentation leads to but one of a number of possible information defects or uncertainties. When the facts of the situation are knowable, managers can usefully employ theory to guide their data collection and make deductions. When the facts are uncertain, management must employ other methods to frame and analyse problems – or else be irrational and, thereby, be beyond analysis.

Classical theory's inability to address uncertainty is so fundamental a weakness that it severely shapes our expectations of managerial theorizing. This criticism is not new, it gives the work of Simon, Child, Shubik, Knight, Thompson and Barnard its importance. As the chapter proceeds, I argue that admitting uncertainty creates a new place for the manager in management theory. The manager acquires a new function, going far beyond the rational data gathering and decision-making defined by classical theory. He becomes the creative artist, the person who uses his judgement to choose to create order out of disorder. In lieu of the classicists' economic or social man, or of Simon's 'administrative man', I propose 'choosing' man. Above all else, this suggests a creative uncertainty resolver who chooses his own versions of reality. As defined by Child's term 'strategic choice', this manager makes choices, for which he, rather than the data, must bear responsibility.

I begin with a review of Simon's concept of bounded rationality. This goes some way to introduce uncertainty at the lower level of the analysis. Child's concept of strategic choice introduces uncertainty at the upper level. Shubik, a mathematician and epistemologist, and Knight, an economist and philosopher, work with more general models which establish a basic typology of uncertainties. I then look at the managerial theory of Barnard, and the further analysis by Thompson. As the hypothesis comes together, it can be seen that it is merely an operationalized footnote to Barnard.

In this chapter I begin to address the research programme's underlying philosophical and methodological issues. As we move from Simon towards Barnard, despite their common commitment to science, we clearly abandon the positivistic approach into which most managerial theorists have been trained. We embrace Barnard's more pragmatic philosophy. I argue that managers are not really interested in the ultimate truth about a situation and assert instead that they are more interested in the 'cash value' of a particular way of thinking, in whether it works and helps them towards their goals.

Rejecting positivism is a serious step which raises many methodological issues. These will be explored in Chapter 4. I make this shift as a matter of strategic choice with respect to the current research. It cannot be justified logically. I might note, however, that although most management academics embrace positivism, most managers profess to being pragmatists. This philosophical gap is intriguing but peripheral to this research. Nor can we point to some 'straw man' barrenness of management theory and conclude that it cannot advance further without drawing managerial creativity into the analysis. Management theory is a large body of established thinking which provides much insight into many problems. My concern here is that it does little to help management deal with strategic problems, especially in uncertain environments; and this view is supported by my own subjective experience.

Within the positivistic tradition the organization is tangible and empirically observable. It is a thing which has substance, history and behaviour, about which there are facts. Abandoning this tradition,

I redefine the organization as the set of ideas which influence individual behaviour. The firm is a body of knowledge, what might now be called a 'knowledge-base'. The entrepreneurial manager discovers, copies, creates and manipulates information and ideas. From these he constructs the firm's unique rationality, vectored towards the firm's purposes and reflecting the firm's situation, as represented within these ideas.

3.2 Bounded Rationality

In Chapter 2 I have shown that in a democracy the role-occupant's relationship with the organization begins with his freely made decision to participate. It is then mediated by several distinct factors: his ability to fulfil the role's requirements, the training he receives and his motivation, whether he be searching for economic, social or emotional rewards.

Simon extends this typology. He argues that the *Zweckrationality* expected of the bureaucratic role-occupant is a demand which, by definition, is beyond any individual's abilities. People, being human, have but limited capacities to understand, remember and reason. Simon explains: 'administrative man is limited by the constraints that are part of his own psychological make-up; limited by the number of persons with whom he can communicate, the amount of information he can acquire and retain, and so forth. The fact that these limitations are not psychological and fixed, but are instead largely determined by social and organizational forces, creates problems of theory construction of great subtlety' (1952b: 1134). Thus, even if they fully intend to be rational, people are only limitedly so. March and Simon go on to propose three models of the individual:

1 functional, considering role-performance alone;
2 attitudinal, recognizing the problems of motivating people to participate in roles;
3 perceptual, recognizing the problems of integrating people of bounded rationality into roles. (1958: 6)

As we saw in Chapter 2, different models of the individual lead to different theories of management or, as Simon puts it, of administration. The adopted model of the individual defines the lower level problem which the theory must solve. Classical theory, assuming an unlimitedly rational individual, deals with motivating people to participate, and, because it separates the role from the occupant, with the design of roles. Simon's theory deals with the design of roles, and organizations, which function properly despite the individual's limitations.

Limited rationality cuts two ways. The more limited the individual, the more closely the role must be specified to ensure that he can handle it. Yet the more complex the specification the more the organization designer must rely on the individual's own, unspecified, responses. Simon's solution revolves around getting the individual to see things from the organization's point of view, sharing its perceptions. 'The elements entering into all but the most routine decisions are so numerous and so complex that it is impossible to control positively more than a few. Unless the subordinate himself is able to supply most of the premises of decision, and to synthesize them adequately, the task of supervision becomes hopelessly burdensome' (1957: 227).

Simon's point of departure is Tolman, the behavioural psychologist who 'treated man, and rat, as a goal-seeking, hence decision-making organism, whose behavior was moulded by the structure of the environment in which he sought to achieve his aims' (Newell & Simon 1972: 874). He neatly inverts Tolman's point, arguing that, since the environment can be controlled, people are thereby malleable: 'the task of administration is to so design this environment that the individual will approach as closely as practicable to rationality in his decisions' (1957: 241). The individual's limitations are a problem because of the discrepancies between the objective environment in which the economic actor really lives and the subjective environment that he perceives and to which he responds (1959).

The solution depends on the individual's ability to learn and internalize the organization's own system of constraints. Simon makes much of a distinction between facts and values. Facts are statements about the observable world and the way it operates. Facts are validated scientifically. Values are arbitrary, either validated socially, by the democratic process, or organizationally, by the policy-making process (1952a: 52). Organizational goals are both factual and valuational.

The notions of limited rationality, and the accompanying concept of satisficing, have not yet been operationalized. Nor have they led to major revisions of classical theory. Nor can they, for implicit in Simon's analysis is a concept of 'total rationality'. It has two components. First, Simon's rationality is to do with the objective facts of the means-ends chains leading to the organizational objectives.

Second, it has to do with the legitimacy of the values implicit in the organization's policy. Simon's assumption of total rationality reveals his hope that the organization designer can intellectually achieve the vantage point from which he can specify the roles, controls, training and information flows that are sufficient to deal with each differently limitedly rational employee. Simon's position is wholly managerial, a neo-Platonist image in which his administrators perform as philosopher-kings. The assumption is that the factual and valuational bases can be reconciled, so creating a coherent organizational rationality on which the design can be based. Ultimately Simon does no more than present Smith's, or Taylor's, science-based social reform theory in new words.

Whatever its shortcomings, Simon's analysis brings out two new points; overall, as Barnard remarks, it has the right feel (in Simon 1957: xii). Both points bear on Simon's great influence in this field. First, he focuses on the gap between total and limited rationality. From the individual's point of view, this captures wonderfully something of the uncertainty we feel about our grasp of the world. Since Simon seems, at first sight, to be dealing with the gap, he legitimates bringing uncertainty into organizational analysis. Second, Simon seems to be working towards a new prescriptive theory of administration. This breathes new life into the positivists' programme – and postpones the day when they have to make a significant place for managerial creativity in their theory. Thus Simon points to the route beyond classical theory, even though his philosophical commitments prevent him from making the journey himself.

3.3 Practical Rationality

Epistemology is the part of philosophy that deals with the structure of knowledge. Much modern epistemology, especially Jamesian pragmatism, focuses on practice rather than truth. It rejects a positivistic epistemology which asserts:

1 the knowability of the universe;
2 the factual nature of scientific knowledge;
3 the irrelevance of value-judgements. (Kolakowski 1972: 16)

Most epistemologists now argue that scientific knowledge is, at best, tentative and limitedly objective, waiting to be displaced by new levels and types of understanding. Even those who adopt the realist position implicit in accepting the eventual knowability of the universe, such as Popper (1968: 111), agree that complete objectivity is probably beyond us. The closest we can come is a relative objectivity, validated empirically against today's accumulated body of scientifically disciplined opinion. Kuhn's analysis of the history of science reminds us that this body changes during scientific crises and 'paradigm shifts' and that current acceptance is no guarantee of future acceptability (1970). However we react to such relativeness, we still depend on rationality to analyse our intentional goal-oriented activity. We see management as rationally directing organizational activity towards defined ends in a real physical, economic and social context.

But if rationality is not to be validated by reference to objective facts, how is it to be tested? Lukes argues that rationality comprises two distinct ideas (1967). First, it is logical, it is a framework for making valid deductions from premises. Second, it goes beyond logic in making assertions about the nature of reality. Positivism presumes these assertions must be grounded uncritically in sensory experience. A broader view is possible, with these assertions about reality being grounded elsewhere; such as by reading a holy book. The result is an alternative rationality. Thus Lukes defines a rationality as the conjunction of an abstract logical language, with which symbols can be manipulated, and some correspondence rules or beliefs relating these symbols to reality (1967: 261).

Simon, as a declared positivist, proposes two rationalities, one total, the other limited; the second necessarily being a subset of the first. Hence he writes of limited rather than alternative rationalities. But once we deny the possibility of total rationality, we must either abandon rationality altogether or open up the possibility of alternative rationalities. Cultural anthropology shows us that there are accepted action-oriented rationalities other than our own (Horton 1967; Horton & Finnegan 1973). Choosing one rather than another is a judgement. Given no clear knowledge of reality, there is no clear distinction between fact and value. Hence the judgement is neither a value-judgement nor a factual judgement.

Given such arbitrariness, we must recognize that when we look behind people's rationality we see interests rather than logical arguments. The notion of scientific objectivity is replaced by a relative objectivity grounded in the individual scientist's interests. If no one is able to achieve absolute objectivity people's choice of rationality must reflect, above all else, their interests. Thus the divergence of individual and organizational rationality, which is the fulcrum of Simon's theory, is the result of a divergence of individual and organizational interests. While Weber sees this as the reason why organizational order presupposes the exercise of power, Simon obfuscates rather than extends classical theory.

Ultimately policy decisions are about selecting the rationality that implements the organization's interests, seen as the value component, and that which allows its decisions to be analysed and conclusions drawn, the factual component. Buried in this policy process are those judgements which select the correspondence rules that management will use to define the firm's situation, what comprises its facts and reality. These are neither given nor self-evident. This is why, for instance, long range planning can begin only after management has laid down a comprehensive set of policies and 'planning assumptions'.

3.4 Strategic Choice

Child's historical researches show that managers make value-judgements about which policies to pursue. They also make choices about purely practical matters without bothering, or being able, to justify themselves (1964; 1968; 1973). Child argues these choices can only be understood in terms of management's interests, extending even to its choosing 'the context within which the organization is operating, to the standards of performance against which the pressure of economic restraints has to be evaluated, and to the design of the organisation's structure itself' (1972: 2). These are management's 'strategic choices'. They cannot be analysed in terms of the data presented to management, for, as Child argues, the data alone are clearly insufficient to determine these choices. A full analysis must reflect what management brings to its decision processes as it manifests its own interests. By recognizing the contextual data as defective and introducing managerial interests, Child introduces a new treatment of uncertainty into organizational analysis.

While Simon's empty arguments are well received, because they support the prevailing positivistic ideology, Child's arguments are both more practical and more radical. He shows that organizational analysis is invalid without direct enquiry into management's own interests and, in consequence, into the organization's political processes. Political theory must be brought into organizational theory to resolve the uncertainties he judges present in the contextual data.

He writes: 'when incorporating strategic choice in a theory of organisation, one is recognising the operation of a political process' (1972: 16). Child's influence is considerable. While not yet gaining him a Nobel prize, it has done much to re-legitimate the longitudinal analyses which alone can reveal the workings of organizational politics. It has also repaired the relationship between Organization Theory and Business History.

3.5 Types of Uncertainty

Simon is suggestive when he talks of different sources of limited rationality; incomplete information, unstable values and inadequate mental capacity (1957: 81). Other writers, unaware of their positivistic philosophic commitments, so misunderstand the impasse into which organization theory has fallen that they define uncertainty as a measurable attribute, principally of the environment (Lawrence & Lorsch 1967; Duncan 1972). Gifford et al. note, after an extensive review of this research, that 'although there is general agreement on the importance of uncertainty in the organisational design literature, there is little commonality among researchers or theorists regarding the meaning of uncertainty or ways to measure it' (1979: 459).

In his classic economic text, Knight differentiates uncertainty from risk (1965). Risk is the result of probabilistic information. Probability theory presumes certainty at the population level. Uncertainty is the result of ignorance, the lack of information, probabilistic or otherwise. Given that uncertainty is not here defined – or definable – theoretically, Knight resorts to a pragmatic test. Risks are those economic events which are insurable, simply because insurers act on the belief that they are certain at the population level. In economic affairs, uncertainty is what cannot be insured.

Others, such as Hurwicz, argue that making any kind of choice requires the decision-maker to evaluate probabilities, therefore Knight's distinction is empty. This criticism is itself empty, a mere presumption of the point these critics wish to prove. If, as they presume, all decision-making is logical, then it follows that all decision-making behaviour must be reduced to terms that allow it to be fitted into that model. Hence these critics presume away Knight's vision of what uncertainty and judgement can bring to economic analysis.

Shubik goes further than Knight. He establishes two dimensions of uncertainty by differentiating between situations in which information is available but incomplete and situations that are inherently unknowable. Our ignorance about things differs from our ignorance about people, for people are creative actors like ourselves. Economic indeterminacy, Shubik argues, is the result of our uncertainty about how others will respond to our actions.

At the 'epistemological origin', the place of total knowledge, incompleteness and indeterminacy are no longer different. We know what determines the other person's behaviour. It is no longer a matter of choice for him, nor surprise for us. If uncertainties merge at the origin, it is because they are not really different. How then can a typology of uncertainties be useful? Here I argue only that it is useful to distinguish these types of uncertainty because they may suggest different uncertainty coping mechanisms. Our focus is on managerial behaviour, and a typology of uncertainties may lead to a typology of behaviours. Thus we adopt a pragmatic criterion rather than a truth or logic based one. The shift from a positivistic framework to a pragmatic one is implicit in the treatment of rationality discussed above. Rather than abandon all criteria, and descend into anarchic relativism, we adopt pragmatic criteria.

But this logically entails two other types of uncertainty. I have already mentioned correspondence rules. If we cannot tell whether our beliefs about reality are indeed facts, we must recognize that our thinking may be irrelevant, that is not attached to the phenomena being analysed. Second, we cannot be sure that our correspondence rules are coherent, that they are consistent with each other. This kind of uncertainty is widely recognized as the problem of comparing 'apples with oranges', of comparing things that are unalike when we cannot quantify our information on a common basis. Coase (1937: 388) and Barnard (1968) deal with it in some detail. Simon also deals with it in an early paper (1962: 2).

3.6 Management's Response to Uncertainty

The typology of information defects runs to four items:

1 Incompleteness – ignorance of what can be known.
2 Indeterminacy – the unpredictability of others.
3 Irrelevance – to the reality being analysed.
4 Incommensurability – of the ideas and measures used.

Each type suggests a different managerial response. Incompleteness can be met by a search for further information. Scientifically trained people have a tendency to spend too much time and money on information search in uncertain situations. They are used to bringing a clear theory to a situation, so they can see immediately where information is lacking. More pragmatic people tend to see costs, both in the information gathering process and in delaying the decision. Deciding that the problem is one of information shortage is, itself, a significant strategic decision. Ultimately, when the costs of further search are too high, management must act on the basis of whatever information is available. Such defects as remain must be dealt with by making intelligent guesses, or with some other stratagem such as finding parallel cases.

Indeterminacy occurs outside the organization – the unanticipatable reactions of those with power over the organization. It is dealt with politically in the policy process. Or it occurs internally – the unanticipated reactions of those in organizational roles. Here it is dealt with by the exercise of power or, given a more Human Relations approach, by winning the hearts and minds of the dissenters and motivating their participation.

Indeterminacy is most clearly explored in political thinking and in game theory, its abstracted form. Game theory has been applied widely to management (Shubik, 1956, 1960; Bierman et al. 1961; Raiffa 1982), although McGuire writes that 'the promise of game theory, foreseen so clearly in 1944, has not yet materialised' (1964: 139). Nevertheless game theory illustrates well how managers cope with uncertainty. When the information about the players is certain, game theory provides perfectly adequate solutions which can be determined by the analyst as an objective third party. But once we move away from two-person zero-sum games towards N person non-zero-sum games, this arm's length thinking breaks down with 'many difficulties that appear most intractable to investigators' (McGuire 1964:156). A two-person non-zero-sum game is actually an incompletely defined situation. Solving it requires supplemental information, provided by the decision-maker himself in the form of his choice criterion. This states his value system with respect to the game. Miller and Starr see four choice criteria: pessimism, optimism, regret and rationality (1960: 86). These convey additional information in that they are equally available within the specification of the game, the player can choose whichever he wishes. Information reduces uncertainty. Completely defined situations contain their conclusions.

The player needs to make a policy choice only when the situation is incomplete, that is when he has alternatives.

Dealing with irrelevance is familiar to anyone who has argued that a situation is a reoccurrence of a previous situation, only to be told that it is a 'new ball game'. Note that the difficulty of correctly characterizing situations is our rationale for exposing business students to as wide a range of models as possible. Given that we can never prove any one model correct, we advise our students to depend on 'gut feelings' to guide their choices.

The earlier chapters focused on incommensurability as the most fundamental type of uncertainty. It is uncertainty that renders managerial theory so problematic as a source of analytic frameworks for practising management. The grandest theoretical achievements we know are the long-term resolutions of uncertainty, specifically of incommensurable frameworks; Newton's bringing together of mechanics and astronomy, Maxwell's resolution of electricity and magnetism, Einstein's resolution of the previous incommensurability of energy and mass. As we have seen in the field of social science, Smith's combination of individual self-interest with ordered markets similarly achieves grand theory. Managers have more modest objectives as theorists, but greater concerns about whether their resolutions lead to predictable consequences and a sense of control. Though the managerial and scientific objectives differ, the process of theory-building is the same, and is equally a manifestation of the theory-builder's interests, be they profit, intellectual delight, fame or worship.

Here we see the organizational version of the general principle of human creativity, that is that managers ultimately cope with the residue of uncertainty in their information by resolving it creatively from within themselves. When the problem is incompletely specified, the manager's choice is a true act of judgement. Locke writes: 'the faculty which God has given man to supply the want of clear and certain knowledge in cases where it cannot be had, is judgement . . . The mind sometimes exercises this judgement out of necessity, where demonstrative proofs and certain knowledge are not to be had; and sometimes out of laziness, unskilfulness or haste, even where demonstrative proofs are to be had' (1928: 298). Another way of expressing this is to describe an uncertain situation as under-determined or open-ended. The act of judgement which resolves the uncertainties achieves logical closure, creating a well-formed closed universe of discourse in which any statable premises can be thought through to an unambiguous conclusion. The administrative problem that Simon describes is that the role situation is open so long as the individual is likely to adopt his own divergent rationality.

The act of judgement can also be seen as superposing a logically complete framework onto an under-specified or ill-structured package of descriptive data. The manager will focus on reaching specific goals in a specific situation; he has measurable responsibility for action and results. Academics have different interests and will choose different frameworks. They are interested in statements, generalization and theory production. Such divergence leads managers to regard academics as unrealistic, while academics view managers as parochial. Neither is more rational or realistic than the other. Both focus on different aspects of the uncertainties in the situation and, in their own ways, attempt to advance to their different objectives.

3.7 Organizational Politics

Several authors, including Child, March and Simon, and Pettigrew see organizational coalition-making as the process by which organizations resolve their uncertainties. This applies especially to the incommensurabilities arising from internal conflicts and differences of managerial interests, and puts the focus on the middle level of our managerial model. Here the theorist replaces the model of the individual creative manager with creative group processes, generally without being adequately specific about the processes of group formation and maintenance. He fails to answer why people should participate in his group process, and so begs the most basic question of organization. But it also suggests, correctly, that an organizational theory that incorporates a strong theory of coalition formation would be able to deal with many uncertainties at the upper level. Business historians typically explain the progress of the firm in terms of the rise and fall of various competing coalitions.

Pettigrew takes this to its logical conclusion, observing the way political pressures influence not only the policy-making but also the formal structure and process of the firm (1973). Politically motivated control of the flow of information affects the reality that people experience. Subordinates' withholding of information, especially bad news, and failing to correct misunderstandings are favourite political attacks on superiors. Conversely, failing to inform and direct subordinates who are later measured on their performance is a different attack. At the extreme, this kind of politicking puts the organization into a state of continuous revolution, with objectives, structure and process all forever under-defined. The firm becomes indistinguishable from society at large, without identity or boundary, and the theory of organizations collapses into a theory of political groups and processes.

There is much organizational behaviour that can be illuminated from this theoretical viewpoint, and it appeals to my own experience of organizational politics. But often speaking of politics is more of a theoretical bolt-hole than a means of illumination. We are seldom sure how 'politics' is defined, and we lose any sense of the organization as an entity separable from the individuals taking part in it. Organizations become societies writ small, rejecting Toennies's initial insight. In this monograph, I treat the organization as something that exists in the minds of its creators and other participants; that behaviour-modifying sense of prior purpose, the separation of role and occupant and ongoing constructed order which, for most authors, defines an organization.

Since March and Simon import politics as the conflict resolver of last resort, where the really wicked uncertainties are resolved, they are able to propose a theory of managers as uncertainty avoiders. They fail to explain how the ever-present informational defects are, in practice, resolved. However, I agree that managers attempt to avoid uncertainties. The stratagems they adopt, copying others who do not avoid uncertainty, are an integral element of my theory.

3.8 The Organizational Boundary

The organization's boundary seems clearly defined in a bureaucracy. The organization consists of defined roles, standard procedures, and an integrated rationality, as well as the resources available to perform in the role. But in Chapter 2 I argued that policy setting takes place outside the logical boundary of bureaucratic organization. Strictly speaking, the process belongs to the owners. They do not act bureaucratically, they create the organization. In practice, the owners generally delegate this right to the senior executives. Fayol remarks that the shareholders' role is 'very restricted' (1949: 61). Veblen, Berle and Means and later Nichols (1969), Child (1969) and Zeitlin (1974) all address the evident transfer of power from owners to managers.

The reasons for this transfer were evident long before the Industrial Revolution. Owners can only retain absolute control by being present and overseeing the day to day affairs of the firm. This is precisely because frequent decisions need to be made to keep the business running. Since many of these are 'wicked' uncertainty resolving decisions, the owners cannot adequately programme them into standard operating procedures. As soon as the owners delegate to others, either because there is too much for them to do, or because they wish to be elsewhere, they lose their intimate contact with the changing terrain of the business. They cut themselves off from the information flows which are the springs and courses of organizational power. They expose themselves to even greater uncertainty.

The availability of authoritively able and trustworthy people, to whom the day to day affairs can be delegated, delimits the pace at which business and industry can grow. Pollard notes that the rapid expansion of industry which we call the Industrial Revolution accelerated delegation and the adoption of new materials and techniques, such as double entry bookkeeping. It also made owners increasingly dependent on a new class of professional managers (1968: 168). This, in turn, profoundly affected national educational systems, which were reoriented towards producing people capable of joining this new class.

The transfer of power weakens our intuitive sense of the organizational boundary, if only because we are confused about whether the boundary is tangible or conceptual. We have a sense that people are either part of the firm or not, resources belong to the firm or they do not. But owners who might be eager to transfer policy-making to managers, use external auditors to ensure there is no similar transfer of resources. Since people are part of the organization only while they are performing in its roles, it seems that it is the roles which define the organization and its boundary. Nor is this quite adequate, for organizational activity also tends to create different kinds of roles for outsiders. A large manufacturing enterprise creates roles for sub-contractors just as military campaigns create opportunities for camp-followers. Long-term customers are embraced in reciprocal behavioural norms. These external roles, which are important to the organization and can frequently be managed to good effect, are evidence that an organization can influence its environment. This complicates the notion of boundary again, suggesting that each theory of the organization carries its own boundary concept. In fact, the boundary is simply a facet of the theory. It cannot be detached from a theory and reattached to the organization in any unproblematic way, because the organization itself is undefined without the theory.

The notion that managers are uncertainty resolvers and theory-builders is part of a theory of the firm as a body of knowledge manifesting a specific and purposive rationality. The organizational boundary is the conceptual divide separating the firm's rationality from other rationalities, those individual and social patterns of thought and behaviour that would remain unchanged if the organization ceased to exist. While strategic decisions are made within this boundary, and so must follow the creation of the firm's rationality, policy decisions are made prior to and without reference to that rationality. In this sense policy is made in the social, technical and political environment in which the organization is embedded. Strategy is the process of articulating the policy choices within the rationality of the business. Thus policy and strategy differ to the extent that these rationalities differ.

The fact that managers might be making policy decisions, along with the strategic, administrative and operational decisions, does not mean these decisions are of the same type. First, they make policy decisions as citizens and are increasingly held accountable for the effects of these decisions. It does not impress us that a substance is a source of private profit, when that fact is offered as a defence against the charge that the substance is a danger to public health.

3.9 Thompson and Systems Thinking

Given the notion of the organization as a knowledge-base, a purely intellectual construct, the organization boundary is really a way of referring to the processes through which the environmental and organizational rationalities interact. The three level model also allows the organization to become manifest as a separable viable system interacting in other ways with its socio-economic environment. Goods and services are exchanged through many external markets. Although I have not stressed these systems aspects, all the theorists discussed, from Smith to Simon and Child, adopt this same image. They vary, of course, in the degree to which their conclusions are determined by systems thinking. Some, such as Dutton (1927) and Fayol, see the organization as a biological organism, and speak of nervous systems. This can usefully extend the mechanical metaphor implicit in bureaucratic theory towards the neurological metaphors adopted by some cyberneticians (Beer 1972). Systems thinking shifts the focus away from structure and substance, and onto the processes of exchange, transformation and order maintenance.

Thompson uses systems thinking to bring uncertainty into organizational analysis in a way that is different from Simon's limitedly rational individuals and Child's political processes. He begins with Gouldner's distinction between closed and open systems. The first models the organization as isolated and manageable, the second treats it as embedded in an active environment and exposed to outside forces. Instead of attempting a theoretical integration, he sees this exposure as a fundamental type of uncertainty which can be used to define a key activity for management. 'Uncertainty appears as the fundamental problem for complex organisations, and coping with uncertainty as the essence of the administrative process' (1967, 159). Thompson's great insight is his proposition that organizational maintenance in the face of ongoing interactions with the environment means absorbing these uncertainties into the organization. The organization becomes less organized and coherent, its rationality becomes less comprehensive. But this must not go too far, to the point at which the inner manageable core of purposes, beliefs and values is disturbed. So Thompson argues that there must be specialized boundary spanning or uncertainty absorbing units.

Thompson sees a two-dimensional matrix of uncertainties somewhat similar to Shubik's with:

1 incomplete information; and
2 contingency (indeterminacy). (1967: 159)

Management's task is 'providing boundaries within which organisational rationality becomes possible' (1967: 162). Unfortunately Thompson does not deal with the process of the boundary spanning units, except to propose a division of managerial labour between 'adaptive' and 'directive' administration (1967: 148). Nor does he deal with integrating the different activities into a theory for the organization as a whole. Though his analysis clearly frames the problem of uncertainty, he does not carry it through to a theory of the open organization. His thinking remains as fragmented as classical theory.

Thompson creates a two domain model with the boundary-spanning rationality enveloping the core rationality. This suggests a two-step process of organizational management. The first step resolves the uncertainties, creating a rational domain in which subordinates can act without exposure to uncertainty. This restates the policy and strategy difference in systems terms, stressing the logical primacy of the policy decisions. The two-step model is also similar to Ashby's theory of responsive systems.

3.10 The Theory of the Executive

Barnard's treatment of uncertainty is by far the most profound of those discussed in this chapter. It is enriched by Barnard's considerable executive experience, for he rose to a very senior level at Bell Telephone and subsequently moved into the Washington bureaucracy. He was also a scholar of high attainment, especially in his study of Pareto. Apart from his interest in Henderson's systems thinking, he felt little need to analyse or refer to other management literature (Henderson 1970).

Barnard builds a new model of the organization which leaves a place for management's creativity. This contribution, which Barnard calls 'leadership', treats managers as the essential mechanism for resolving uncertainty. He focuses on the fourth kind of uncertainty, incommensurability. His model consists of three subordinate systems or 'economies': the physical resources, the individual employees and the relationships between the organization and its environment. We might call these the physical, the motivational and the social sub-systems. These are part of the environment. They exist irrespective of whether the organization exists, they are logically prior to the organization. Barnard argues that management brings these three together into purposeful and co-ordinated activity, and thereby creates the organization as a viable self-sustaining system (1968: 251). The uncertainty with which management must deal arises from the incommensurability of these systems. While each sub-system is coherent and analysable in itself, the interactions which make up the organizational system are at a different level of complexity and subtlety. Barnard writes: 'the respective economies are heterogeneous between themselves, and widely variable as between the corresponding economies in other coöperative systems. They do not admit of quantitative comparison' (1968: 287).

Barnard does not provide a theory to address this uncertainty and so proscribe management's reaction; quite to the contrary. He argues instead that organizations experience limitations, which he calls their 'strategic factors'. These can arise in any of the four systems. But, he argues, the most crucial and typical limiting factor is leadership, and its absence is typically experienced most sharply in the organizational system (1968: 288). Barnard implies that leadership ability is a personal trait or ability to cope with uncertainty, particularly with that of bringing the sub-systems together. Barnard adds: 'these conceptions are, on the whole, new and not now understood or adopted. They are theoretical and their role is limited to the present analysis and description of coöperative systems. They are, however, taken into account in specific situations by those skilled in the executive arts' (1968: 287).

Here Barnard succeeds in bringing management's contribution into the centre of the analysis in ways the positivist tradition can barely express. No other writer addresses the question of managerial judgement quite so directly, and Andrews writes: 'Barnard's purpose is to provide a comprehensive theory of co-operative behaviour in formal organisations . . . his business has not yet been completed or his conceptual approach rendered obsolete' (in Barnard 1968: vii, xxi). Simon, who is significantly influenced by Barnard, touches on this kind of uncertainty when considering whether economics and organization theory are, in fact, commensurate (1952a: 41). Thompson, more obviously following Barnard's line, displays a clearer desire to carry his model further (1967). Few other authors choose incommensurability as the vehicle to bring uncertainty into organizational analysis, perhaps because they are trained to focus only on positivistic notions. They may also be overly sensitive to the difficulty of operationalizing Barnard's concepts.

The study of leadership, like that of creativity and entrepreneurship, is paradoxical. The concept is so powerful that it is both a cause and an explanation of everything we want to know about society and, maybe, ourselves. As cultural anthropologists and other students of myth know, we cannot approach this topic too directly. We need some way of testing rather than assuming the idea that the leader's contribution differs materially from that of the led. Here Thompson's work is valuable, for he talks of creating domains of activity so conceptually ordered that they are materially different from normal social life. This takes us back to Weber, but focuses greater attention on the substance and process of developing a *Zweckrationality* and of making it manifest as a social belief system. Barnard argues that the leader's raw material is in the organization's environment, logically prior to the business. The leader draws the socially given constituents together and transforms them in some way so that they synthesize into a new, distinctive rationality or universe of meaning.

3.11 Another Look at Policy and Strategy

In this chapter I explore criticisms of classical theory's principal defect, that it excludes uncertainty and so excludes managers as contributing agents. These criticisms are productive because they shift the focus onto managers as resolvers of many types of uncertainty. Management is now given the task of generating conceptual order in an environment disordered by the uncertainty introduced by each author. Simon's source of disorder is the unpredictable rationality of the limitedly rational employee. Child's source is the political process through which managers make their interests felt. Thompson's source is the environment, which displays uncertainties the organization must internalize. Barnard's source is the same environment, but with the uncertainty spelt out in terms of the incommensurabilities of the sub-systems that bring the environment together with the firm.

These criticisms, in suggesting a new theory of organizations, also suggest a new answer to why organizations exist, something left unclear in classical theory. As quoted previously, Barnard writes: 'coöperation justifies itself as a means of overcoming the limitations restricting what individuals can do' (1968: 23). It is now clear that Barnard is not here referring to the mechanical aspects of co-operation, as one might in talking about how a gang of men can move a rock a single man has no chance of moving. He is referring to intellectual co-operation, the process of transforming our ideas and knowledge about problems. Simon grasps only part of this when he writes: 'it is only because individual human beings are limited in knowledge, foresight, skill and time that organisations are useful instruments for the achievement of human purpose; and only because organised human beings are limited in their ability to agree on goals, to communicate, and to co-operate that organising becomes a problem' (1952b: 1134). Barnard sees leadership as the final component in a theory of the organization as a knowledge making system.

Any benefit from organizations is completely balanced by the difficulty of creating and managing them. The two aspects are completely interdependent. Such balance, or double edgeness, is a general truth of all technology. We adopt technologies because they transform rather than solve our problems. We exchange one problem, which we find difficult, for another we judge easier to handle. Being optimistic about our ability to control the world and our future, we tend to ignore the downside. So technology gives us many unpleasant surprises; we discover it is difficult to control and we generally fail to extract its expected benefits.

Introducing uncertainty in these ways gives new meaning to the terms 'policy' and 'strategy'. Both are uncertainty resolving processes, different from the administrative and operational decisions which take place within the organization's defined rationality. Equally, Child's concept of strategic choice has force because the uncertainties resolved in the policy process are different from those resolved in the process of making strategy. This difference becomes institutionalised when there is a division of managerial labour within the firm, along the lines suggested by Thompson, with policy and strategy made by different people. This is typical of the divisionalized firm.

Policy is framed in terms of the alternative objectives which can be legitimately pursued within the socio-economic context. Policy choosing is inherently political and takes place within the partly legally structured but multiple rationalities of a capitalistic democracy. The policy process reflects the separate interests of the firm's owners and those others with legal or other powers over the firm. These interests can be commensurable, but still contradictory or mutually exclusive, in which case resolving them is not a matter of coping with uncertainty, it is more of a political contest. Uncertainty arises when these interests are incommensurable or are incompletely presented, incompletely understood, produce disturbing reactions when presented, or are irrelevant or unrealistic given the firm's context. Neither the policy process nor its output is necessarily rational in Lukes's sense of being both logical and realistic.

Strategy-making takes place within the context of these already made policy choices. Its output is the constructed rationality which is the intellectual essence of that organization, its roles, processes, standards and procedures. The strategic process is creative in the sense that theory-building creates knowledge from data. Strategy creates order in a disordered environment. The result of the process is the theory of the firm which, in Thompson's metaphor, surrounds the core of rational activities. The strategist creates order and predictability for those whose functions are either administrative, applying the technology of administration, or operational, applying the technology of production.

Strategy is the process which creates the middle level of the three level model with which I began this enquiry. It brings about what, following Toennies, was previously presupposed, that is that organizations are analytically unlike either societies or individuals.

I have now framed a theory of management which is actually a theory of managerial cognition focused on the managerial response to organizational uncertainties. Of the various types of uncertainty, incommensurability is that which stands most clearly in the way of creating a context for subordinates' rational activity. Irrelevance remains the deepest epistemological problem, but that does not stand in the way of constructing a rationality based on false beliefs about reality. Indeed, most employees have experienced that sense that the company's decision-makers live in a different world to the one they experience. We can only see when management fail to resolve the problem of relevance, in the sense of choosing policies and strategies appropriate to what the organization eventually experiences, after the fact.

3.12 Theory Building

Implying parallels between Barnard's concept of leadership and conventional concepts of theory-building requires us to look carefully at the relationship between data and theory.

We use theory to make sense of, or information out of, data which is otherwise raw sensory experience. The pragmatist's view differs from that of the positivist. Without philosophizing more than necessary to bring out a few essential differences, we can say the pragmatist sees no necessary relationships or consistency between his ideas about reality. His universe does not have to be logically constructed. Such ideas as we do hold are conveniences. Even though they work, in the sense that they allow us to predict our experience of the universe, they may still be fictions. Theories become statements about the relationships between ideas, not statements about reality.

Tarski points out that theory-building draws previously unrelated ideas into a logically consistent relationship (1965: 130). For example, prior to Maxwell's theory of electromagnetism, its constituents, electricity and magnetism, were known but not logically or mathematically related. Experiments did not create the theory, they only suggested a relationship. An inductive generalization is not a theory since, without the constituent ideas being logically related, we cannot be sure it is internally consistent.

The theory-building process cuts two ways. It produces closure onto an internally consistent system of meanings, but it also separates the constituent ideas off from their previous meanings. Each of the ideas produces terms whose meanings are wholly defined by the other terms. Thus force, acceleration and mass are co-defined by Newton's Laws of Motion. The previous meanings of 'force' and 'mass' were abandoned. A theory expands when it is integrated with others which share the same definitions. But the process of enlargement is generally one of synthesis, and only achieved along with some adjustment of previous meanings. Thus Einstein again redefines mass, indicating relativistic rather than Newtonian mass, when relating mass and energy.

Another illustration of the process of theory-building, which does much to explain the persistence of two by two matrices in management literature, is Lazarsfeld's property-space (Lazarsfeld & Rosenberg 1955:40n). Here we have an area defined by the conjunction of two variables, say P and Q. These are displayed as the axes of the matrix. All events that can be mapped into the matrix (the property-space) must be measurable in both P and Q terms. In a two by two matrix the scoring is binary, but in principle the scoring can be binary, integer or continuous. The scoring of P is completely independent of the scoring of Q.

We can use the property-space to illustrate some of the counter-intuitive aspects of the universe of discourse which now lies within it. First, it does not contain the events, merely their representations as scores in the P and Q languages. They are separated from the scores by our methods of observing and scoring. Prior to our theorizing, the property-space is open and purely descriptive. The matrix is a way of displaying and categorizing the scores. It also is specific to these (P, Q) events, so implying the existence of other events which cannot be referred to or categorized in the matrix. A descriptive matrix presents data such as 'the number of (P, non-Q) events is 27'. Any statements we make are grounded in the world that precedes the matrix. We cannot make statements about the relationships between the different domains of the matrix.

A theory proposes relationships between the different parts of the matrix. It puts us in a position to make new statements which could not be made until after the matrix was created. Such statements are instances of the theory, members of an infinite family of possible logical entailments of the theory. The statements are tautologies, correct only if they can be proven from the assumptions of the theory.

They are not statements about reality. The process of theory-building redefines the P and Q languages, making them independent of the correspondence rules which previously gave them meaning. P and Q are now redefined in terms of each other. The previous universe of discourse was descriptive, grounded in inductive generalizations whose meanings were based in observational procedures. The new universe of discourse is a logical one, bounded by these new languages. There is no necessary relationship between statements in the previous languages and those in the new universe of meaning. Similarly, no other language can be admitted, an issue explored in epistemology as Hempel's Paradox (1966). Since we have severed the connection with the empirical bases of the previous languages, if we assert that our theory says something about reality, we imply a different set of correspondence rules. These are developed as we test the new theory.

This indirect interaction between the theory of observation, which is the 'old' language that allows us to make statements based on these correspondence rules, and the 'new' language of the theory being tested is generally overlooked. It makes Baconian critical experiments impossible to assess. There are not even, as Popper would have it, conclusive refutations. Einstein captured it clearly in his alleged remark that 'if the facts don't fit the theory, change the facts'. The traditional positivistic attitude to observational data leads to much unnecessary confusion about testing a theory. Popper's falsificationism is naive and only tenable to those who accept empirical evidence uncritically, as if no correspondence rules, procedures and observational theorizing were involved. Our confidence in the impact of evidence on theory arises because we believe the experiential and analytic contexts to be well matched. These issues, which are also explored in Bridgman's Operationalism, can only be matters of judgement.

3.13 Shared Judgements

A judgement, according to Kant, is a conclusion drawn from premises. Judgements may be 'analytic' or 'synthetic'. When the premises are complete and consistent, they contain the conclusion. The process of drawing out the conclusion is analytic, strictly logical and closed. Locke terms this 'demonstrable proof'. The process is objective and independent of the deducer who must not add anything to it. 'Synthetic' judgements are open; the conclusion is not contained in the premises alone. As Ayer argues, the conclusion goes beyond the premises (1946: 77). This is not quite right. For there to be a conclusion, there must be a complete set of premises. The question is about where these premises come from, and their logical status. In an analytic decision the 'decider' and the process of decision are passive. There is no addition to the data. A computer is such a decider. It cannot cope with incomplete data.

In a synthetic decision there must be an active decider. The person judging supplies premises additional to those given in the data, and the conclusion manifests him rather than goes beyond him. He and the conclusion become part of each other. The seeming objectivity of the analytic process disappears. Such creativity brings something of the synthesizer's private self into the social world. Having no 'self', a computer cannot make synthetic decisions, though we might make the computer appear more active by programming it to access and search a database for additional premises whenever it is asked to reach a conclusion with incomplete premises. This gives the computer a piece of the programmer's 'self'.

If, as I surmise, policy and strategy decision premises are incomplete in any of the ways suggested by the previously established types of uncertainty, then it follows that these decisions are synthetic rather than analytic. Operational and administrative decisions, as I define them, are analytic. Such theory as might be advanced about these decisions must capture this vital distinction and so avoid a categorical error of the most major kind.

The work of Barnard and Thompson shows that the first step in organizational management is the resolution of uncertainty alone, so creating a coherent and closed rationality. The problem, taken as a whole, must be broken into its components, differentiating the synthetic and analytic components. The second step is then analytic, strictly logical within that created rationality.

Creating a new rationality creates, at the same time, problems with establishing its logical and empirical status. We can test the resulting rationality for internal consistency, that is logicality. But we are in much greater difficulty when we consider the implicit correspondence rules. We must assure ourselves that we are considering the correct rules before we can usefully research this two-step process. In the absence of a secure test against reality, we can only test this correctness against our own subjective choice or that of the decision-maker being investigated. Clearly, we cannot dismiss another's beliefs simply because they differ from our own, so this seems to be no test at all. I discuss the questions of integrity and validity in Chapter 4, which focuses on research method.

The most immediate difficulty is with operationalizing the theory of the manager as a creative uncertainty resolver. So long as we focus on a single person's creative judgements, we are perilously close to destructive relativism and we have to find some method of controlling this.

There are several alternatives, all of which are visible within the literature. First, we can presume that judgement is a personal quality, inhering in the person and unrelated to the substance of the decision process. This is sometimes called 'traitism'. It proposes that if we show good judgement we do so in all our decisions, whether it be in choosing spouses, Derby winners or our company's products. Thus we can record the outcome of several decisions and regard them as members of a single population which we associate with a particular decision-maker. Second, we can categorize decisions on structural grounds, arranging them on a spectrum of, say, ambiguity. We can record the outcome of different types of decision and draw conclusions such as Person A does well with low-ambiguity problems, while Person B does better with high-ambiguity decisions. Thirdly, we can categorize decisions on content, arguing perhaps that Person C is good with customer complaints while Person D knows how to write good advertising copy.

All of these alternatives treat the individual as an isolated decision-making unit. Another dimension of alternatives opens up as soon as we consider group processes. These can cause individuals to share their judgements. We can see group decisions emerging after strict parliamentary procedure, or after informal polling of various members' positions, or after scientific analysis of the alternative outcomes, etc. However shared judgements are developed, we can discover this by researching the group's members cross-sectionally, treating them as representative members of a supposedly homogeneous decision-making body.

If, as I argue, analysis follows synthesis, we can separate the two steps. We can apply different models of individual process to the different parts. My research hypothesis is that managers facing the synthetic step of the problem, having to create a rationality for the firm, have a choice. They can either synthesize a new rationality for themselves or they can communicate with others facing similar problems and search for an existing group solution.

A group-oriented strategy is more than simple uncertainty avoid-

ance. The test of a rationality is experience, whether it works.
Managers also learn, adjusting or abandoning prior rationalities as
they reflect on their experiences. The group is a resource because it
has a much wider body of experience than the individual. Note also
that when individuals adopt rationalities that lead to the demise of
their firm, the group learning is strong, maybe even stronger than
when they see success.

Each firm's circumstances will be different, so the group process
will function only as advice, not as a completely prescriptive solution.
Thus my hypothesis is that individual managers will make up their
own minds, but will recognize the need to:

1 be logical in drawing conclusions within their chosen rationality;
2 accept the useful opinions of their referent groups;
3 modify their beliefs in the light of their experiences.

This reshapes the hypothesis into one that can be operationalized by
researching the group's shared rationality.

3.14 The Industry Recipe

Much research has investigated shared meaning structures, especially
within the phenomenology of everyday life (Schutz 1967, 1970a,
1970b, 1972). Berger and Luckman, following Schutz, argue that
social interaction inevitably builds up a set of mutual expectations
which, when confirmed, are treated as social understanding. Interaction leads to communicating and, maybe, a sharing of judgement
and rationality. This is the process of socialization which produces,
inter alia, an understanding of how others deal with uncertainty.

Schutz sees discrete bodies of context-oriented understanding into
which the individual must be socialized if he is to meet his fellows'
expectations and so form part of any organization. He calls these the
'recipes' of everyday life (1944: 505; 1967: 13). When the organization is created for a chosen purpose, directed towards an agreed
objective, the resulting recipe is a human artefact. But the individual
already socialized into a recipe is unaware of the processes by which
it is generated and modified. It becomes 'common sense', an
uncritically accepted body of scarcely articulated knowledge. In this
sense, the sciences are a collection of heterogeneous recipes for dealing
with the problems defined by the current conventions of the science.
The science's objectivity is relative, measured by the extent to which

the discipline's characteristic recipes are shared.

Recipes apply to and are grounded in particular contexts of experience (Glaser & Strauss 1967). Each socially adept individual becomes familiar with a variety of recipes, each corresponding to a different organizational or social role. Clearly, individuals apply different patterns of belief to family life, religious affairs, the workplace and so forth. So long as each context brings him into contact with a different set of people whose expectations must be met, he will need to sustain different roles.

There is still a tension between any recipe, the individual's independent sense of self and his ability to respond creatively to uncertainty. The individual will disaggregate his experience and judge different parts relevant to different contexts. He can then achieve some degree of objectivity, setting his own experience against the shared beliefs of that context. Cognitive dissonance may result from divergencies and contradictions between different contexts. This may cause the individual to abandon his independent belief, or to involve others in resolving that dissonance. As others begin to share the individual's view, the dissonance can develop into a publicly accepted anomaly, and eventually lead to changes in the recipe (Kuhn 1970: 77).

For Schutz, the recipe is a shared pattern of beliefs that the individual can choose to apply to his experience in order to make sense of it, so that his response can be rational. Its four-fold function corresponds directly to the four types of uncertainty. These are resolved by specifying:

1 acceptable amounts of data;
2 ways of forecasting unspecified responses;
3 relevant contexts of activity; and
4 ways of drawing the various considerations together into a coherent rationality.

Schutz's use of the term 'recipe' is similar to Kuhn's use of the term 'paradigm'. However, as Masterman notes, there is considerable ambiguity about Kuhn's meaning (1970). There is closer convergence with the term 'heuristic'. Newell et al. defined this as: 'any principle that contributes to a reduction in search time' (1958: 22). Alternatively, Kuehn and Hamburger note that a heuristic adds something to the problem definition, so making it solvable. However, the heuristic's defining characteristic is that it is not logically connected to the problem. The solution's status, whether it is suboptimal or even legitimate, cannot be established (1963: 645). Simon, and later Clarkson, researches methods of making heuristics explicit by getting decision-makers to verbalize their process. The result is a decision protocol, defined as 'a transcript of the verbalised thought and actions of a subject when the subject has been instructed to think or problem-solve aloud' (Clarkson & Meltzer 1960 : 474n). Clarkson subsequently expands this to analyse investment activity. The trust officer is asked to read articles from financial journals and analysts' reports and to comment on the ideas, forecasts, facts, and so forth presented (in Cyert & March 1963: 256).

A recipe is not a theory. Nor is it a formula, which is a statement of a theory. Theories, and the tautological statements that articulate them, are closed. A recipe is open; it does not resolve the uncertainties at the individual level, only some of those at the group level. It is a guide to action, not an abstraction. It assumes correspondence rules which tie it to a specific context or universe of action. It is not a protocol, which is an articulation or an instance of an action-oriented and contextualized rationality. It is a set of heuristics, rather than a single heuristic in Newell et al.'s sense. It does not simply complete an otherwise understandable description. Kuehn and Hamburger accept the meaningfulness of their data too uncritically. They need a framework to make it into information. A recipe is a complete framework, in the sense that it indicates the data necessary to make up a complete description of a situation.

So far I have focused on rationalities shared with those outside the organization. The work of all the classical theorists, as well as that of Simon and Barnard, stresses the importance of shared rationality within the firm. The process of establishing this is not the subject of this research, nor is it much commented on in the interviews, though I will touch on it later in this chapter when discussing planning. No theory of management which claims to cover all the levels in our model can ignore this task. This is not the same as that implied in the individual's decision to participate, which is a matter of his personal policy. Having decided to participate, the individual is a *tabula rasa*, waiting to be given his organizational basis for action. However, as Simon points out, there is little to be gained by developing a coherent corporate rationality if it cannot be articulated into a coherent organization, that is one in which the role-occupants share the organization's rationality.

3.15 Conceptual Closure

A theory indicates a logically closed universe of discourse. A recipe, in contrast, is both contextualized, dependent on some correspondence rules, and open, resolving only part of that context's uncertainties. Its closure mechanisms are neither logical, like a theory, nor contextual, for it does not contain everything that can be said about that context. The research hypothesis is that recipes are closed by the decision-maker, who simply judges the recipe to be adequate to his needs. The inherent relativism is controlled by the group process and its collective experience. The recipe evolves as an accepted rationality. It is effective in that its guidance is seen as relevant. It is efficient in that it recognizes the context's search costs and decision-pressures.

Here we imply the same process theory of human cognition that runs throughout Gestalt psychology. The model is bi-phase; a period of openness, data gathering and exposure to the environment, followed by a period of closure during which the data is reconstructed, made into information and conclusions are drawn (Lewin 1935; Klapp 1975). The *Gestalten* which make up the individual's world-view are essentially closed theories. Gestalt theory is about exploring and, where appropriate, repairing and reconstructing world views.

Starting from a similar phenomenological position, George Kelly arrives at a significantly different interpretation (1955). He argues that a normal person's world-views are open and ambiguous. It is closure that is temporary, done only at the time of decision and action when the purposive actor cuts himself off from the situation's ambiguities and uncertainties: 'the person commits himself to a choice. He chooses sides. He jumps in with both feet' (1955: 1061). Rejecting the closed *Gestalten*, Kelly is obliged to find other units of analysis from which the actor's ambiguous conceptualization is constructed. He calls these elements 'personal constructs' and builds a philosophy of 'constructive alternativism' around their acquisition and manipulation (1955: 12). The actor's set of personal constructs is tested continuously against his experience of living in the world. Thus Kelly defines mental disorders pragmatically, in terms of the adequacy of the actor's ability to deal with the world. Normality means:

1 the constructs must adequately correspond with the person's experience;

2 their interrelation must adequately explain their experience;
3 the world view must be open enough to allow surprise;
4 the world view must be simple enough to be closed off for action.

Mental disorders disable the patient by leading him to adopt a world view that does not meet these criteria. Although Kelly agrees with the Gestalt view that too complex a set of constructs produces schizophrenia, he differs when he argues that too closed or simple a set is equally abnormal, producing dysphasia, a condition of excessive isolation from the world.

As a clinical psychologist Kelly is especially interested in the context of everyday family life. His constructs identify the elements of family relationships; units such as parents, friends, siblings and so forth (1955: 20; 1962: 225). We are interested in a different context, that of organizational life. But Kelly's empirical research establishes the number of constructs necessary to form an adequate world-view. Physiologists are prone to remind us of the enormous quantity of data which bombards our senses. Yet, as Simon notes, our capacities are extremely limited. Kelly finds that 20 or so constructs are adequate for handling family life. There is a trade-off between, on the one hand, the richness and precision resulting from a broader vocabulary, and on the other, the task of achieving closure for action.

The idea that 15–20 constructs are sufficient for the construction of an actionable characterization of reality occurs in other research work. Bougon et al., adopting the phenomenological viewpoint, attempt to draw the 'cause maps' or characterizations shared by members of a jazz orchestra. Using non-directive interviewing, they establish that 'seventeen variables were identified that all the UJO musicians agreed could be punctuated out of their experience' (1977: 608). On the subject of openness they write: 'paradoxically, sense-making requires inconsistencies among the participant's beliefs, since to make new sense one has to be inconsistent in that he must actively discredit past wisdom' (1977: 621). Similarly, Blau and McKinley study the 'work motifs' or ideological structures of a large sample of New York architectural practices. Using open-ended questionnaires they develop an inventory of 16 constructs (1979: 206).

Likewise, among the managerial theorists, Fayol relies on 14 principles to describe the administrator's world (1949: 19), Pugh et al. end up with 14 empirically distinct elements to depict the organizational design problem (1968: 96), Montanari uses 14 dimensions of organizational structure to operationalize Child's concepts (1979: 204), Grinyer and Yasai-Ardekani employ 19 dimensions in their analysis of organizational structure (1978), Assael characterizes the political activities of trade associations with 16 constructs (1968: 24), Andersen finds 15 variables sufficient to characterize a diversification target industry (1959) and so on.

3.16 Context and Content

The psychological theory of closure advanced above assumes corre spondence rules are included in the recipe. They define the context in which the recipe is considered relevant. They identify the data that must be collected before the manager can develop any sense of knowing what is going on. The recipe indicates how the data are to be interrelated and evaluated and is thus specific to a particular context.

Of several possible organizational contexts, that of its industry seems historically and empirically the most important. The notion that business life can be usefully organized along industry lines is wholly conventional. Stockbrokers, executive recruiters, consultants, and other service professionals segment their markets this way. Most managerial theorists accept this, along with the significance of the manager's industry knowledge (Fayol 1949: 7; Simon 1957: 85; Child 1968: 234). Donham remarks that the precedents a manager uses as the basis for his decisions are 'limited mainly to the industry of which his concern is part' (1922: 2). Industrial economists view the world this way. They also observe the tendency of firms within an industry to copy each other, which Florence calls 'swarming' (1961: 89).

The research hypothesis, that recipes are shared and significantly influence managers coping with uncertainties, can be broken down into several constituent parts:

1 that there is a pattern in managers' responses to uncertainties;
2 that managers appear to be rational in their own terms, and that their rationality –
   (a) is of limited complexity,
   (b) displays partial closure,
   (c) defines correspondence rules,
   (d) is shared along industry lines.

The industry recipe introduces a fourth and intermediary level into our previous three level model. The organizational and social levels are now separated by the industry level, which becomes the organization's primary analytic environment. The broader socio-economic environment is secondary, acting on the firm through the recipe, the industry's collective response. Similarly, while the recipe is crucial to the formation of strategy, it influences policy by demarcating what the industry thinks operational and professionally acceptable. Stressing the industry recipe as the rationality which managers use to resolve the firm's strategic uncertainties is not to deny the existence of other rationalities. I have already mentioned the significance of the manager's own interests. There are also economy-wide and society wide issues.

3.17 Planning

Many authors think of strategy as the explicit overall plan to reach the objectives chosen in the policy process. The strategic decision process produces this plan. This is unfortunate on two counts. First, it should be noted that many successful companies operate without such plans, though they do spend time discussing strategy. Second, this definition misses the point. Although we cannot produce a logical plan without a coherent rationality, so demonstrating that strategy has been made, the organization's rationality can, indeed must, be made manifest in many other ways.

Planning, especially the variety called strategic planning, has a chequered history. Scientific Management depends on planning, but is itself only a stage in the long history of scientific analysis of the processes of production (Hoagland 1955; Litterer 1961). Church and Fayol plan for the firm as a whole, but do not see the elaborate interweaving of financial, marketing, production and labour plans to which we now have access through the power of computer modelling. Fayol suggests 'sizing up' the company's overall situation (1949: xi). After World War II, Gilmore writes: 'the job of sizing up . . . was growing more complex and critical as technological change accelerated and as environmental factors affecting the ability of the firm to survive in a more competitive world increased in number and complexity' (1970: 15). Attempts to make this job more systematic followed the 1955 Harvard conference on strategic planning and Drucker's work (1954). As an academic subject area, strategic planning really begins with Ansoff who sees a need systematically to integrate production, administration, finance, marketing and R & D (1957; 1958; 1965).

The value of a formal systematic plan is far from clear. Grinyer notes that the idea that planning pays is endemic to the literature (1973: 3), and Glueck cites extensive research (1976: 7). But there is equal evidence that planning achieves little (Rue & Fulmer 1973; Grinyer 1973; Grinyer & Norburn 1974).

We can separate the planning process from the plan itself and find total agreement with the old military maxim: 'plans sometimes may be useless, but the planning process is always indispensable' (Steiner & Miner 1977. 172). Whether or not the plan is important, we can see the process as one of a number of ways of developing a shared rationality among those involved. This is crucial to the effective control of any distributed decision-making. The theory of bureaucracy assumes that the chosen rationality is readily distributed around the organization and, as a result, that inter-role communications are perfect. Simon draws attention to the uncertainties which interfere with organizational communications, so making individual judgements necessary . Training, company meetings, house journals and newsletters, etc. are all alternative communication channels. No set of these can ever ensure perfect communication. Participation in the planning process, because it refers back to the policies so frequently, and because it focuses on resource allocation and performance, proves to be a powerful method of communicating the firm's rationality.

The planning process also creates communication between the owners, and those other outsiders who take part in the policy process, and the management, to whom the policy process may well have been delegated, at least in part. When there is a division of power over the firm, policy needs to be negotiated and these negotiations become the ultimate source of order within the firm. Politically adept management can employ these negotiations to their advantage, to control, for instance, political struggles between different owners or to co-opt the outsiders into the executive's chosen rationality.

3.18 Conclusion

I have now constructed the research hypothesis. Chapter 2 reviewed classical theory and its conventional criticisms; they leave it unaffected. This chapter began with a different critique, focused on the fact of uncertainty and on classical theory's inability to deal with it. I have categorized uncertainties and introduced a variety of sources, the most penetrating being the inter-system incommensurability which is central to Barnard's theory. I argue that uncertainty is resolved by the manager using his judgement to supplement the description of the decision situation.

Such judgements are personal and inherently unresearchable unless we can construct a suitable population of like cases. Rejecting the idea that an individual's judgement is stable across decisions of different types, I propose that managers draw their judgements from a shared pool which I call an industry recipe. The others who draw from and contribute to this pattern of shared judgements are managers from the same industry.

4

Research Methodology

4.1 Introduction

At the end of Chapter 3 I focus on the industry recipe, the shared knowledge-base that those socialized into an industry take as familiar professional common sense. This is the central component of my theory of strategic management as uncertainty resolution. Following Kelly, I argue that the recipe is made up from around 15 distinctions or 'constructs'. These are synthesized together to create a universe of discourse attached to a particular industry, so making statements about the firm's situation and experiences possible. I hypothesize (a) that the recipe is a group level concept, evident as a shared rationality, and (b) that it is the major contributor to the manager's constructed theory of his situation.

In this chapter I describe a method for researching an industry's recipe. I borrow primarily from the social anthropologists, who are trained to penetrate and explicate unfamiliar cultures and alternative universes of discourse. I also consider the similar phenomenological methods which are applied in ethnology, interpretive sociology, psychology and psychiatry. I discuss these methods and their shortcomings, and determine what is appropriate for this research.

Abandoning the conventional positivistic arm's length relationship between the researcher and the subject material, phenomenological procedures create problems with direction, control, validity, and with the notion of a research result. In Chapter 3 I argue that scientific objectivity is relative, grounded in the shared views of the scientist's professional group. Not simple myths, these views are shared and so judged 'scientific' because they are underpinned by the reproducibility of the research results. Interpretive methodologies call for quite different tests, and for different concepts of validity.

In Chapter 3 I also argue that a recipe is not a closed universe of discourse. It remains ambiguous, ready to be closed off for action in the particular context of the decision-maker's chosen policy and circumstances. In this sense a recipe is beyond being completely understood, much as our own culture cannot be completely grasped simply because its remaining openness permits surprise and adaptation. But such ambiguity exacerbates the methodological problems. How are we to know when to stop researching? When do we have a result? My answers are tentative proposals for clarity in this controversial area.

Although these concerns cannot be resolved in any absolute fashion, except by strategic choice, I adopt the cultural anthropologist's method and conduct unstructured interviews. While I argue that these are fundamentally different from the more familiar structured interviews, I also argue that there are no wholly unstructured interviews. Inevitably there is structure in the conduct and direction of any social interaction. These issues are dealt with fully by Merton and Kendall (1946), whose lines I follow.

This chapter also covers various practical matters, such as selecting the sample, and setting up, conducting and analysing the interviews. It closes with a discussion on the problems and advantages of phenomenological methods, especially those of researcher-respondent relations, on the idea of industry membership and on interpretation.

4.2 Problems with Interpretive Research Methods

The real problem with interpretive methods is the lack of common ground between the researcher and his audience. The positivist researcher shares extensive ground with his audience because both agree to a common rationality, that is a commitment to science generally, and to a shared definition of the research objective and methods in particular. The positivistic researcher states a hypothesis, which logically entails an observable consequence. He chooses an established method to make the proposed observation. His argument is based on shared premises, shared method and deductive logic. He can say 'if you accept this hypothesis and this method, then you must accept this conclusion'.

The positivist's hypothesis actually demands more than this. It entails his rationality; accept the hypothesis and one perforce accepts the entire rationality. Thus the cautious positivist never goes beyond the current conventions of his discipline's accepted research rationality, objectives and methods. Using Kuhn's terms, he engages in incremental rather than critical science, exploring accepted anomalies and extending the current body of accepted knowledge. As his pupils, we understand when we see how what we already know is extended by his arguments.

The phenomenologist could not start from this position even if he wished it. His purpose excludes it. His research objective is to encourage the sceptical listener into a new way of looking, into an unfamiliar rationality which probably includes unfamiliar premises and objectives. He is trying to educate the unconvinced. Consequently, there is no common ground on which he can stand and say 'because you accept that, you must accept this'. He must limit his demands to logicality alone. As his pupils, we begin to understand only after we have grasped the researcher's decision premises, objectives, and patterns of causality. The nature of that understanding is different, involving a novel rationality, not just a further consequence of a familiar rationality. Frequently this type of understanding comes suddenly, as a holistic experience, an 'aha', a 'shock of recognition'. The meaning lies in the totality of the inter-relationships, not in the elements or constructs. We can learn this way only by exposing ourselves, displaying a certain innocence. We are too often trained out of this natural interest in the unfamiliar, this readiness to be surprised and affected by other people's lives and ways of seeing.

The interpretive scientist's research result is an unfamiliar rationality, a complete universe of hypotheses. It may be one he has created, as an original creative scientist, or it may be some other person's, now revealed by his research. Since, as I argue in Chapter 3, one's choice of rationality is beyond both logic and empirical evidence, so accepting an alternative rationality is ultimately a matter of the listener's judgement. The achievement of the interpretive social sciences is two-fold. First, to grant us a sense of humility about other peoples and cultures and their different way of seeing the world, but second, to give us the ability to objectify ourselves and see how significant a part judgement plays in our own lives.

Positivist training, which leads us to expect proof to every type of explanation, inhibits such openness. As Popper points out, the positivistic researcher generates hypotheses – makes guesses – which he then checks, rather than making discoveries during his research (1969: 115) He must anticipate his every finding, basing his thinking on an increasingly closed and mature rationality. He makes no attempt to find an alternative novel rationality. Similarly, he will never question the meaning of data or his sense of data as facts.

An enquiry into judgement and alternative rationalities must treat the meaning of any data as problematic. The researcher cannot pre-empt the subject's own meaning system or rationality when it is the actual target of the research. The researcher must remain open to the subject's own method of explanation and conclusions, provided they conform to logic. Until the researcher finds otherwise, he is forced to assume the subject is logical, and therefore, by his own lights, rational. Here the subject has the initiative, especially in the process of constructing the meaning of his world. Walsh writes: 'the failure of positivistic sociology lies in its inability to grasp the meaningful constitution of the social world and its consequent reliance on a methodology inadequate for the exposition of that world' (1972: 18).

4.3 The Interpretive Method

The purpose of these non-positivistic methods is to elicit unfamiliar meaning-structures, rather than to extend familiar ones. While they have a long history, contemporary interpretive anthropological research originates as a reaction to Tylor's prescriptive approach to culture. He proposes a fixed categorization scheme covering weapons, textile arts, myths, rites, etc; a scheme which implies that cultures are readily comparable (in Bohannan & Glazer 1973: 67). Similarly Frijda and Jahoda argue that Tylor's comparative method presumes that all human cultures are instances of a species-specific but nevertheless universal culture, and that they all develop with the same sequence of stages.

Boas, with greater humility and respect for the integrity and uniqueness of other cultures, rejects this presupposition. He insists that the first step into another culture is to learn the local language, so that the researcher can begin to confront the world in the same way as do his subjects. Accepting the primacy of the subject's view, with its evident strangeness, brings uncertainty, and the subject's part in its resolution, into the centre of the analysis (Benedict 1959: 22).

While the ethnologist proceeds on the assumption that there is a culture to research, the interpretive sociologist is more interested in the processes of communication which lead to shared meanings. We assume there are two ways of discovering a symbol's meaning, ostensive definition, pointing to the physical object-symbol, or verbal definition. Boas argues that both are necessary to full understanding; the researcher must both learn the language and must live among his subjects with their objects, artifacts and symbols. The first familiarizes him with their thought, the second with their contexts of activity. As Evans-Pritchard writes: 'to understand a people's thought, one has to think in their symbols. In learning the language one learns the culture and the social symbols which are conceptualized in the language' (1951: 80).

4.4 The Return Journey

The interpretive scientist's first problem is to enter into the unfamiliar meaning-structure. His second problem is to bring that understanding back to his audience without subjecting them to the same rigours as the researcher underwent in the field. This implies an appeal to some framework common to the researcher's subject and audience. Malinowski and Radcliffe-Brown argue that all aspects of human culture are functional, thus rejecting the extreme relativism of Boas's views. They adopt an essentially Durkheimian view of the universality of human sociology (Beattie 1966: 49).

Evans-Pritchard notes that this refocuses the research away from the culture and its unfamiliar rationality and onto the presumed functions (1951: 56). He argues for a different solution to the researcher's problem of communicating with his audience, proposing a three phase method. 'In the first phase, as ethnographer, he goes to live among a primitive people and learns their way of life. He learns to speak their language, think their concepts and feel their values. He then lives the experience over again critically and interpretively in the conceptual categories and values of his own culture and in terms of the general body of knowlege of his discipline. In other words, he translates from one culture to another. In the second phase of his work . . . he tries to go beyond this literary and impressionistic stage and discover the structural order of the society, so that it is intelligible not merely at the level of consciousness and action, as it is to one of its members or to the foreigner who has learnt its mores and participates in its life, but also at the level of sociological analysis . . . Having isolated the structural patterns in one society, the social anthropologist, in the third phase of his work, compares them with patterns in other societies' (1951: 61).

This is a perfectly adequate description of the methods adopted in the present research, so long as we remember that Evans-Pritchard is a strong critic of functionalism and that his notion of structural order is neither closed nor coherent, but is an open adaptive system. The three steps are:

1 entry;
2 translation;
3 comparison.

The process of translation depends upon using small pieces of common ground rather than, as the functionalists assert, a comprehensive common structure based on function. The interpretive researcher has to illustrate his points with something recognizable in his audience's world, much as one communicates about food, drink, laughter and sleep with a person who does not speak one's language. As the pieces of common ground and verbal points build up, they become a series of constructs in a new rationality. Eventually the audience gets a sense of understanding. But since the recipe is open, the process of translation is never complete, and can be heightened by comparisons between recipes.

4.5 The Research Method

My research focus is the interplay of the firm's individual differences and the sense of group membership implicit in the body of familiar and taken-for-granted common sense knowledge. The practical research problems are two-fold. First, people have difficulty articulating what they take for granted so long as they are without an alternative intellectual vantage point. It is like trying to imagine oneself in outer space or dead. We deal with this by getting as close as possible to the actor's vantage point by observing him acting in his own professional context. We observe him acting out his rationality rather than intellectualizing about it and verbalizing his observations. He remains within his own familiar professional context, in contact with that context's social interactions and shared meanings. The artificiality of putting the subject into an entirely new context, in an unfamiliar laboratory, is avoided. The second problem is that of the researcher's impact on the situation. This is minimized by unobtrusive methods, which means keeping the research process out of the subject's field of attention, ensuring that the subject's behaviour is the result of familiar stimuli, rather than those generated by the researcher.

At first sight, an interview must necessarily appear on the field of attention. But our research is to do with the processes of uncertainty resolution and so long as the subject is faced only with the familiar, the interview will not trigger these creative processes. As we shall see, the interviewer must strive for transparency, imposing neither language nor direction. The unstructured interview leaves the respondent to choose his own language and topics, thereby staying within his familiar rationality. A structured interview, in contrast, controls the language, format and topics, thereby presenting the respondent with uncertainty, a puzzle to be decoded and solved.

As the researcher tries to penetrate his subject's rationality, his behaviour converges on his subject's, he enquires into learning how to behave like his subject, that is grasping the rationality and meaning-system which makes the subject's analyses and decisions understandable. As Giddens remarks: 'immersion in the form of life is the necessary and only means whereby an observer is able to generate such characterisations . . . To get to know an alien form of life is to know how to find one's way about in it, to be able to participate in it as an ensemble of practices' (1976: 161).

In practice, the techniques used by interpretive sociologists vary widely from one extreme, with the researcher as an active participant standing *pari passu* with the other participants, to the other, in which the researcher is an unobserved and passive observer. McCall and Simmons note: 'participant observation . . . refers to a characteristic blend or combination of techniques and methods . . . it involves some amount of genuinely social interaction in the field with the subjects of the study, some direct observation of relevant events, some formal and a great deal of informal interviewing, some collection of documents . . . and open-endedness in the directions the study can take. Because of this rather omnibus quality . . . it has not lent itself to the standardisation of procedure that social scientists have come to expect of their methods, as in testing, survey and laboratory work. Profound questions of reliability, validity and generality of results have thus been raised' (1969: 1). Here McCall and Simmons are missing the real differences between a structured interview, which has the subject dancing to the researcher's tune, and an unstructured interview, which challenges the researcher to make sense of the subject's responses.

Because they force the researcher into the subject's rationality, unstructured interviews are fundamentally different from structured interviews. Unstructured, the interview is a deliberate social interaction, set up to communicate unanticipated meaning from the subject to the researcher. It is quite different from, for instance, Mintzberg's passive observation of managerial behaviour within pre-established categories. Here Mintzberg assumes the meaning of his categories and thus, in fact, of managerial work itself (1973).

The unstructured interview relies on the manager's verbal communication skills. Everyday experience, and Mintzberg's work (1973: 39), show that about 60 per cent of a typical manager's time is spent communicating verbally, so we are reasonably confident in depending on his verbal facility. Second, the researcher acts as a pupil rather than as a ring-master forcing the manager over a set of prepared hurdles. This allows the manager to retain a familiar authority relationship with the researcher. This transfer of initiative is engagingly summarized for psychiatrists as Kelly's First Law: 'if you do not know what is wrong with a person, ask him: he may tell you' (1955: 322).

4.6 The Sample

The sample selection followed an exploratory phase. Five local companies were contacted to test the procedure for getting and conducting unstructured interviews. These visits confirmed the general methodological approach.

Three target industries were then selected to reflect a variety of concerns. First, given a focus on industry recipes, I wanted to avoid conglomerates and other complex enterprises which span several industries. Second, I wanted to look beyond the few dozen large and international firms who have been the target of much strategic planning research (Fouraker & Stopford 1968; Wrigley 1970; Berg 1973; Channon 1973; Rumelt 1974, etc.). The idea of industry recipes is applicable to ordinary managers who do not have MBAs or similar qualifications, who have given no special thought to how other businesses are run. Small firms thus became the target of the research. Third, it cannot be argued that the industry recipe is the major determinant of strategy if the firm is being used to implement government policies which are not applied to the industry as a whole, such as regional development policies. Fourth, given that the research method is cross-sectional, sampling several firms within a single industry, I needed industries that have a reasonable population of firms. To prevent other distortions I also preferred industries which are not dominated by monopolistic or oligopolistic concerns.

Finally, it is clear that the recipe offers a way of classifying firms according to which recipe they adopt. Traditional classification methods, such as SIC numbering, tend to be based on the materials processed rather than on the body of knowledge being applied. These methods break down completely in the service sector. Therefore I chose both manufacturing and service industries in order to test, in a preliminary way, the possibility of a classification scheme based on recipe adoption.

As a result of these deliberations, the three industries chosen were:

1 the most traditional sector of the UK iron foundry business;
2 the liquid milk processing, bottling and distribution business;
3 the industrial fork-lift truck rental business.

The first was chosen after discussions with Professors Lupton and Gowler, then both at the Manchester Business School, and with the Foundry Industry Training Committee (FITC), with whom they had been working on a business and skills classification scheme.

In the interpretive programme the statistically based norms for sample selection which are normally applied in positivistic research are replaced by different concerns. The positivist selects from a population whose relevance and representativeness are assumed. The validity of his findings is a function of the variability of his data, the number in the sample and the number in the population. The interpretive approach is radically different. It simply requires sufficient data for a rationality to emerge. At the extremes of social anthropology, the data for an entire culture are often revealed, along with extensive field work, by a principal respondent. Ishi does this for the Kroebers. Similarly, Benedict advises researchers to seek out the deviant or marginal members of a culture, who are often able to act as translators.

In this research, I sought a cross-section of apparently representative companies, rather than a single correspondent. Instead of using a single company to generate the final recipe, I used each to add to a partial picture. I moved from company to company until the picture became sufficiently complete, though I will deal with what constitutes 'sufficient' later in this chapter. I had to remain open to finding that the company being researched had adopted an alternative recipe and did not belong to the sample population.

Once a particular industry is chosen, the firms to be sampled can be found by looking at trade publications, such as buyers' guides and the yellow pages, noting who advertises in trade journals, and by asking managers about their competitors. In my three target industries, the sample of iron-founders was found with the assistance of the FITC, the dairies from the yellow pages, and the fork-lift truck rental companies from advertisements in the materials handling trade press.

Some cultural anthropologists regard prior knowledge of the target culture as essential to research (Evans-Pritchard 1951: 76). Nevertheless, there is something to be said for not preparing for an unstructured interview. Even a passing familiarity with the industry's history or background, or the firm's situation, is likely to be reflected in attempts to guide the interview. If required, information can be gathered from Companies House, from trade directories such as Kelly's and Compass and, in the case of quoted companies, from Extel cards. But it should be remembered that all this information has been abstracted for a particular purpose. This purpose may differ from our own and the information may be categorized under schemes which are wholly different from those which managers use for their own industry.

4.7 Getting the Interview

This seems relatively straightforward and may be a reflection of the ordinariness of the firms being investigated; bigger firms' senior managers may be less accessible. Letters are too easy to ignore, so all the interviews were set up over the telephone. The crux of getting an interview seems to be legitimacy. This can be established in several steps. First, asking for the senior manager by name, which can be obtained from the reference books or from the firm's switchboard, will increase the chances of being put straight through. If the secretary asks about the purpose of the call, there can be problems. The researcher, who has spent a lot of time thinking about his work, is inclined to give anyone who asks a full synopsis, forgetting that few people, even fellow academics, share his interest. The researcher must remember that the objective at this stage is to get an interview, not justify his whole programme.

The second step to legitimation is to stress the association with an academic institution, and the non-commercial and confidential nature of the work. The third step is to make the research sound unthreatening and simple, couched in words such as 'I am looking into the problems of running firms in this industry and wonder if I could come and talk to you about it for half an hour?'. It seems that the more senior the manager, the readier he is to grant an interview. This makes it easier to get to the strategy-makers. It is extremely important to avoid being deflected into interviewing a junior manager on the grounds that he is more familiar with the details.

4.8 Running the Interview

Most of the extensive interviewing literature is based on the structured approach, its intent being to confirm or reject hypotheses about a population. There is rather less written about interpretive methods (for example, Lofland 1971; Olson 1976). The present research is guided by Katona's analyses of business location decisions (Katona & Morgan 1952) and, to a greater extent, by Merton and Kendall's work (Merton & Kendall 1946; Merton, Fiske & Kendall 1956).

Merton and Kendall call their method 'focused interviewing' and it combines unstructured interviews with a loose pattern of agreement with the interviewee about the context of enquiry. Their subjects are young soldiers off to fight in Europe, their enquiry is into the effects of propaganda films. The context of activity, watching the film, is quite clear and within it Merton and Kendall minimize direction. They write: 'the value of non-directive interviewing has become increasingly recognized, notably in the work of Rogers and Roethlisberger & Dickson. It gives the subject the opportunity to express himself about matters of central significance to him rather than those presumed important by the interviewer. In contrast to the polling approach, it uncovers what is on the subject's mind, rather than his opinion of what is on the interviewer's mind . . . Private definitions of the stimulus situation are rarely forthcoming when directive techniques are used' (1946: 545).

This is the counsel of perfection, of course, since setting up or opening the interview is clearly directive. Merton et al. note the danger of setting the wrong tone and structure with one's opening remarks (1956: 171). The problem is reduced in the present research because managers will generally take the initiative and ask 'What is this all about?'. Again there is a temptation to justify the research programme, but the objective is now to get the manager talking freely about his view of the firm's world. Experience shows that two starters work well; first, asking the manager what he does for the firm, or second, and generally better, who reports to him and why. Once started, most managers will talk freely. In fact, as many interpretive researchers discover, subjects often talk so much that they are forced to intervene. Few managers, it seems, have the opportunity to talk over their work with an intelligent and sympathetic outsider who is powerless and therefore neutral in their world.

Many interviews take on a therapeutic quality as the manager exposes his doubts and vulnerability. But this will not happen unless the researcher appreciates that he bears the burden of comprehension. The manager is comfortable with his own jargon, and breaking the flow to check on what he means will diminish the interview's usefulness. The researcher is in foreign territory, struggling to make sense of the incomprehensible and to absorb a huge quantity of what appears to be ill-structured information. If he cannot bear the burden and, at the same time, sustain the necessary delicate social interaction with the subject, the rapport will be lost. Many researchers find this extremely discomfiting and take to structured interviewing to relieve them of this burden and to protect them against being surprised by their own research process. The researcher's preparedness to be surprised and discomfited is, of course, a measure of his ability and commitment to enter into an alien rationality.

It may be necessary to intervene if the subject wanders too far from the context on which the research is focused. If intervention is necessary, a surprising amount can be achieved with body language alone. If some verbal intervention seems necessary, there is a temptation to use leading questions. As Lofland points out, these are quite different from remarks designed to prevent the subject digressing (1971: 81). Leading questions are dangerous where there is a risk that they will draw the interviewee out of the context and pattern of attached judgement that is being explored. This is especially true where the subject is led out of a context of which he has practical experience into one of which he has no practical knowledge and therefore no grounded sense of judgement. This is the argument against 'scenario testing', which was tried during the exploratory phase and rejected. Unless all the judgements being revealed are attached to the target context, the programme gets completely out of hand.

Merton et al. suggest four intervention criteria related to range, specificity, depth, and the 'personal contexts' being covered (1956: 12).

Range is focus on the context, which should be broad enough to explore the extent of the subject's responses to the stimulus situation. Specificity is a matter of ensuring that the conversation is precise enough to draw out the constructs, rather than showing up broad non-operational generalities. Depth is appropriate when it reaches the interviewee's subjective involvement, rather than some arm's length objectification. By personal context, Merton et al. mean something close to our concept of judgement, that is what the subject adds to his knowledge of the uncertain situation to characterize it. They note two dimensions of addition: 'idiosyncratic', which is personal and derived from experience, and 'role', which is built up from the experiences of those others around the subject who are sharing similar experiences. They write: 'The role context helps account for the relatively frequent, if not actually modal, responses to a situation' (1956: 116). They conclude that 'the focused interview results in an inventory of personal contexts found to govern responses to a particular type of situation' (1956: 117).

The interviews are focused in several ways before they start. First, by introducing the interview as 'about the problems of running the firm'; second, by insisting on meeting senior managers with strategic responsibilities; third, by interviewing the managers at their workplaces, keeping them in the physical context of their organizational role. Like the use of body language, physical location is a major determinant of behaviour. Managers behave one way when behind their desks, and quite another when acting as hosts in another room.

4.9 Collecting the Data

The complexity we find in the world is a reflection of our data categorization scheme. If the scheme is weak, we feel overburdened by what we see going on, and by change. If our scheme is powerful, as are our visual ordering schemes, we absorb huge quantities of data without distress. At the beginning of the enquiry, the researcher's scheme is weak, almost non-existent. The researcher cannot absorb or see the significance of anything. Even sticking to a pre-arranged procedure, Mintzberg finds note-taking a burdensome full-time activity (1973: 271). This is dangerous because the researcher will concentrate on making notes rather than on developing rapport with his subject; and without the rapport, the interview does not work properly. Once the researcher becomes familiar with the industry jargon, and the accompanying concepts, he will find it a highly efficient data reduction and categorization scheme.

Faced with exploring the taken-for-granted in a conversation that he both participates in and reports, the researcher has little option but to use a tape recorder. There is plenty of literature on this (for example, Schegloff 1971; Lofland 1971: 88; Bowey 1976: 73; Salaman 1979: 192). A recorder leaves the interviewer free to concentrate on the subject, but it produces data which must be analysed without the interviewee present to settle questions. Tape recording requires careful management for there are many ways of producing useless recordings and many managers find the experience distracting or threatening.

1.10 The Interview Data

Of the 34 interviews in the sample, 25 were recorded at least in part. These were made into transcripts. During the exploratory phase, some of the transcribing was done by assistants. This proved unsatisfactory, for a transcript is unable to capture the data as fully as the recording. There are important data in the respondent's intonations, hesitations, etc. which need to be available as the researcher begins to work on the interpretation of the recordings. Everyday speech is highly ungrammatical and much of its meaning arises from the context in which it occurs. The recording can help recapture the actual data, which is neither the recording, nor the transcript, but the researcher's experience of the interview in its own context.

The positivistic methods of content analysis presume the meaning of the data by imposing a predetermined coding and classification system onto the material (Olson 1976: 71). The analysis focuses on data content rather than on meaning, for content analysis breaks down completely if the material fails to conform to the anticipated linguistic structure (Giglioni 1972: 13). Similarly, Schegloff argues that everyday speech is unintelligible until both speaker and listener are socialized into the same meaning structure which covers the vocabulary, syntax and common sense knowledge. Clearly this requires some familiarity with the taken-for-granted experiences in which the normal patterns of judgement are grounded (1971).

For the interpretive researcher, getting at the meaning of the dialogue means probing through the actual language used to get at the pattern of judgement made manifest in the interview. There is no need to see the interview as anything other than a straightforward social event, with the obvious meaning being the most important. The researcher's data is his total experience of the target culture. It comprises all of his interactions as well as field-notes, photographs, artifacts and memorabilia. Only after establishing an understanding of the alien rationality can interpretive researchers begin to probe for further subtleties and motivations to form hypotheses and test the culture's integrity and consistency. Thus Merton et al. and Bowey take the data at face value, following Kelly's First Law

Many researchers are exercised by the risk of the respondent falsifying evidence, telling lies (for example, Vidich & Bensman 1954). We have no reason to suppose managers have time for this. In fact, unless there were a conspiracy across the sample, so that the same untruths appeared generally, the effect would be lost in the noise. In the event such untruths were shared, they would be elements of a recipe, and as I noted in Chapter 3, there is no reason to think of a recipe as a 'true' representation of the industry's 'reality' or policy intents.

Having agreed the context of discussion, the manager's responsibility for the firm as a whole, the researcher prompts the manager to talk, listening and responding in order to keep the one-sided conversation flowing. Eventually the researcher begins to pick up some of the meaning. Part of it is a feeling for the range of the pattern of judgement, part is grasping the meaning of two or three key terms. Evans-Pritchard notes: 'the most difficult task in anthropological fieldwork is to determine the meanings of a few key words, upon an understanding of which the whole investigation depends' (1951: 80). This is made simpler by the cross-sectional method. The contrasts between interviews throw the shared terms and meanings into sharp relief. Within three or four interviews, provided the interviews are mutually reinforcing, the researcher has a preliminary grasp of the industry's rationality.

4.11 Validity

The next problem for the researcher is to determine when he has interviewed enough. This is the question of validity. Positivistic enquiry stops when the discipline's conventions for statistical significance and objective certainty are met. These define scientific understanding. The interpretive basis for knowledge is quite different, essentially defined by the point at which the researcher feels competent to act as a member of the alien culture. The sample size necessary is that required to give the researcher this confidence. The notion of a statistically valid sample is quite meaningless in an interpretive programme. The kind of validity that the anthropologist demands is that which makes data itself meaningful. The positivist, in contrast, accepts the meaning of his data without discussion and turns to checking whether it confirms or contradicts his generalizations. In the present research we must regard all data as problematic, focusing instead on how managers give it meaning. We reject the positivist's authority to decide on the meaning of the data to which the manager responds.

At first sight, this seems philosophically acceptable but overly pedantic and dismissive of the practical problems facing the researcher. Schutz struggles with these problems, emerging with three validity criteria:

1 logical consistency;
2 subjective interpretation;
3 adequacy (in Phillipson 1972: 150)

These are an inadequate attempt, somewhat in line with McCall and Simmons, to present the phenomenological programme as some kind of alternative to the positivist one, as if they were both directed towards the same objective. The crux of understanding the interpretive method is seeing that it is directed towards a different objective, a set of problems dismissed by assumption in the positivist approach. Equally, the phenomenological programme makes assumptions about the representativeness of the respondents and the resulting data which are regarded as problematic within the positivist programme. Thus the two methods are directed towards different objectives, even though these different objectives are interlinked and mutually supportive (Spender 1979).

Reading Husserl and Heidegger and exploring the foundations of contemporary phenomenology teaches us that if there is anything corresponding to the positivist sense of validity, which is based in the professional group norms, it must be wholly subjective (Lauer 1965). Writers who appreciate this, such as Nagel (1963), Gidlow (1972) and Pivcevic (1972) conclude that phenomenological methods are not only not alternatives, but they are actually discontinuous with positivistic science. I agree, but argue there is more to it.

Although discontinuous as universes of discourse, they are related by practice. The methods are simply different facets of the same search for knowledge, a recognition that all enquiry must take something for granted if it is to avoid a crushing solipsism.

Phenomenological or subjective validity is not the point where some conventions oblige us to accept whatever is being demonstrated, it is the point where we become willing to act on the basis of the knowledge presented. Goodenough argues that the researcher's objective is to learn 'whatever it is one has to know or believe in order to operate in the manner acceptable to the group's members and to do so in any role that they accept for anyone of themselves' (1966: 36). This presents validity as like 'satisficing', a subjective confidence level 'of being sufficiently consonant with an object of our experience for the actual purposes at hand' (Schutz 1970: 61), and 'when further research is deemed unnecessary' (Schutz 1970: 142).

This is the point of closure, when the constructs have been communicated and have synthesized into the recipe. Clearly there must be some number of constructs, between two and, say, several hundred, which can give the researcher this sense of sufficient knowledge and confidence to act. Following Kelly, I guess this to be around 15–20. But the real number is that which the researcher experiences as he proceeds with his research. This refers to the common experience we all have when we ask someone about something. We reach the point where we have heard enough, we get a feeling of understanding, and we want the talk to stop. This feeling is shared when two people are being adequately sensitive to each other. During the interview, the researcher and the subject find a point at which the conversation has covered the subject adequately and that they have arrived at a natural conclusion. The interview can be continued only by raising an entirely new topic or by investigating a revealed construct in much greater depth.

The practical issue, of course, is the difference between the researcher's confidence and that of his audience. The interpretive method is a two stage one. The entry stage is followed by the researcher's re-emergence with something to say. The audience can accept the researcher's willingness to act on what has been discovered, without, of course, sharing the same confidence. The positivistically inclined audience wants an objective test that forces it to accept the researcher's conclusions. It cannot have this within the interpretive programme, because it is faced with its own interpretive task, to try and penetrate the researcher's own unfamiliar rationality. In the same way that Popper points out the infinite regression of the positivist programme, so the interpretive programme is viciously circular. The outcome of the programme is each individual's subjective confidence that he has learned something. He follows the trail of evidence left by the researcher as he shows off cultural artifacts and tells stories of life in the target culture. The researcher must recreate his experience in ways that the audience can share, and so be led through the same learning process. The novelist or case-writer works the same way. We cannot measure objectively whether he has captured or created a situation, all we can do is express our subjective response to what he has written.

We might call the researcher's bluff, watching how well Kelly gets on with his patients, or seeing whether Evans-Pritchard can really find his way about in Anando society. As Filmor et al. illustrate, this test offers no escape from circularity, for how do we know how to make sense of what we see (1972: 10)? How do we know that Evans-Pritchard is truly socialized and is not simply being humoured as an eccentric Englishman? Here we have become interpretive researchers, which is exactly what Kelly assumes we all are as we struggle to make sense of our lives. Having the researcher check with the subject is no way out either, for how is he to evaluate the subject's responses?

Ultimately we have only our own judgement to go on in deciding whether to believe the researcher who tells us he understands some other culture or rationality. The audience must draw its own conclusions on the basis of the evidence presented, without the customary positivistic dependence on assumptions shared with the researcher. The audience cannot be forced, with the power of logic, to certain conclusions. The audience, engaged in its own interpretive research, must reach its own point of closure. The researcher must be able to sense when this has occurred and have sufficient resources, as a story-teller, to be able to lead the audience the whole way.

Perhaps surprise, in the sense that Shackle uses the term (1961: 67), is the key concept here. The audience must be prepared to be surprised, to go beyond its own rationality and system of views and relationships. Individuals in the audience must be sympathetic and see surprise as evidence of something new. As one surprise follows another they begin to reconstruct the evidence and new meaning emerges. Eventually they have a novel comprehensive rationality at their disposal. They have learned.

4.12 Communicating the Research Data

Given a common sense approach, the researchers' initial task is to immerse themselves in the data until they begin to achieve some sense of understanding. Then they must analyse their growing meaning-system, breaking it down into its basic distinctions or constructs.

The next step is to bring their understanding back with their presentations or writings. They will find it easier to communicate the unfamiliar constructs when they can embed their explanation in the audiences' rationality, or one that lies outside the recipe and is somewhat familiar to their readers. If we say 'the firm was losing its labour to other employers who were paying higher wages' the audience will generally accept the point without further debate because it accepts the significance of personal financial interest. Novelists, journalists and case-writers use this technique, as do writers such as Merton et al., Bowey and Kelly.

In the following chapters, I present a trail into each of the recipes. The trail consists of separate points of meaning supported by dialogues drawn directly from the interviews. Each construct depends on some familiar rationality for its presentation. But as the narrative builds up a new sense of meaning emerges until finally closure occurs. The reader must judge for himself whether the recipe is complete. Where the research succeeds the reader will have a sense of power, of knowing that were he suddenly, for instance, to be given a dairy to run, he would know what questions to ask. He would know how to discover what was going on and whether the new-found enterprise was healthy or not.

4.13 Cluster Analysis

In the dairy and fork-lift truck industries the pattern emerges readily. Indeed, I might suggest that the distinctiveness and clarity of a recipe is a measure of that industry's maturity. As time proceeds, so the recipe becomes more coherent and more of a closed universe of discourse. The more closed it is, the less opportunity there is for those adopting it to be surprised, since they increasingly reject what does not make sense. This produces the familiar 'bunker' mentality. People whose way of looking at the world does not give them adequate power over their situations often retreat into denial, externalizing the fault and avoiding the challenge to look at their experiences in an unfamiliar way. This stage, which prevents adaptation in a changing world, will inevitably be followed by a critical phase of cognitive reconstruction which, in an organizational setting, might involve abandoning one recipe in favour of another (Grinyer & Spender 1979a; 1979b).

In the case of the foundries, there is more change going on in the industry and less clarity in the recipe. Because they can help reveal patterning, techniques such as cluster and factor analysis are useful.

Cluster analysis is a technique for systematically exploring similarities in a body of allegedly comparable data. It contrasts with many techniques, such as factor analysis, which explore differences. The latter are essentially positivistic in the sense that they require prior commitment to the dimensions in which differences are to be examined. While cluster analysis is not interpretive, it makes fewer logical demands on the data and can be used to examine poorly structured data, data whose meaning is uncertain. It also admits a wide variety of structures, so the bias introduced by one can be assessed by comparison with another (Sokal & Sneath 1963; Everitt 1974; Shepard et al. 1972, etc).

Like participant-observation, cluster analysis or numerical taxonomy is an omnibus collection of similarity seeking techniques. Each analysis focuses on a different kind of similarity. As Everitt points out, most writers' definitions of cluster analysis gloss over the 'strategic choice' of similarity or 'distance' criterion (1974: 43). For these reasons, the conclusions that can be drawn from cluster analysis are of questionable validity (Green et al. 1967; Miller 1977). Nevertheless, they can help the researcher move towards his point of closure and actionable confidence. They cannot supplant the trail of meaning which the researcher uses to communicate to his audience since, on its own, cluster analysis is an abstract process of data manipulation and presentation that adds no meaning whatsoever to the data. In the case of the foundry industry analysis, clustering the data helps illuminate that the industry is in transition from one recipe to another.

4.14 Industry Membership

As we look at the research into recipes, a vicious circularity emerges between our sense of an industry and the group of companies who adopt a given recipe. The definition of industry membership has troubled economists for a long time. There are especially wide differences between the definitions of those working within an industry and those looking on from without. Triffin remarks that economists' definitions are related to the materials processed, the commodities produced or the technologies applied (1962). None of these are necessary determinants of the way the industry, or its constituent firms, are organized.

We can see obvious paradoxes in every industry's situation. We see the 'motor industry' as made up of assemblers, sub-component manufacturers, and vehicle sales and service outlets. Yet tyre manufacturers are treated as part of the 'rubber industry' and sheet steel manufacturers as part of the 'steel industry' In the absence of a standardized definition of, say, the percentage of throughput that goes to another industry, which would re-define the supplier as being part of the consuming industry, we use whatever definitions suit our purposes. Triffin writes: 'the value of these groupings is an empirical one. It is never useful to speak of industries or groups in a general, abstract way, but it may be very helpful to speak of the oil industry, coal industry or steel industry etc. A careful enquiry, however, cannot blindly trust traditional classifications and terminology as a safe method for building up these groupings' (1962: 88).

Similarly, Robinson writes: 'it seemed at first glance that it would be possible to define an industry as a group of firms producing the same commodity for the same market. We must now recognise that to define it either by the commodity produced, or the market for which it produces, is in many cases either impossible or at least unsatisfactory. In practice all we can do is follow the example of those who are actually engaged in the industries. Certain employers find that they have a bond of common interest with certain other employers, and come to regard themselves as composing an industry . . . Industries as such have no identity. They are simply a classification of firms which may, for the moment, be convenient. A change of technique or of organisation may require a new classification and a new industry' (1958: 8).

This illustrates the fluidity of the concept of industry membership. The point is that the term actually derives whatever meaning it has from the user's analytic structure. There is no empirical correlate, the industry cannot be reified. Focusing on strategy-making, we are necessarily defining industry membership in terms of perceived groups of competitors and of relations with customers and suppliers, and of alternative ways of looking at these, that is in recipe terms. We can hypothesize connections between the markets, materials, technologies and so forth and the resulting recipes, but we need first to establish the recipes and see how they define industry membership.

4.15 Conclusion

In this chapter I have argued that exploring an industry recipe is an interpretive or phenomenological task. The conventional positivistic methods are inappropriate because they presume the meaning-structure that is here problematic and the actual target of the enquiry

The researcher, having established the recipe to his own satisfaction, then faces the daunting task of communicating it to the audience He must lay out a trail of meaning for it to follow. In my case, each construct is illustrated by analogy with the audience's familiar world. The recipe itself emerges suddenly as the separate constructs coalesce into a meaning-system.

In the next three chapters, I construct trails into three industry recipes. In each case the presentation is a narrative, itself a precis of all the conversations and interactions which make up the research data. I begin with the most complex, that of the iron founders.

5

The Iron Founders

5.1 Introduction

The truth of meaning leading to the iron founders' recipe is really no more than a synopsis of the research interviews. The results are presented as an invitation to the reader to share the researcher's interpretive process. At first sight the data is like a case study and can be formatted in the customary way:

1 General economic, social and technical background to the industry.
2 Summary history of the particular firm being considered.
3 Detailed analysis of the firm's decisions.

But this research differs in that it is cross-sectional. This allows us to focus on the intellectual context in which the firm's problems are framed rather than on the actual decisions made. The recipe emerges in a series of characteristic steps suggesting Barnard's four sub-system model:

1 The environment is segmented into a recognizable product-market structure. The firm's place in economic society becomes clear.
2 The firm's technological, human and financial structures and commitments emerge. The sub-system input and output flows are identified.
3 The problems that must be coped with if the firm is to be synthesized into a coherent rational entity emerge.

At each level the analyst is tempted to call a halt and explain the situation in terms of what he has done. Thus we find many cursory analyses offering explanations in terms of environmental events alone, as if the firm were a passive victim of external events. The next temptation is to explain the firm's condition in terms of one or other sub-system. In this analysis I imply that both the environment and these sub-systems reflect management's strategic choices. Whether these choices are wise and effective depends on management's ability to understand the implications of these choices and address the challenges they present. While these are many and varied, my focus is on the task of creating a coherent rationality which alone enables the firm to grasp the opportunities opened up by these strategic choices. The rationality is neither abstract nor static. It is forged and refashioned as managers respond to specific problems.

5.2 The Industry Background

Modern foundry practice is still rooted in the technology developed around 1720 in Coalbrookdale. Here the Darbys discovered how to smelt iron with coke rather than charcoal, an invention of enormous consequence. Many of the firms in my sample use technology only marginally different from that of the late eighteenth century.

Foundry work is hot, physically exhausting and dangerous. Pig-iron and scrap is melted in a three-stories high coke-fired furnace called a 'cupola'. The whole foundry revolves, as in a ritual, around the operation of the cupola; loading it, firing it, and eventually 'tapping' or draining the molten metal from it. Because of the intense heat inside the furnace, the refractory materials which line its walls must be inspected, repaired or replaced after each firing. Most foundries fire their cupola every other day. The cupola is charged and lit early on the first day. After lunch it is ready to pour. The cupola cools overnight and on the second day its lining can be repaired. The next day it can be charged again. The two day cycle means many foundries operate cupolas in pairs.

The molten metal is tapped into a 'ladle' which is carried by crane or by hand to the point at which casting takes place. While in the ladle the metal's composition can be altered by 'inoculation', adding pinches of other elements, so making other 'grades' of iron. Casting means pouring the liquid metal into a cavity formed within sand. The metal takes up the shape of the cavity and solidifies as it cools. The sand is contained in 'boxes', the cavities formed by 'moulds'. The sand is packed under pressure so as to stand the heat and weight of the metal. The molten metal is poured in through 'runners' and the air escapes through 'risers'. Most casting is in totally enclosed moulding boxes, which separate into halves to allow the sand to be moulded before the metal is poured. The resulting casting is 'knocked out' of the moulding box after cooling.

The sand is moulded with the aid of moulds or 'moulding patterns', wooden or metal pieces shaped the same as the desired finished casting. A pattern can be 'loose' and lifted out after the sand has been packed around it. A pattern can also be 'plated', mounted onto a board and pressed mechanically into the sand to both pack and shape it. This allows some mechanization. Moulding can be done in 'lines' as moulding boxes come up to a 'squeeze' or 'roll-over' press which carries a plated pattern. Loose sand is fed in by hand or by a 'slinger' system. In a mechanized foundry, the finished moulding box is conveyed to a pouring point and thence to a cooling area. When cold enough to handle it goes on to the knock-out. The casting is separated from the moulding box and the sand, and goes to be 'fettled'. There the excess metal which filled the runners, risers and other 'flashes' is removed. The sand, though coloured black, is called 'green' and is generally recovered and cleaned.

Mechanization calls for heavy capital investment. In the days before mechanization the moulders worked very independently, bargaining with the foundry-masters for a rate of so much per casting. The moulders prepared their own sand, boxes and metal. They poured their own castings and knocked them out. Over the years the moulder's ancillary activities have been cut back and mechanized so that he now spends the greater part of his time on the most skilled part of his job, that of preparing and hand finishing the packed sand after using the pattern, to produce the best possible cavity. The final cavity can be further modified with 'cores' which produce penetrations and cavities within the final casting. Core-less casting is simpler than cored casting, in which the cores are also made of green sand and require delicate handling. Chemicals are often added to the sand to help it bond, giving it greater strength and allowing closer moulding tolerances.

Many foundry activities have been mechanized to the point where, in appropriate circumstances, it is possible to load the sand, set the pattern and cores in, pour the metal and knock the box out without much manual intervention. Those who operate the machines are regarded as semi-skilled workers, unlike the moulder or pattern-maker who is a skilled craftsman. Only fettling, cleaning up the finished casting, has resisted mechanization. The occupational dangers are considerable, not only from molten metal, but also from the risk of explosion which follows if metal is poured into damp sand.

Ferrous foundries differ from those which cast steel (and serve an entirely different market) and from those which cast non-ferrous metals such as bronze, aluminium and zinc alloys. These other technologies operate with different temperatures and metal qualities. Many ferrous foundries used to be 'tied' to engineering companies which manufactured railway engines, electrical machinery, machine tools and so forth and so consumed large quantities of iron castings. As the UK engineering industry has changed, so the foundry industry has been restructured and few tied foundries remain. Among the causes of change are losses from the substitution of other materials, such as plastic guttering and drain pipes. But there are also gains, such as the development of cast-iron crankshafts for mass-production cars

Overall the industry has shown a persistent decline in output tonnage, employment and industrial significance. The steady decline noted in the 25 years prior to this research is complicated by a trade cycle of between six and ten years' duration. The post-war peak of 4.2 million tonnes output in 1964 was followed by a peak of 3.8 million tonnes in 1970 and a 25-year low of 3.2 million tonnes in 1974. The number of foundries has fallen steadily from about 1,370 in 1962 to about 700 in 1974. While the numbers of every size category fell, the decline is most marked among the smallest foundries, those employing less than 50 people. The industry is concentrating, with 80 per cent of total production now coming from those foundries that are highly mechanized and employ over 1,000 men. There has been a rise in per capita output from 28.8 tonnes per man per year in 1962 to 38.6 tonnes in 1972. .

The industry is widely regarded as of strategic, technical and economic significance. The National Economic Development Organisation (NEDO) first published its analysis of the present and future state of the industry in 1974. It has been updated periodically since, and continues to make gloomy reading. The level of capital investment persists at 5 per cent or less of turnover. The return on capital employed varies from a high of 9 per cent to substantial losses. Most foundries are struggling to survive in this declining industry. An understandable strategic response might be to diversify out of the industry, maybe into substitute materials. The NEDO report, committed to keeping the UK foundry industry alive rather than being concerned about any particular firm, calls for a 60 per cent increase in investment, greater control over the trade cycle, better working conditions and the rapid recruitment of better qualified managers and technologists (1974: 52).

The Foundry Industry Training Committee (FITC) segments the

industry into seven ferrous material clusters according to metal quality, casting weight, end-user, and production volume (1974: 2). Cluster 5: Iron, medium or heavy jobbing, loose pattern moulding, for unspecified engineering markets, was chosen for further investigation. This cluster has the largest number of establishments, is the most traditional and is relatively stable without rapid changes in market or employment. The FITC statistics show the cluster is far from uniform. It shows a positive correlation between establishment size and the number of administrative personnel (0.52) and a negative correlation between the number of craftsmen and the total number of operators. As the number of operators increases so the number of 'moulder/coremakers' decreases (−0.71) and the number of other craftsmen decreases (−0.60). The implication is that the sample includes foundries that employ different technologies. Instead of maintaining a constant ratio between the numbers of craftsmen and the number of semi-skilled men over various establishment sizes, some establishments have many operators and few craftsmen while others have a more conservative mix with fewer operators and more craftsmen. However, as the total number of operators increases, so the ratios of the various operator categories remain constant: machine moulders (0.55), plate and loose moulders (0.50) and other operators (0.50). Despite including some foundries with many operators and few craftsmen, Cluster 5 shows the highest percentage of skilled employees (28 per cent), with moulders/coremakers accounting for 16 per cent of total employees.

5.3 The Research Sample and Interviews

Of Cluster 5's 44 establishments, five were considered overly special cases and unrepresentative, leaving a preliminary list of 39 foundries spread throughout the UK. To save travel expense, those in three areas, London and Kent, the West Midlands, and Mid-Scotland were targeted. Of the 25 firms in these three areas, 23 were contacted. Though one firm refused outright, 18 were eventually visited. One further foundry close to Manchester was included, making a total sample of 19.

In all cases the interviewee was a senior executive, in 16 the Managing Director, in two the Executive Director, in one the Marketing Director. In some cases the Managing Director was joined by the Financial or Sales Director.

Table I The foundries

Case number	Foundry	Location
1	Bo'ness Iron	Bo'ness, Stirling
2	Chatwin's	Tipton, Staffs.
3	Wm Coupe & Sons	Preston, Lancs.
4	Cruikshank & Co.	Denny, Stirling
5	Dudley	Brierley Hill, West Midlands
6	Forth Alloys	Cumbernauld, Dunbartonshire
7	Fullwood (Hamilton)	Hamilton, Lanarkshire
8	Fullwood (Motherwell)	Motherwell, Lanarkshire
9	Hemel Hempstead Engineering	Hemel Hempstead Herts
10	Henley	Halesowen, Worcs.
11	H & J Hill	Willenhall, Staffs.
12	Ed Matthews	Bilston, Staffs.
13	Jas Maude	Mansfield, Notts.
14	Newcast	Silverdale, Staffs.
15	Thos Perry	Bilston, Staffs.
16	Thos Seager	Faversham, Kent
17	Shaw & McInnes	Glasgow
18	Steel & Garland	Worksop, Notts.
19	Wellman Incanite	Smethwick, West Midlands

I expected some resistance to my tape recorder and on two occasions decided against using it, taking notes instead. On two other occasions the conversation seemed rather stilted until I switched the recorder off. Invariably there was considerable unrecorded discussion, especially during my visit to the moulding shops and over the lunches which most firms generously provided. These remarks were normally an elaboration of what I had already been told. However, as I shall show in the analysis, every construct is supported by recorded discussion; none is introduced with interview notes alone.

Introducing the interview, I often implied that I was not very interested in the detailed figures, rates of production and scrap, the margins, costs and so forth. I tried to make it clear that I was searching for the managers' ways of thinking about their activities and difficulties. Few interviewees thought their replies confidential; they thought what they had to say was well known to other founders. They recognized that much of what they said might be controversial, especially their comments about Government support. They also took a managerial attitude, associating themselves with the owners rather than with the customers, employees or general public. They were surprisingly frank. Their infrequent attempts to rationalize ex-post stood out. Some were quite happy to go into detail on costings, profits, rates of return and so forth, and had these figures at the ready. In every case this information filled in their strategy, never determining it. I was twice asked to keep something confidential; once when discussing a technical innovation, the other occasion when discussing a foundry closure. Most interviewees seemed glad to be able to talk over their concerns, and kept the interview going far longer than I had planned.

5.4 The Foundries

Case 1 – Bo'ness Iron

A traditional private firm owned and managed by experienced foundrymen. Open site by the Firth of Forth in a small declining industrial town. Specializes in man-hole covers, drainage traps, grills etc. – articles which range from the medium (1 tonne) to the very light (1 oz). The bulk of the sales is to the Scottish Local Authorities who use their own designs rather than the British Standard designs which are mass-produced by the larger foundries. Although Bo'ness foresees the end of its protected niche, it feels it does not need to act yet.

The foundry is not mechanized. All moulding is on the floor, with primitive cranage and storage. There is a fine pattern shop and some trial use of carbon-dioxide setting sands for core-making. There have been persistent difficulties with labour, the long local foundry tradition eroded with the closure of the two other local foundries. Although Bo'ness retains a core of skilled men, it finds it very difficult to replace them, being forced to fill in with transient semi- and unskilled labour unfamiliar with foundry work and who hinder the skilled men. No shortage of orders but struggling to contain rising materials costs.

Case 2 – Chatwin's

Small autonomous subsidiary of a major metal manufacturing group. Modest mechanization with small roll-over presses, but majority of the work done with traditional 'snap-flask' and floor moulding boxes.

Real nineteenth-century works buried in the heart of a traditional foundry area. The manager, brought in to save the company from bankruptcy in the 1971 downturn, has redirected it from machine moulding to light delicate work, such as architectural pieces which can be done by only a few other UK foundries. Intimate management style with the skilled moulders negotiating piece rates with management. No shortage of orders. Increasingly severe shortage of moulders.

Case 3 – Wm Coupe & Sons

Private company owned and managed by four foundry-trained sons of the founder who rotate management duties. Restricted and awkward site in an inaccessible village with one alternative employer. Current management style the consequence of the 1971 crisis, resulting in a new consultant designed computerized piece rate system. Speciality medium weight castings (up to 3 tonnes) with 'reasonable' repeats (around 100 per annum) for printing, carpet manufacturing, laundry and general equipment engineers. Considerable mechanization, with special machines from the US under consideration. Emphasis on pattern-making and further mechanization to relieve the shortage of moulding skills.

Case 4 – Cruikshank & Co.

Wealthy, privately owned company in open country with excellent local foundry traditions. Accent on skilled work, that is high quality floor mouldings for pump and compressor manufacturers, crane makers, etc. Limited mechanization, but lavish equipment for metal quality control, including computerized spectrographic analyser. Extensive use of CO_2 and self-setting sands for moulding and cores. Shortage of labour following the rise of the school-leaving age and the trend to earlier retirement. Considerable attention to apprenticeships.

Case 5 – Dudley

Private company owned and managed by experienced foundrymen, who bought the previously tied company out during the 1971 downturn. Extensive mechanization, excellent pattern-shop, widespread use of setting sands for moulding and cores. Special shell moulding section. Computerized accounting and production costing, with variances available two days after the end of the period. Specialities are medium to lightweight semi-mass produced articles for most engineering sectors. Some labour shortage but no desire to draw on the local pool of immigrant labour with mass production foundry experience. Actively considering diversifying into non-ferrous casting and proof-machining on adjacent sites. Aggressive and involved management.

Case 6 – Forth Alloys

New firm established in 1959 by very experienced foundrymen. Attracted to Cumbernauld by the Special Area Development Grant, but also by being close to a traditional foundry labour pool. Extensive mechanization, including automatic fettling booth. Skilled moulders treated as technological advisers to a largely semi-skilled workforce. Specializing in special alloys and ultrasonic testing for the earth moving, bus and truck equipment manufacturers. These engineers pay over the odds for highly accurate, high quality castings which can be set up without proof machining or risk of post-machining rejection for casting flaws. Second speciality in high quality cast compressor crankshafts so competitive that they can displace forged crankshafts in overseas markets.

No cupola, electric furnaces only, supplying two separate shops. One skill oriented floor moulding, the other completely mechanized with automatic sand handling. Ample orders, liaising closely with their customers through two technically qualified sales engineers. Highly profitable, ploughing everything back and intent on steady expansion.

Cases 7 and 8 – Fullwood (BSC Hamilton) and Fullwood (BSC Motherwell)

These two tied foundries turn out all the pig-iron ingot moulds used by British Steel. Though the production process is somewhat different from that of the other firms in the sample, the moulds are handbuilt. The technical control is much greater than in most heavy floor moulding. Each mould is tested and carefully tracked through its entire life. The manufacturing techniques are updated constantly in a search for greater ingot mould life. The Fullwood foundries monopolize the ingot mould business. They typically plan a slight surplus over BSC requirements, selling the margin not required to the Scandinavians. They face eventual closure due to the introduction of continuous casting. The employees are not likely to get other work within BSC, nor do their skills match other foundries' needs.

Case 9 – Hemel Hempstead Engineering

A newly re-equipped foundry, purchased by a successful group specializing in motor components. New management team, familiar with the new market. All jobs introduced through parent company. Job costing and estimating done by computer. Excellent open site Solid core of skilled men, but high turnover among the semi-skilled. Accent on pattern development, generally in metal, to ensure the mechanized moulding plant can be operated without skilled men. The motor industry sets tough standards on speed, quality and price, and these generate a characteristically tough management style.

Case 10 – Henley

A subsidiary of GEC–AEI, recently re-equipped with new management. Labour force reduced by 30 per cent. Redirected out of the declining market for core-less fuseboxes into general engineering. Immediate problems are lack of skills, poor local employment reputation and shortage of orders. New management from the motor castings trade has succeeded in stabilizing employment, regenerating pattern and core-making, introducing some counter cyclic business and laying out a recovery plan.

Case 11 – H. & J. Hill

Small foundry, subsidiary of an industrial group with many interests in other fields. The foundry business was once central to the group. Previously managed by an autocratic manager who died without warning. He had initiated a major investment programme without any other executive being fully aware of its nature or purpose. Subsequently run by a non-foundry accountant who invested in mechanized plant without focusing on particular markets, so taking the company into direct competition with the large-scale mechanized producers. Under utilization for several years, followed by price cutting to win orders. The group has decided to make no further investments and close down when appropriate. Few skilled men remain.

Case 12 – Ed Matthews

Same parent group as Chatwin (Case 2). Small foundry, but extensively mechanized for the volume production of small items. Some rationalization of facilities and personnel between the two companies with the intention of sustaining investment in both. A portion of the output is for Chatwin's parent company, transferred at below open-market prices. Emphasis on pattern development, to facilitate intensive production, and on industrial relations to increase per capita productivity.

Case 13 – Jas Maude

Same group as Steel & Garland (Case 18). Both foundries run by young, foundry-trained management. Modest mechanization, specializing in high quality, high accuracy castings in a wide range of metals for technologically sophisticated customers who need gearbox, compressor, pump and valve castings with reference faces cast in. Medium weight range (100 lbs to 2 tonnes) with medium production runs (around 40 off per week).

Case 14 – Newcast

Substantial foundry established in 1947 under the present Managing Director. The company changed hands in 1962 and in 1969. Now part of a major UK engineering group which has ensured substantial investment and demanded high commercial performance. General jobbing in the medium weight range (100 lbs to 8 tonnes), both one-off and repetitions. Piece rates negotiated with management. Semi-mechanized with customers among the pottery, valve and colliery equipment, compressor and diesel engine manufacturers. Intensely concerned with training because of the shortage of skilled men, though many leave for more money as soon as their training is complete. Also concerned about management succession for many of the industry's senior managers retire in the next few years.

Case 15 – Thos Perry

Tied foundry, the subsidiary of one of the two UK roll-makers, whose work since 1810 has consisted entirely of casting and machining rolls for the rolling-mills which manufacture tinplate, railway rail and steel section. With mill costs soaring, down-time is more and more expensive. Roll quality, measured in terms of the tonnes rolled before roll replacement, becomes the major determinant of operating profit. As in the Fullwood foundries, a very specialized technology.

Case 16 – Thos Prayer

Private company formed in 1964 to produce high quality castings for the hydraulic, valve, machine tool and general engineering markets. Open site but residential development closing in on the foundry. Mechanized with plant-wide automatic sand recovery, cleaning and delivery system. Geared to semi-mass production rates of 1,000 items per week. Highly profitable with full order book. Determined to expand entirely out of profits. Skilled men are company trained, there being no pool of local foundrymen. Extensive use of labour saving techniques. Computerized costing system and quality control laboratory. Company objective to make 15 per cent net on turnover in good times, over double the industry average, and to keep break-even volumes low to shield profits during bad times.

Case 17 – Shaw and McInnes

Almost the last surviving Glasgow foundry, established on the present, now awkward site in 1846. Now a subsidiary of one of the UK's largest trading companies. Extensively re-equipped five years ago, with a shift to electric melting anticipated to enable it to handle a wider range of metals. Speciality supplier of iron pipework from inches to several feet in diameter for power stations, chemical and sewage plants, etc. Huge order book. Extensive use of setting sands. Special machining and flanging facilities required for this market. Managed by an accountant who has been with the firm 40 years, broken only by his war service. Most items are one-off. Though skilled labour is short, the rate of foundry closure in Glasgow has ensured a recent surplus.

Case 18 – Steel & Garland

Run and owned in conjunction with Jas Maude (Case 13); same comments apply.

Case 19 – Wellman Incanite

Nickel-chrome alloy foundry specializing in internal parts for marine and power station boilers, and other high temperature applications. An interesting comparison with green-sand foundries; the techniques are similar but the necessary levels of skill are significantly higher because of the trickier metal and finer tolerances. Considerable investment, mechanizing moulding and core-making, sand handling and electric melting. Risk of losing skilled workers rules out relocation. Huge order book gained in a global market in which each major industrial country has no more than one or two suppliers, all equally flooded with work. Managed by a team of technically qualified professionals.

5.5 Interpreting the Interviews, 1: Introduction

In Chapter 3 I argued that the firm's policy choices are limited by what can be legitimately pursued within the firm's socio-economic context. These choices resolve its political freedom of manoeuvre. The policy choices need not be rational, coherent, realistic or consistent. Strategy-making, not policy choosing, is the process of creating the firm's rationality, resolving the uncertainties and implementing the policy choices in the firm's situation. The strategy is rational when it reflects the external influences and constraints over which the firm has no control. These influences and constraints are the 'facts' of the situation. But they are not self-evident, readily obvious to outsiders. Their identification, selection and evaluation is part of the strategy-making process.

The most obvious feature of the foundry industry is its decline. Prior to World War II the industry supplied a wide variety of castings for subsequent machining by all manner of engineering manufacturers. Architectural castings were widely used. But all showed the engineering design fashions of the time. The castings were heavy, lightly stressed, inaccurately cast and inexpensive. They deadened sound and vibration, and were of such massive proportions that they tolerated considerable internal defects. But they also required considerable machining to remove excess metal. These design fashions have changed. Modern engineering calls for lightweight, highly stressed, accurate castings which cannot tolerate internal defects. Thus the total weight of castings must continue to fall, even if the castings market does not shrink because of competitive pressure or other causes.

5.6 Interpreting the Interviews, 2: General Environment

Declining general demand (Construct 1)

The first construct is that of declining general demand. It appears in such statements as

We feel that the foundries will be down to 400 within the next five or six years, and we want to be one of the 400. (Case 16)

Foundries are closing rapidly. There are not a lot of us left and we are lucky to have survived. (Case 17)

I think in future we must look at spheroidal graphite because the growth in that type of casting is rapid and there is contraction in the remainder of the industry. (Case 11)

These are extremely mild comments when we consider the extent of the decline in grey iron tonnage and the modest growth of the quite different spheroidal graphite (SG) market. The first surprise is the discovery that few managers associate their own circumstances with the appalling industry situation revealed in the NEDO report. This is even more surprising when we recognize that Cluster 5, the research sample, is the most technologically conservative and least capital intensive part of the industry. We might have expected this to be the part most affected by the decline. Clearly we need to distinguish most carefully between what managements say about their own firms and what they say about the industry. Cases 11 and 16 suggest they see niches which offer them chances of survival and prosperity. We must suspect that managers see a much finer level of market segmentation than suggested either by the FITC clustering or the NEDO report.

Cyclical market (Construct 2)

The foundrymen take the cyclical nature of their markets for granted. But the pattern of leads and lags, as it works through from engineering orders to castings orders, leaves them at the 'end of the line'. This exaggerates the cyclic nature of the business. There is disagreement in the industry about whether the cycle is regular and a feature of the foundry business, or whether it is determined by the overall economic fluctuations.

This cycle has been on a long time. It is difficult for one to say what is the cause of it. The supply and demand, that sort of thing. (Case 4)

We are quoting 6, 7 sometimes 8 months because we have a long order book, but it is peaks and troughs. Three years ago we were quoting 6 to 8 weeks. It just depends on how demand and supply equate. We were really working hand to mouth in 1971. (Case 17)

We used to have three reps but cut that down to one when things were tight in 1972. Sometimes you lower your prices, you make at breakeven point. And I see this situation could well arise in two years' time. But when you are at capacity you can extend delivery dates. Delivery has gone to 16 weeks and that has never happened before. (Case 3)

Some companies allude to cyclicality as they explain their attempts to balance their turnover.

The markets that contract the least when there is a recession are the compressor people, printing people, the people that sell beer and the people that sell newspapers. Refrigeration plants, we did get into that market, but unfortunately they could not pay the price we needed. But we have got into the compressor market and printing. (Case 3)

We've got a big spread of customers through industry generally on the basis that if the machine tools are down then probably control valves are up and that sort of thing. (Case 16)

It is as well to recognize that some of these managers only tried to find counter-cyclic work after reading the NEDO report, which was familiar to most. Yet the only firm which felt that it had successfully established a broad anti-cyclic portfolio had done so already, before the report was published. Many who tried after reading the report decided it inappropriately distorted their customer portfolio.

Tied foundries (Construct 3)

The third construct alludes to one traditional source of insurance against cyclical downturns. This is for the foundry to be tied, to become a subsidiary of a parent who is also a customer. This arrangement shields the foundry from open market conditions.

The group as a whole doesn't encourage . . . by all means, everything else being equal, go to a company within the group, but you have got absolute freedom of choice where you buy and where you sell. (Case 17)

We've tried to stop trading within the group because the transfer pricing was very much to our disadvantage. (Case 2)

We find quite a lot of these tied foundries, when they are busy everything is all right. But as soon as their own engineering work gets short, then they go out onto the general market. They they are told, keep your foundry going at all costs and they come in with a reduced price. That can affect us quite a lot, but as soon as they get busy they literally go and leave their customer. Well, they have kept their foundry going, but they do a lot of damage to the price structure of the industry. (Case 4)

They were told by their friends at Vauxhall Motors, particularly in the purchasing department, that if they could get hold of a good foundry somewhere they would fill them up with work. There's never been any question that if we found hard times Vauxhall would pull work out of other places and put it in here. Even pay a little bit more for it because of the very close ties we have got. (Case 9)

Segment-specific under-supply (Construct 4)

The market is segmented in many ways, not only in the degree of protection. Some foundrymen perceive that the decline of their particular market segment is not as fast as the shrinkage of total foundry capacity. They separate demand from supply in each segment.

We tended to get the benefit of those foundry closures in other areas because the work has still got to be done. We ourselves are pretty convinced that for the years ahead there is a definite shortage of good foundry capacity, not just in the UK, but in the Western world generally. (Case 6)

We are pinning all our faith on foundries closing. We are very busy at the moment, the same as nearly every foundry in the country. But we feel, with the Health & Safety Acts and the Clean Air Acts and all the rest of the legislation that is hitting foundries on the head, that enough people will say it is not worth the investment. We've only got to concentrate on one foundry, because that is all we have got. There are foundries that can afford it, but for everyone of us there are going to be four or five who cannot. (Case 16)

You find that a lot of foundries down South have lost their skilled floor moulders and they have kept their machine moulding sections going and they don't have the capacity for the jobbing type of work any more. (Case 4)

Well, you can't go wrong in the casting field at the moment. Let's face it, half the foundries in the country have shut down and the rest are ready to. There's a fantastic market here. (Case 9)

This is more evidence of the fine degree of market segmentation apparent at the managerial level. Successful managers have to have a subtle feel for the various kinds of work available within the generally depressed situation. They also have to understand the resources and capacity necessary to win and meet these orders.

The need to solicit business (Construct 5)

These foundrymen concentrate on their own businesses rather than on the state of the industry, especially if they have plenty of orders on hand. Traditionally, the length of the order book is short at around six weeks. The crucial indicator of the individual foundry's relationship with the market is less a matter of the order book length than of whether it needs to go out and solicit enquiries.

We have a Sales Manager who has an assistant, but we keep them locked up here most of the time because over the past 7 or 8 years we have had either enough orders to cope with our planned expansion or, in the bad times, so much new work coming in from existing customers because of the closures of other foundries. (Case 16)

Since 1971 the sales rep hasn't been out. He doesn't need to. (Case 2)

Rather than how do we select our facilities to fall into line with the motor trade's requirements, it is more a case of them, because of the very close relationship between our company and General Motors . . . selecting the jobs they are in trouble with. (Case 9)

Even in this declining industry, most of the firms sampled felt it unnecessary to sell actively. Those that had had to do so understood that they had become exposed and seriously threatened.

We, in our wisdom, set about making manhole step-irons on this plant, which is an ideal running line for this equipment, and then we set out to market them. (Case 11)

We may have been supplying him with a certain type of roll which is going to be 30% more than he has been paying before. He usually throws up his hands in horror, so we may guarantee it gives you 30% in performance over the other one. You've got to do that else you would never sell it. (Case 15)

Customers' long-term prospects (Construct 6)

Finer market segmentation means greater reliance on one's relationships with a smaller group of customers. The supply and demand patterns change segment by segment, so foundries which want to retain the initiative will explore the long-term prospects of their potential customers. This is especially important if a major proportion of capacity is tied up with one customer.

On two occasions in the last 18 months we have done our own market survey, taking all our customers who took more than 1% of our production and we have analysed where the bulk of their stuff goes to. A very large part of those customers are related to the energy industries and this gives us considerable hope because whatever happens, no matter what Government we have in power, it must support the development of energy and power. (Case 6)

We've got a broad decision that we won't do more than 12% for any one customer . . . the latest figures I've done for last year, there were two customers who had more than 10%. Nobody gets more than a 10% slice of our cake. Several people have said to us 'we want more'. (Case 16)

5.7 First Summary

A product-market analysis characterizes the firm's market. It leads to decisions about whether to sell the existing products to more customers or to widen the range of products which can be produced from the firm's existing resources and sold to the existing customers, or a mixture of these. The first six constructs tell us something about the way foundry managements view their markets and customers. Most seem satisfied that they can survive in their niches and do not feel they have to diversify into unfamiliar businesses. Although the industry is in decline, the pressures seem to be coming from elsewhere, and suggesting different strategies.

Material supplies and costs are not a major issue. There is no desire to integrate backwards to absorb supplier uncertainty. All raw iron is supplied by British Steel at fixed prices. All fuel comes from the Coal or Electricity Boards at fixed prices. There is some uncertainty about the supply of scrap-iron, exacerbated by the UK's membership of the EEC and the collapse of the UK scrap market, previously stabilized by the DTI. Cost inflation is a problem, but raw materials and fuel together only account for around 26 per cent of the sales value of the industry as a whole. It should be somewhat less when, as in Cluster 5, the accent is on maximizing the skill content of the final casting. Being oil derivatives, there are some uncertainties about the supply and pricing of the resins and the other sand setting chemicals.

5.8 Interpreting the Interviews, 3: Labour

The local labour pool (Construct 7)

The decline in the workforce is a completely different matter. As the NEDO makes clear, there is a continuing decline in the numbers employed in the industry, and in the available skill-base.

But no firm deals with the labour market in general. The market each experiences is finely segmented to its geographical locale. Some firms find a local pool already trained, and a tradition that allows it to continue.

Basically it is all floor moulding. We are still fortunate to have quite a few skilled moulders in this area. (Case 4)

We inherited a good supply of skilled men here. (Case 2)

It was the nearest place to the foundry area of Falkirk, Bonnybridge, Denny and so on where there was a pool of foundry labour. (Case 6)

Some foundries might previously have had access to a pool, but now that has gone and they sometimes have to struggle to retain their skilled men.

Labour is the real raw material. We had a very bad reputation locally. Now I emphasize stability. (Case 10)

They can't just walk out of here and go across the road and get a job. There used to be a dozen foundries within a mile of here, now there is only one in Glasgow. These things help to make life that bit easier. (Case 17)

Training the available labour (Construct 8)

The traditional source of skilled men was the apprenticeship scheme which each firm ran. After the war, the in-company and day release schemes were reorganized under the FITC. The result is a Training Levy and considerable expenditure by Local Authorities. Some companies make this work for them.

I have got 14 moulder/coremakers on day release. (Case 4)

We have apprentices. They have got to serve . . . I think it is 4 years now. (Case 3)

Other firms are disappointed.

We can still attract young fellas into the industry. We do have apprentices, but we don't send them on day release. The type of labour you get, unfortunately, just is not interested. They are glad to get away from school and they are not going to go back. If you insist, well, they just pack up and go elsewhere. (Case 17)

Apprentices just want to go on and teach. Young men who do come into the industry want to get into management. Ultimately, shortage of skilled men will kill the business. (Case 2)

Other firms provide for themselves, doing their own training.

There isn't another foundry of our type nearer than High Wycombe, so that if we want anything, we train it. We have something like half a dozen on our books, two of those have qualified by experience and are every bit as good. We don't really see that we shall take any moulders or coremakers on for a long time. (Case 16)

But this may dilute the bargaining power of the conventionally trained skilled moulders.

When I talk about a skilled moulder, I'm talking about someone who holds a union card. We have, this year, come to an agreement with the union that we can upgrade a general labourer to do moulding duties as long as he joins the union etcetera. We paid quite a lump sum out to each existing moulder for them to accept this. It had to be done, we were losing money, we couldn't produce enough castings. Eventually we agreed to pay them £100 tax-free per man, and £2 per week on their wages. (Case 3)

Given the relative lack of concern with materials, we now have constructs enough to cover the inputs and outputs, and so encompass the operation. In fact, we have just about enough to describe the traditional foundry. The nineteenth-century firm was little more than an administrative and marketing channel for the skills and efforts of the men on the shop-floor. It was a simple framework for bringing customers, moulders, and casting facilities together. The business was driven by the customer's need, and customers would sort out any technical details directly with the moulders. The firm, which took the order, effectively sub-contracted the work to the shop-floor workgroup, which would include moulders, pattern-makers and labouring apprentices. The appropriate piece rate would be negotiated, the margin between the piece rate and the price covering the moulder's rent of floor space and facilities, costs of administration and the foundry's entrepreneurial profit.

This arrangement meant the firm need take little interest in or responsibility for the way the work was done or organized. But this is no longer the case.

5.9 Interpreting the Interviews, 4: Technological Environment

Managing the foundry's technology (Construct 9)

There have been enormous changes in the relative costs of the plant and the labour. Management's financial risk is now so high that it feels obliged to control the work more closely. A substantial degree of technological control has to be imposed onto the shop-floor, whether the work is skilled or not.

You can't be producing SG castings weighing 3 tons and water pumps of one-eighth inch section from the same base material because you've got to make molybdenum and nickel additions to tighten the grain up. (Case 9)

In a cupola, if you've got a charge on, you don't know exactly when the metal is going to appear. So you might overlap one lot or another lot. And you could possibly be in trouble casting a thin section job in grade 20, so we try to inoculate in the ladle which is more expensive. (Case 3)

Our general overall strategy is to aim for the higher grades of metal. We have got the control, we have got the metallurgists, we are carrying the overhead to make these higher grades which a lot of people do not want to take. (Case 16)

Mechanizing the traditional process (Construct 10)

It can be seen that the modern type of foundry can be distinguished by the way it does, or does not, manage the skilled men and the technology. The old style moulder accepted or rejected work, took the molten metal made available at the cupola and inoculated it according to his own ideas. He built his own patterns, set his own runners, risers and cores, and did his own knock-out and fettling, etc. The modern foundry is no longer controlled by the moulders. It is controlled by the managers who determine the scope of business as described by the first eight constructs

Today's customers, production systems and design fashions demand predictability rather than creativity. Modern castings are highly stressed and cast in exotic materials. Management controls the technology through its investment decisions and by establishing operational standards. As the contingency theorists point out, the consequent changes of production technology force changes in the administrative technology. Some managements have been able to codify, capture and optimize the appropriate technology of administration in the ways sought by Taylor and Fayol.

Technological control can be achieved in two ways. Mechanization has de-skilled much of the work, so that suitably equipped semi-skilled men can be integrated into a powerful and easily controlled productive force. But the technological advances have also substantially leveraged the skills of both moulder and pattern-maker. This uses technology for control in a different way, and is also a strategy for dealing with the shortage of skilled labour.

We don't just have one moulder for one job. He gets half a dozen jobs and if there is any holdup on one job, he goes onto another. So he has no downtime at all and we are producing a vast amount of tonnage and standard hours' work per moulder by virtue of this. (Case 3)

We still keep a few floor moulders, but they're less and less available. In fact I don't know how a number of competitors and foundries are managing in the business because they are only working at half-cock, because they just will not do the job. (Case 11).

We are putting in plant to assist the moulders, but not moulding machines. (Case 4)

We can't make a reasonable profit off the very easy castings, we must accept a modicum of difficulty. The skill is all done in the pattern work. You don't rely on the skill of the moulder. More and more you are coming to the point where you take all the work and get the machine to do it. (Case 3)

We try and do as simple methods as possible. We spend a lot of money on our patterns, we charge the customers twice as much for the patterns as anyone else does, not only because we like a bigger cut, but we like to make them the way we want them. We've standardized with bolsters and pattern-plates. We like to get it so the patterns sit in open prints and close over with bags of clearance. Generally we have tried to standardize and simplify so that even my kids could come and put cores in. And, let's face it, some of the people who work for us are no better than kids, so you have to try and take the human element out of it as much as you can. (Case 9)

New process possibilities (Construct 11)

One side of new production methods is the need for a new administrative approach. The other side of changing the technology of production is the new product possibilities that are opened up. Technology that de-skills generally means building a special purpose system designed to do specific work. In effect the system will be programmed and optimized for that work. Flexible systems, which are unspecialized and can be turned to a variety of tasks, are quite different. Far from taking the 'human element' out of the work, they add to the range and power of a skilled man's artistry.

What we are finding as time goes by is that the foundry industry is becoming de-skilled to a certain extent, so it really doesn't matter quite so much about the skilled men . . . with the advent of the air-set process, which has de-skilled it further and further, it is a perfect way to make a one-off. (Case 16)

From the constructs above we know foundries are not all looking for a way to diversify away from the traditional lines of business. On the contrary, even though there is overall decline, the demand for high quality product often outstrips the skilled men available. New technology, however, is expanding the boundaries of the business. The one-off comment above applies to the manufacture of production prototypes for engineering customers who are looking for lightweight, highly stressed, complex shaped castings with lots of internal structure which must be produced with cores. This technology captures business from the highly specialized prototype machining shops who normally manufacture these prototypes from solid stock.

The new metallurgy also opens up the possibility of capturing business from the forgemasters. Twenty years ago no one would have dreamt of casting a lightweight engine or compressor crankshaft, which would have been drop-forged. Now the escalating cost of dies and forge time, and the consequent expense of incorporating design changes into ever lighter, more highly stressed and accurately produced forgings, exposes the forgemasters to the founders.

5.10 Second Summary

The first six constructs make it possible to characterize the foundry's general environment. Constructs 7 and 8 capture the founders' definitions of the principal consumable resource, labour. The last three constructs (9, 10 and 11) describe the founders' technological environment. The main options are beginning to emerge. We are beginning to get an idea of how the successful foundry must deal with and balance off the strategic choices which determine these sub-systems. In short, assuming reasonable policy choices, we have reached another point of possible closure on a strategy.

Assuming we intend to maximize profit, we can systematically:

1 look for market niches with minimal decline or even growth possibilities (Construct 1), and ensure that the customers who are our channels into these niches have reasonable long-term prospects (Construct 6);
2 select from these niches, avoiding those which are excessively cyclic (Construct 2), preferring those which offer under-supply and thus less competitive pressure (Construct 4);
3 make some estimates about the cost of getting orders by aggressive direct marketing and competitive pricing (Construct 5);
4 identify and avoid the markets served by tied foundries who will disturb the market when times are tight (Construct 3);
5 having identified the market needs, draw up the production options and the alternative technologies which can be applied, select those which combine low cost with quality adequate to access the high margin business, or select those which lead to unique production capabilities on which super-normal profits can be reaped (Constructs 10 and 11);
6 identify the labour necessary to run and operate this plant, assess the skills available locally (Construct 7) and the possibilities and costs of adding to the local supply as necessary;
7 given an understanding of the union activity and the workplace

expectations, determine appropriate technologies of administration and control (Construct 9).

Now we can 'do our sums', set sales and profits targets and see whether the project meets our investment criteria.

Although this is an over-simplification of a true investment evaluation, it covers most of the territory, with the possible exception of the recruitment of the management team. The sketch above seems an entirely acceptable basis for enquiring into a foundry's strategy.

5.11 The Next Level of Analysis

Maybe this kind of investment analysis goes on when a new foundry is being considered, but it does not seem to capture the way the managers were thinking. We might conclude that this, more than anything revealed so far, shows their lack of professionalism. On the other hand, we might show more respect and suspect that we have to do further research before we can be sure of what the managers are really doing. We might better interpret our sense of their shortcoming as evidence that we have not yet grasped their rationality.

The analysis above actually illustrates the investor's cast of mind. We are still in the realm of policy, out of touch with the firm's rationality and with the strategy-making processes which create it. We have yet to grasp the rationality the managers impose on and articulate through the firm. The managers are committed. Their point of view is necessarily different from that of the investor trying to evaluate the risks of getting involved. The investor presupposes competent management who will bridge the gap between his investment and the resultant revenue. He has no knowledge of how this will be done. That is what we must now explore.

The investor presupposes profit as the goal. As much debate within micro-economics shows, there is little empirical evidence that managers are profit maximizers (Alchian 1965). Without this assumption, I could not have brought the 11 constructs above together. Part of the interpretive method, therefore, is to avoid over-hasty closure by assuming too much about the problem being researched. We can see the problem in terms of the amount of interview evidence that can be encompassed by our framework. If we assume the managers are profit maximizers, too much of what they say must be left out. We must expand and enrich our conceptual framework so that we capture more of the data. While we will never

capture it all, we are now at the point of which Barnard wrote when
he said that analysis reaches the edge of the organization and then
retreats (1938 : ix).

5.12 Interpreting the Interviews, 5: Management Mechanisms

Management of the customer portfolio (Construct 12)

Any foundry, even when mechanized, has an extremely broad
capability. Though cranage and pour capacity may imply upper
limits in the size of piece that can be cast, the principal limitation
is the craftsmen's skills. In this business, these skills are relatively
general. But, if it is to serve its customers effectively, the firm must
focus itself onto specific parts of the markets to which these skills
could be applied. There is a considerable need to limit the work
accepted to that which can be performed profitably. The technology
does not limit the work adequately. Without focus, the ongoing
interaction between the work undertaken, the mistakes made and the
lessons learned is insufficient to ensure mastery of the production
process and continued profitability. Far from dealing with the whole
market, the management must focus the firm sharply with specialisms
for a highly segmented market.

It has several mechanisms for doing this. It can control the
acceptance of new business. This is easiest if all sales·activity is
handled in the office. When the foundry puts salesmen on the road
there is an immediate loss of control. When there is a surplus of
enquiries, the foundry can specialize further and accept only the
business that best suits its strategy. When orders are short, it becomes
difficult to resist the temptation to take any work that will occupy
unused capacity.

Broadly speaking, profitability is always a function of a firm's
control over its market. At the extreme, when the firm has total
control over its market, it has a true monopoly. While no foundry is
likely to achieve such control, we can reasonably suspect that market
power is a more likely managerial objective than profitability. Such
power can be gained. The crux is the firm's relationship with its
customers. The firm seeks a 'special relationship' which, like all
power, needs to be exercised with discretion if it is to endure.

Part of a special relationship is its reciprocal nature, its pattern of
mutual involvement in a shared world. It becomes visible as the

foundry's willingness to take on undesirable work, even sub-
contracting it out, to keep the relationship from turning 'sour'. This
shifts the analysis away from the work and onto the customer. The
foundry management really controls whom it works for rather than
what work it does. Thus Construct 12 refers to the portfolio of
customers rather than to the portfolio of tasks or capabilities. Here
a 'market-driven' style of thought contrasts with the alternative 'task-
driven' or 'technology-driven' styles.

We don't go out to get jobbing work from anybody as a policy, but if
someone is giving us a reasonable crack of the whip on their machine
moulding, then we'll throw in the odd bit of jobbing work if it helps them.
(Case 16)

Let's say we have become more selective in the business that we take than
we were originally, on the grounds of suitability, continuity, always with the
factor in the back of our minds, that we may take certain work on that is
not, if it stood on its own, entirely the sort of work that we would select,
but in order to give a good customer in other fields of production what he
requires, we will put that through for them and take it. (Case 6)

Inevitably, because we are their main supplier and the main turnover with
them is the jobs that we want and need, they do say 'Ah, you must make
us some of the stuff you don't really want because we have difficulty getting
it anywhere else'. (Case 3)

Foundry work is generally contracted for on an item by item basis.
Selective pricing is another way the foundry can manipulate its
customer list, though most managers find it an unsatisfactory
mechanism.

If it is a job of Grade 17 or above that particularly suits our type of
production, we will look at the quote extremely carefully. If it is Grade 14,
we will make sure we get a good price for it. Probably they shouldn't buy
from us anyway, but we still get the orders. We have marked up our 14 to
the stage where we shouldn't get it, so if we do, at least we are getting the
return per ton that we are looking for. It appears to be working slowly,
although in the last year there has been one of the unfortunate situations
where we seem to have too much Grade 14. (Case 16)

We then realized that we were dealing with some firms unprofitably and
always had been doing. It was then my job to go to these firms and tell
them that that was what we had been doing and that we needed, possibly,
150% increase on certain articles and a minimum of 50% on others. Once
we found out what our true costs were, we had very little difficulty bumping
up the price to realistic levels. Inevitably we lost one or two jobs that went
to fabrication. (Case 3)

Management's involvement in the special relationship
(Construct 13)

Because of the subtlety of the special relationship and its importance to the firm, maintaining it becomes a strategic matter. It cannot be delegated to sales or technical staff. Management is intimately involved with the customer. Every interaction becomes part of the delicate process of managing the bi-lateral relationship. This is a far cry from the arm's length pre-WWII foundry-master's style.

Two of the three directors, no one else in the place has the authority to take on any new work. Normally we do it that we take a weekly look at the quotes that have been prepared and we say 'No, not interested in that one' or 'Yes, we'll go for that one, send that out but follow it with an immediate phonecall and say we are really interested in this sort of work if you'd like to come and talk to us about it'. (Case 16)

It is processed and examined by the methods engineers, they come up with their recommendations. It may stop at that point, but normally it would go on from that point to costing and it would be costed out on a cost card at that stage. When it gets finally to that point it is examined by Mr Dawson, who is the Managing Director, and his sales coordinator, Mr Wright. They sit down together, along with, probably, the works manager and they pat the ball around and decide what the answer is. That is the general method of handling it. (Case 6)

The time when management exercises its greatest power over its customers is when it decides to close down capacity. Thus this construct also deals with senior management's co-ordination of the order book and its capacity planning decisions. Setting up additional capacity is largely a matter of expanding the moulders' and pattern-makers' skills.

There is always one new job going through the foundry for Caterpillar. There is always one new pattern going through, either being made or being sampled. As soon as one is approved and in production, we get another from them. The account is building up that way because they want high quality castings. (Case 16)

You know doorknobs. They are tricky little castings and there is a big market for them and I thought 'We could make doorknobs'. So I went along to a customer and got an order for thousands of these, but in a light section. We fiddled about, we put patterns down at our own expense, and we made a complete hash of it. And we couldn't make it. (Case 2)

While mechanization is a method of control over the workforce, it can put management into the hands of the firms supplying the equipment. It also makes management more dependent on the new class of foundry technologists who know how to make the increasingly sophisticated equipment operate.

It is a simple rule with brake-drums, there is no contraction in the vertical plane. It took us four months to find that out – and a lot of scrap brake-drums. We altered the patterns and made some more and it was different. We altered the patterns again and made some more. We made the mistake of altering some very expensive pattern equipment on the strength of a dozen bloody castings, instead of fifty castings. Eventually we had to cut the top off the pattern and put a piece in because we had taken so much off and it was undersize. But we have now realised that if you make a pattern to standard rule instead of to contraction on the height, you get it dead right first time. These things are that if we'd had a chap with the right experience at the time we would have known, but our chap on the brake-drums didn't come till after that. (Case 9)

The problems of developing skills are matched by those of sustaining existing skills. A moulder loses his touch quite fast. Skills cannot be put on a shelf as can the tape of a numerically controlled machine tool.

We are finding that quite a lot of people from the South come up here looking for this type of capacity. You find a lot of foundries down South have kept their moulding machine sections going and they don't have the capacity for the jobbing type of work any more. (Case 4)

The change in the industry's skill base is not a simple matter of the decline in the number of skilled moulders. The workforce's skills are always a consequence of the work managements give them to do. The decline in the industry's ability to produce ornate architectural castings is directly balanced by its growing ability to produce the highly stressed, lightweight and accurate castings required by other types of customer.

The management of the customer portfolio and its co-ordination with capacity planning is the detailed tactic of repositioning the foundry, moving it from one market segment to another. It is the crux of the marketing strategy. The foundry cannot assume that buying new capacity, be it machines or moulders, enables it to do new business with any degree of success. The possibilities for moving the foundry away from its present lines of work, or its specialities as seen by its customers, are severely limited. Given a choice, the foundry would change its customers before it risked changing its capacity.

Constructs 12 and 13 deal with the delicate balance between marketing a general service and being a speciality supplier. Managements may try to control this balance, but they must adapt as the market conditions their customers face change (Constructs 1, 4 and 6), as the technology which defines their capacity changes (Constructs 10 and 11), as the scarcity value of their shop-floor skills changes (Constructs 7 and 8), and so forth. So long as they experience a surplus of orders (Construct 5) and are free to make their own product-market decisions (Construct 3), they have power over their markets and are 'ahead of the game'. From this position they can afford to try and anticipate developments and move out of declining market segments into ones with better prospects.

Managing capacity changes

The notion of maximizing market power seems sufficient to pull the constructs together. But it is difficult to see how Construct 2 fits in, how the emerging rationality takes care of the cyclic nature of the business. Most foundries, even those with most success in establishing these quasi-monopolistic special relationships with their customers, have to find a way of coping with the periodic downturns. When business is slack, the thought is to go out and get other business. This is now getting close to the heart of the managerial rationality, understanding how the firm's freedoms of action are charted and navigated.

If you go out and sell, when it does pick up we are really going to let people down, and they have long memories. Better to struggle through at just above break-even point than go and commit ourselves to work that in six months' time we are going to let everybody down on and lose them forever. So it's a conscious decision. We don't always take work on when some people would say we should be taking work on. So we have made a conscious decision to take on work that we can do at all times. (Case 16)

I have a basic philosophy towards acquiring work. No new customers are taken on when the industry is slack. When the industry is busy, you are busy, but then is the time that you must expand to take on the work that is available. Because you are not going to get work when you are slack. I suppose that applies to every industry anyway, not just foundry jobs, but I have proved it to be quite true. (Case 3)

I have been in this game for so long and it is not policy to completely ignore the less profitable people. For the time might come when you are right at the bottom, when you are thankful to get this sort of thing to keep you going. So if you want them to do that, then you must respect them when you are busy too. (Case 4)

This is the other side of the special relationship, the reciprocal part of market power. In practice the relationship only survives because of its mutuality, its even handedness. The market's cycles mean that during the downswing, the power passes from the founders to their customers. When business is booming, foundry capacity is hard to find and the initiative returns to the founders. But now the engineers are in dire need of castings, running short at the time their own margins are strongest and their orders most valuable. The dimensions of the special relationship are that, when the business peaks, the founders will service their customers' needs, and when the business troughs, the customers will give their founders sufficient work for them to survive. The founders cannot expand or re-equip when business is down, simply because their thoughts are on survival. They can only expand when at their busiest because they must be able to carry their customer portfolio through the whole trade cycle.

Pursuing a quasi-monopoly and avoiding competition (Construct 14)

The foundry's technology is flexible enough, in a purely technical sense, for it to be applied to almost any part of the grey iron market, as the story of the doorknobs (Case 2) illustrates. The most efficient foundries should be able to capture more business, exploit economies of scale and expand using a very competitive strategy. Yet it is clear that these managers are working hard to avoid this kind of competition. Indeed they know that the customers who send work out for competitive bid, and then choose suppliers on price alone, are to be avoided. But the founders compete instead for the right to serve their customers in the way that panders to the customer's belief that his work is special, that he differs from his other engineering competitors.

We are not the sort of foundry to put a foundry in and go and say, look what we have got, come and take up our capacity. We would far rather go to somebody and say, look, what do you want us to produce. And if you want it that badly, are you prepared to come along with us and put some money in on it? You nearly always find that people are. (Case 9)

But only part of the market will feel this way. Other firms, in other clusters in the FITC analysis, may perceive the situation quite differently. The motor manufacturers, for instance, are going to be double sourcing mass production items on the basis of tendered bids under extreme price competition. But even when serving the motor industry, as Case 9 illustrates, there are indications of a special relationship.

We probably get 30% higher prices from the motor trade than any other foundry in the country. And this is simply that we are prepared to take the crap that nobody else wants, the jobs that nobody else can make, that nobody wants because there is better work around. (Case 9)

The specialism (Construct 15)

I am almost at the point of closure where there seems to be little more that can be said at this level of abstraction. But I have yet to deal with the problem of the industry's decline. When I looked at Construct 1, it seemed that these managers were not seeing the decline in the same way as, for instance, the authors of the NEDO report. In fact these firms are already responding to the decline. They see that the traditional Cluster 5 business, the rough and ready, unsophisticated, generalized grey iron casting trade, has gone.

Indeed, it may be a crude analyst's stereotype, it may never have existed as something that foundry managements actually created strategies for. There is every reason to think that the pursuit of quasi-monopoly has been a feature of the foundry industry ever since the Darbys managed to keep their coke-smelting process secret for almost half a century. Then, within a few years, the industry segmented itself around the markets then available, specializing in casting parts for steam engines, stoves and grates, bridges and other civil engineering uses, and for the manufacture of artillery. These specializations protected the founders against the explosive increase of capacity which we now call the Industrial Revolution, and which caused the price of pig-iron to drop from £12 per ton in 1728 to £6 per ton in 1802 (Bernal 1971: 596).

The issue that the managements of my research sample face is purely strategic. Do they have a view of the world that offers their firms a viable route into the future? That has little to do with any set of objective facts about the foundry business. One firm says the business will disappear (Case 2) while another says you cannot go wrong (Case 6). Both are right, for each expresses a tenable judgement about an uncertain future.

For most of these companies the perceived survival routes are into specialisms. The alternatives, broadly presented in my analysis of Constructs 10 and 11, revolve around technology. They can choose technology which allows substantial de-skilling and is mass production oriented or they can choose technology which further leverages the skills of the modern moulder.

The first approach is typical of the companies serving the motor trade. The strategy requires high capital investment in volume production machinery. It also requires extensive investment in a technology of administration which can control the labour force of semi-skilled labourers. The second approach is well illustrated in Case 6, where the moulder is more of a technician and less of a labouring craftsman. He uses real-time spectrographic analysis to control his metal, chemically set sands to achieve high tolerances, machined metal moulds to ensure reproducibility and controlled prototype development, fully automatic sand-handling to control sand quality and automatic fettling to finish his work. Companies that choose the first strategy actually respond to the pressures of the Cluster 5 environment by exiting to another cluster. As I have argued above, this requires taking the gravest risk of all, of abandoning one's customers.

5.13 Taxonomic Analysis

I could take the analysis of the interviews further, but the returns are diminishing rapidly. I have come far enough to get a sense of the managerial rationality governing Cluster 5. But there is ambiguity about how these constructs are threaded together. Cluster 5 is under pressure and the market for general jobbing is declining. There is a clear historical shift into capital intensive mass production. Yet Cluster 5 persists. These foundries supply one-off and limited run castings for the prototypes and new machines that eventually become the engineering industry's bread and butter. This requirement will not disappear until an alternative technology overtakes casting. There are also technological and design changes which are affecting the industry's labour force and radically altering its management and technology of administration. To press the analysis further, we can apply taxonomic analysis.

The constructs

The constructs I have identified are as follows.

Construct 1   The declining demand for general jobbing.
Construct 2   The cyclical nature of the business.
Construct 3   Whether the foundry is tied.
Construct 4   The shortage of specific casting capacity.
Construct 5   Whether the foundry needs to solicit enquiries
Construct 6   The long-term prospects of the customers.
Construct 7   Whether there is a local labour pool.
Construct 8   Whether the foundry trains its own men.
Construct 9   Whether there is active management of the tech-
                   nology of production.
Construct 10   The extent of de-skilling, the mechanization of the
                   traditional process.
Construct 11   The use of technology to explore new product and
                   production processes.
Construct 12   Whether the customer portfolio is actively man-
                   aged.
Construct 13   Whether order acceptance is centralized and co-
                   ordinated with capacity planning.
Construct 14   Whether the management seeks a quasi-monopoly
                   or 'special relationship' with the firm's customers.
Construct 15   Whether the company is moving into mass pro-
                   duction or into other specialisms.

A number of other constructs, such as management succession, occur
in occasional interviews, but not with sufficient frequency to warrant
being brought out as major constructs. The list is long enough for
us to see what needs to be brought together in a managerial rationality
or recipe. But we still see a variety of futures. It is not clear whether
the industry brings them together in a single way or whether there
are equally viable alternative ways of thought. Comparing Cases 2
and 16, for instance, suggests alternatives. The first is anxious to
reduce the quantity of mechanizable traditional work, but can only
go so far because of the shortage of skilled men who can do the high-
margin skill-oriented work. The second is anxious to eliminate the

skill consuming jobbing work and is concentrating on getting high-margin mechanizable work for its tightly controlled production lines. At the same time Case 2 has abandoned training its own skilled men, while Case 16 has set about doing just this. It is not simply a matter of alternative answers to the same situation. These managements are seeing their situations differently, reaching for different futures by different paths.

Cluster analysis

We can probe these differences with cluster analysis. Ideally we would be working with triads and trinary data rather than the cruder binary data, but this requires a burdensome a priori structure such as the Repertory Grid. So long as we are looking for patterns, the a priori assumptions must be minimal and binary data in a hierarchical linkage analysis gives us maximum freedom.

The construct scoring is not about whether the managers respond this way or that to the question the construct poses. The score is binary, whether or not the construct occurs in the discussion. We can take Construct 6 as an example. This concerns the customers' long-term prospects. If we had trinary data, we could score 0 for 'theme not known', -1 for 'theme known but does not help analysis' and $+1$ for 'theme known and does help analysis'. With binary data we have much lower information content. We can only differentiate between 'theme occurred' and 'theme did not occur', presuming that occurrence means the construct is useful.

Despite these shortcomings, clustering the data is quite revealing; though it must be borne in mind that clustering will not prove the existence of or explain a pattern. Its purpose is to help us clarify our own ideas.

The scores are shown in Table 2. They were processed with the CLUSTAN v. 1c, the programme developed by Wishart (1969). This offers 40 different similarity coefficients that can be used with binary data. ICOEF 2 (Squared Euclidian Distance), ICOEF 18 (Pearson Phi), and ICOEF 40 (Information Statistic) were chosen, somewhat arbitrarily. It is probably less important to understand the difference between these coefficients than to note the uniformity of the results generated. These are shown in the accompanying tables (Tables 3, 4 and 5). On each the cluster structure is roughly the same, demonstrating the relative insensitivity of the analysis to the coefficient

Table 2 Binary data on construct appearance

Construct number	1	2	3	4	5	6	7	8	9	10	11	12	13	14	15	16	17	18	19
15	•	•	•	•	•	•			•	•	•	•	•	•		•		•	•
14	•	•	•	•	•	•	•	•	•	•		•	•	•		•		•	•
13	•	•	•	•	•	•			•	•		•	•	•		•	•	•	•
12		•	•			•	•						•			•		•	•
11			•		•	•			•		•		•			•	•	•	•
10	•	•	•	•	•	•			•		•	•	•			•		•	•
9		•		•	•	•	•	•	•		•	•		•	•	•	•	•	•
8		•	•	•	•				•			•				•		•	•
7	•	•	•	•	•	•			•	•	•	•	•	•		•	•	•	•
6		•	•		•	•			•		•	•	•					•	•
5	•								•	•	•		•	•		•			
4	•	•	•	•	•				•			•				•		•	•
3		•		•	•		•	•		•		•		•	•				•
2		•	•	•	•	•				•	•	•	•	•		•	•	•	
1		•		•		•	•		•	•			•			•			

Case number

chosen. As noted in Chapter 4, there is little understanding of the meaning of the differences between the various splitting criteria.

The A-group industry recipe

The cluster analysis shows the sample separating into a principal group (Group A), which has some peripheral members (Group A'), and the rest. Some cases appear to have been misclassified by the FITC procedures and really have little in common with the Cluster 5 pressures and strategies. I put these into Group Z. The remainder is loosely grouped into various kinds of Group B.

The splitting criteria are shown on Table 6. They illuminate the various possibilities open to the Cluster 5 managers. The decisive Group A constructs picked out by ICOEF 18 and ICOEF 40 are Constructs 4, 6 and 9. Construct 4 notes that there is a scarcity of a specific type of casting capacity. Construct 9 specifies the scarcity as that which can be pursued by adopting a highly managed technology of production. The analysis also masks Construct 11, which each member of the A-group shares, and this further specifies the technology as de-skilling. But movement into this type of technologically sophisticated capacity must be accompanied by

Table 3 Cluster analysis: ICOEF 40

Group	Case number	Foundry
A	5	Dudley
	19	Wellman
	3	Wm Coupe
	6 13 16 18	Forth, Maude, Seager, Steel & Garland
A'	9	Hemel Hempstead
	2	Chatwin's
	4	Cruikshank
B	14	Newcast
	10	Henley
B'	12	Matthews
B'	1	Bo'ness
B"	11	Hill
B"	17	Shaw & McInnes
Z	7 8 15	Fullwood, Perry

60.22

Table 4 Cluster analysis: ICOEF 18

Group	Case number	Foundry
A	5	Dudley
	19	Wellman
	3	Wm Coupe
	6 13 16 18	Forth, Maude, Seager, Steel & Garland
A'	9	Hemel Hempstead
	2	Chatwin's
	4	Cruikshank
B	14	Newcast
	10	Henley
B'	12	Matthews
B'	1	Bo'ness
B"	11	Hill
B"	17	Shaw & McInnes
Z	7 8 15	Fullwood, Perry

Table 5 Cluster analysis: ICOEF 2

Group	Case number	Foundry
A	5	Dudley
	19	Wellman
	3	Wm Coupe
	6 13 16 18	Forth, Maude, Seager, Steel & Garland
A'	9	Hemel Hempstead
	2	Chatwin's
	4	Cruikshank
B	14	Newcast
	10	Henley
B'	12	Matthews
B'	1	Bo'ness
B"	11	Hill
B"	17	Shaw & McInnes
Z	7 8 15	Fullwood, Perry

Table 6 Key constructs in hierarchical linkages

Group	Case number	Foundry	ICOEF 40	ICOEF 18	Salience θ	Group	ICOEF 2
A	5	Dudley	1 3 6 9 4	3 2 6 9 4		A	4 6 8 10
	19	Wellman	1 3 6 9 4	-2 6 9 4	6		13 14 15
	3	Wm Coupe	-1 -3 6 9 4	-3 2 6 9 4	9		-10 4 6 8 13 14 15
	6 13 16 18	Forth, Maude, Seager, Steel & Garland	-1 -3 6 9 4	-1 -3 6 9 4	1		-8 4 6 10 13 14 15
A'	9	Hemel Hempstead	-6 9 4	-6 9 4		A'	-6 4 8 10 13 14 15
	2	Chatwin's	6 -9 4	6 -9 4	4		
	4	Cruikshank	-6 -9 4	-6 -9 4			
B	14	Newcast	8 -1 3 7 -4	8 1 10 -4		B	-14 15 13 7 -4
	10	Henley	-8 -1 3 7 -4	-8 1 10 -4	7		
B'	12	Matthews	-1 3 7 -4	-1 10 -4 7	0	B'	-4 13 14 15 7
B'	1	Bo'ness	-1 -3 7 -4	-1 10 -4 7	4	B'	
B"	11	Hill	1 -3 7 -4	1 -10 -4 7		B"	-13 7
B"	17	Shaw & McInnes	-3 7 -4	-1 -10 -4 7		B"	-15 13 7
Z	7 8 15	Fullwood, Perry	-1 -7 -4 -1 -7 -4	-1 -7 -1 -7	-7	Z	-1 -7 -1 -7

Construct 6, the identification of the customers for whom this work is to be undertaken and an examination of their long-term prospects. Thus the A-group recipe is oriented towards developing a special relationship with defined customers whose needs are technologically demanding and whose prospects are good. The managers of these foundries need not concern themselves with the overall decline of the industry.

We can strengthen our appreciation of this recipe by looking at the members of Group A'. Each is excluded from Group A for a different reason, although their scores on the remaining constructs indicate A-group membership. Case 9 shows zero on Construct 6. This is the firm set up specifically to serve Vauxhall Motors (a subsidiary of General Motors). It has no interest in Vauxhall's long-term prospects because it does not choose its customers. On Constructs 4 and 9 it separates itself from the price-competitive market addressed by the members of the FITC cluster serving the motor trade (Cluster 1).

Case 2 shows zero on Construct 9, the technological management construct. This is the firm focused on cornering the complex architectural castings market with its small body of highly skilled moulders. It has no intention of installing de-skilling capital equipment. Although its market is small it will persist, and its grasp will increase steadily. However, the firm is prepared to close the foundry should it be unable to retain or replace its skilled men.

Case 4 shows zero on Constructs 6 and 9. This makes its membership of the A-group highly arguable, indeed it may be better classified into a B-group. This case is the Scottish company which has maintained a fairly traditional approach, but has backed up its skilled moulders with spectrographic analysis for tighter metal control on the higher grades. This enables them to work at the upper end of the traditional market, with more exotic alloys, tighter tolerances and so pick up work displaced from the closing foundries further south. They have not de-skilled the work. The company is wealthy and can afford to be somewhat less involved in a special relationship as its prime insurance against bad times. Because of its geographical location it can temporarily reduce its variable costs without losing its men to other employers.

The essence of the A-group recipe lies in achieving a quasi-monopoly through careful management of the enquiries placed on the foundry, coördinating these with investment and training, and recognizing and fostering the subtle pattern of reciprocity. There is a rich mixture of ingredients, some related to the firm's organization, some exploiting the way the market allows itself to become segmented, others recognizing the changing abilities and expectations of the employees. The supply of skilled moulders is failing, partly because of the inadequacy of the industry's training and apprenticeship schemes, partly because of the determination of the craft unions to protect their members from dilutees and others even less qualified. The industry's young people want to be technologists not skilled craftsmen, they want to be managers of capital intensive production facilities that employ only semi-skilled men. Technology now allows such facilities to produce high quality castings which are accurate, have good surface finishes and are free from defects.

But the A group's organizational and managerial system is different from the traditional foundry's. Technical control and effective co-ordination of the customer portfolios and the production capacity are crucial. The lead times lengthen, the foundry must spend more time and money on developing patterns, chills, alloys, testing techniques and on achieving the requisite quality. But the up-market demand is such that many customers will share or even completely underwrite these costs.

The B-group industry recipe

The A-group is focused on niches and its members are relatively unconcerned with the overall industry trend. The B-group, on the other hand, is vitally concerned and is struggling to deal with this problem. The decisive constructs are Constructs 7 and 10. We can get at the essence of the B-group recipe by seeing how these two interact. It is simpler than the A-group's more aggressive approach.

Construct 7 deals with the dwindling supply of skilled men who, the management assumes, control the company's turnover. Management's response is to mechanize the production process, or rather, take on only the work that can be handled by the traditional process as currently mechanized. This leverages the skilled men without, for instance, re-directing the foundry into de-skilled work.

The difference between the two recipes can be illustrated by Case 5. When this company was bought out by the present management, it switched from the B-group recipe it had been using as a tied foundry. Although new technologists and marketing men came in, it was the senior management who had been with the firm previously who master-minded the switch. It was able to do so because its previous work with the new sand and metal technologies had shown it that there was another way. After the transfer of ownership, it took the skills developed in using resin-bonded sands for coremaking into the moulding process itself. This enabled it to de-skill. These changes, which shifted power from the shop-floor to management were fiercely resisted. The new management eventually prevented any backsliding to previous methods by coming in over the weekend and physically destroying all the old moulding boxes and patterns. This burned the company's boats, committing it to the new A-group recipe.

The B-group recipe leverages the skills of the remaining men so that the foundry can sustain its place in the traditional market. With close attention to detail and good management, B-group firms can uuvmvlvv und vivun fluunduh. With the vivovpilvn vf Cuuv 11, whvvv management has given up the struggle, the B-group firms sampled are reasonably satisfied with their financial performance. Although they know there is trouble in their market, they feel they can survive. Few have been able to earn sufficient to increase their capital base, do research or replace their worn-out equipment. Perhaps they should switch while they still breathe. But it is the same for all of us. Grim facts are ignored until they stare us in the face. Only then do we get down to the serious strategic business of changing our personal recipe, our habitual way of doing things. These managers know plenty about the A-group, and they know its recipe does not ensure success or even survival. For many B-group firms, the risks of change still far outweigh the risks of staying put.

5.14 Conclusion

The acid test is whether the reader is drawn into the analysis sufficiently for him to accept its conclusions as unremarkable common sense. The analysis performed above is brief and there is still a healthy gap between what the reader has picked up and what is necessary to run a foundry successfully. But we have moved a long way from the conclusions available at the first point of closure, where we looked at the foundry business as if it were any other, where we were thinking from the conventional investor's viewpoint.

We now understand that technology does not determine the product, nor is the product just a casting. Management has wide options, which can be used to advantage, but which, like all freedoms, must be set aside in the pursuit of rational goal-oriented action.

The common-sense nature of the conclusions causes some curious side-effects. Once we have grasped the recipe we tend to forget that the industry once seemed confusing. We look back at the conclusions and begin to suspect that we could have arrived at them directly by doing a simple market analysis. But now we have the industry management's view of itself, we can see how important segmentation is and along what dimensions it is effected.

At the time of this research, NEDO researchers were thinking out a plan of government intervention designed to save the industry. Over £80 million had been committed to foundries as capital grants covering 25 per cent of the cost of new capital equipment, particularly the fume scrubbers required by the Clean Air legislation. In most cases, these funds were going to B-group type foundries, so supporting the declining part of the industry. Many of the A-group firms had actually ignored these grants. They were generally doing so well that they had installed all the capital equipment forced on them before the grants appeared. By and large, the inability to distinguish the A and B groups rendered these grants socially counter-productive. The funds flowed selectively into the least viable part of the industry, preventing change, and subsidized competition with the A-group, so slowing its growth.

Those who take the investor's view and look at the industry statistics must conclude that there is little future in foundry work. We now see this conclusion is just a result of their analytic framework. When foundrymen are asked why they continue to invest, they say they have no option but to stick to what they know. This is no stubborn streak, for the research tells us a lot about what this reply really means and the circumstances under which it seems both rational and extremely optimistic. We have arrived at this understanding only because we reversed the conventional method of enquiry, ensuring that the framework of analysis actually comes from those whose actions are to be explained and not from our own social or disciplinary preconceptions.

Having done the analysis, we see what the pressures and risks are. We see the difficulty of developing practical strategy. We see how much the foundry managers depend on their industry recipes. We see how much they are able to achieve in a somewhat intractable situation. We also see that foundry managers often underestimate themselves and their creative contributions.

6

The Dairymen

6.1 Introduction

In Chapters 6 and 7 I analyse less complex recipes. Because the methodology was fully worked through in Chapter 5, these next analyses will be briefer. Instead of buttressing each construct with quotations, each analysis will be presented as narrative alone, so moving us closer to a conventional case study. The full transcripts are shown as the Appendix to Spender (1986). In Chapter 5 the final conclusion was unclear until the cluster analysis revealed the intertwining of two different recipes. We saw that two earlier attempts at closure were possible, but would have been inappropriate. We saw that neither the product-market analysis nor the investment analysis provided much information about what managements were doing. The next two recipes are simpler to grasp.

While the foundry industry is under considerable pressure, the dairy industry seems serene. Managements seem more organized and the market behaviour is predictable. There are some important technical developments and these have considerable impact on management and the way the dairy operates. But these are also available to everyone in the industry. While profitability is not high, there is a general sense of adequacy.

I have used the same format as in Chapter 5, beginning with some industry background before moving on to the research sample and the interview analysis. The industry is regional and tends to be organized around the major conurbations. Economy dictated that the research focus on only two urban areas, London and Manchester. Three of Manchester's five major dairies are included, as are four of London's five, bringing seven dairies into the sample.

6.2 The Industry Background

The British liquid milk industry is the product of some of the most sophisticated government intervention into private industry in the world. Although the milk business is truly ancient, the legislative origins of the present arrangements date back to the Agricultural Marketing Acts of 1931 and 1933. As a result of these Acts, the government undertook to regulate the production and distribution of liquid milk in the UK. The intervention policy emerged from the damaging competition of the Depression era. Four regional Milk Marketing Boards (MMBs) were set up, one covering England and Wales, three covering Scotland. A fifth Board, covering Northern Ireland, was set up in 1955.

The Boards act as a compulsory farmers' co-operative. Any milk producer wishing to offer milk for public sale must register with the appropriate Board. Registered producers may sell only to that Board. The Board, for its part, has a statutory requirement to buy all the milk offered. It is also obliged to market it, provided it conforms to a complex set of quality standards. The Boards are the bureaucratic instruments of the government's Milk Marketing Scheme. They also provide a compulsory negotiation structure to bring the various parties involved together. The producers elect members to represent the interests of the farmers, processors, manufacturers and distributors. The government appoints others to represent the consumers' interests.

The industry's statistics are published by the Federation of UK MMBs (1974). The Boards manage the daily collection of nearly 8,000,000 gallons of milk from 81,000 producers. About a third of this milk is hauled in vehicles belonging to the Boards. The remainder is hauled by sub-contractors. The haulage rates are negotiated regionally and applied to all sub-contractors, whose routes are also agreed.

The Board's first priority is the liquid milk consumer. Once this demand has been met the surplus is delivered to 'manufacturers' who make butter, cheese, fresh cream, skimmed milk powders, skim concentrate, yoghurt, UHT milk, UHT cream, dairy ice-cream, cream cheese, cottage cheese, soured cream, soursip, buttermilk, whey cream, whey powder, whey butter, whey glucose concentrate, casein and sodium casienate. Skim powders are used in flour confectionery, bread, margarine, chocolate and sugar confectionery, ice-cream mixes, soup powders, cooked meat products and as an egg albumen substitute. They are used extensively in the catering trade in tea, coffee, cocoa, cakes, custards, puddings and sauces. About 75 per cent of the total milk volume handled by the Boards goes to liquid consumption. This compares with an EEC average of 15 per cent to their liquid markets and the remaining 85 per cent to manufacturers.

During the life of the Boards, the industry's structure has altered significantly. Per capita consumption increased 60 per cent between 1934 and 1950, partly as a result of the government's school milk programme. Over the last ten years average consumption has remained roughly constant at five pints per week. There have been technological changes at the farm and at the processing plant. Both production and processing have become much more concentrated. The number of producing farms has fallen from 128,000 to 81,000 as the average herd increased from 25 to 38 cows, and the annual yield per cow from 765 to 875 gallons. Farm facilities have also changed. Milk-churns have been replaced by bulk storage vats which now account for 72 per cent of the milk collected. The number of private hauliers has dropped from 1,800 to 750. In 1974 there were, in total, 419 milk processing establishments in England and Wales. Of these, the Milk Marketing Board for England and Wales owned and operated 49. The Boards also spent around £7 million per annum on advertising and sales promotion.

Concentration has been accelerated by changes in the milk handling, storing, processing and bottling technologies. Bulk facilities are more widespread. Milk processing, which is primarily a matter of heating, has become faster and more energy efficient. There are various types of heat treatment. Pasteurizing is the least severe and is a simple protection against disease. Ultra Heat Treatment (UHT) is the most severe and is designed to preserve the milk. It extends the shelf life to three to nine months. Eighty-five per cent of the liquid milk for consumption is pasteurized, 8 per cent is sterilized, 6 per cent is homogenized and about 1 per cent sold as UHT. As treatment technology has improved, the optimum plant size has increased dramatically. Bottling and capping plant is faster, increasing from a conventional 200 bottles/minute (bpm) to around 600 bpm for the most advanced plant.

Comparing the UK and EEC consumption figures shows us that milk occupies a special place in the British lifestyle. About 32 million bottles are delivered daily to households. Milk is an important food, inexpensive in comparison with many. One pint supplies a quarter of the daily protein requirements, as well as all the calcium. Eight pints, at 380 calories a pint, will supply the calories required daily by a moderately active man. In real terms milk's retail price has dropped steadily. The minutes of work of the averagely paid worker required to earn the price of a pint dropped from 12 minutes in 1960 to around 3.5 in 1974. The average per capita milk consumption in the UK is 30 gallons a year, compared with 38 in New Zealand, 35 in Sweden, 25 in the US, and with 15 in France, Belgium, Germany and Italy. Butter and cheese consumption in the UK is 28 pounds per person per annum, compared with 49 pounds in France and 29 pounds in Germany and Italy. One gallon of milk produces about one pound of cheese.

The Milk Marketing Boards are also involved in price control. Milk's retail price is controlled by the government. The price paid by the wholesalers and processors who buy the milk is controlled by the Boards. The result is that the processing and distribution establishments operate between fixed limits, which in 1974 were about 19.3 pence per gallon. This margin is the subject of an annual review between the Boards, the government and the Dairy Trades Federation, who more broadly represent the processors, manufacturers and distributors. Until 1975 these negotiations set prices for three years at a time, but the pace of inflation made more frequent adjustments necessary. To provide a 'factual' background to these negotiations, the government regularly reviews the accounts of 60 selected processing establishments to assess the trends of profits and capital investments. These negotiations set the standards which all other producers must strive to match or better if they are to reach or exceed the planned profit levels. These standards are also applied to the selected producers, who thus toughen conditions in the entire industry as they themselves improve.

Although these arrangements are widely recognized to be less than perfect, most parties seem relatively satisfied. Of all parties, the farmers feel hardest done by, though their position has improved under the Common Agricultural Policy. Although the industry's return on capital has been modest and, like the bulk of UK industries, insufficient to sustain real values during inflation, the dairies have been able to continue investment in processing plant. The distribution side has fared less well. The fleet of milk-floats which the roundsmen use is aging, in part because there is no allowance for them in the 'costings'. The costings also severely limit the way rising labour costs are passed through to the consumers.

Table 7 The dairies

Case number	Dairy	Location
Case 20	Clifford's Dairies	Bracknell, Berks.
Case 21	Express Dairies	Ruislip, Middx
Case 22	Heald's Dairies	Didsbury, Lancs.
Case 23	London Co-operative	Southgate, London
Case 24	Unigate	White City, London
Case 25	United Co-operative	Hyde, Lancs.
Case 26	Co-operative Dairy	Wythenshawe, Lancs.

6.3 The Research Sample and Interviews

The sample comprises three Manchester dairies and four which service the Greater London area (Table 7).

Cases 20 and 22 — Clifford's Dairies and Heald's Dairies

Clifford's and Heald's are basically family firms, though Clifford's is now public with the founding family still in control.

Cases 23, 25 and 26 — The Co-operative Dairies

The three co-operative dairies are large regional firms and the result of a lengthy series of mergers among the original local co-operative dairies. The co-operative movement grew up between the world wars, contemporaneously with the development of the Milk Marketing Scheme. While the 'co-ops' supplied all manner of everyday goods, including furniture and clothing, the dairies and the animal feed mills were the jewels in their crown. Large numbers of small scale plants were built, operated by the local co-operative society. After the Second World War economic pressures forced the movement to restructure, partly because of changes in spending patterns, partly because of the inherent inefficiencies of small scale operation, but mostly because of the growth of supermarkets. Most manufacturing plants and many stores were eventually closed. The societies that survived did so by merging and radically restructuring their resources.

Cases 21 and 24 — Express Dairies and Unigate

Express and Unigate are large firms with almost complete national coverage and many other trading activities. The most significant omission from the list is the other large London firm of Job's Dairies. This also supplies much of the Home Counties. After raising the question of my visit at a Board meeting, they declined to see me. This was a pity since they have an excellent reputation, apparently combining high quality and good service with being amongst the most technically aggressive dairies.

In each case I was able to meet with the people responsible for managing both the processing plant and the liquid milk distribution channels. All the dairies organize themselves on a regional basis, with the processing and bottling plant as their hubs. In the case of Express Dairies, which also has area managers, I met with the Managing and Financial Directors. In the case of Unigate, I met with the General Manager of the London Milk division.

6.4 Interpreting the Interviews, 1: General Environment

Increasing gallonage (Construct 1)

The structural changes since consumption levelled off in the 1950s have put considerable pressure onto the processing and distributing establishments. Successive governments have wanted the dairy industry to remain in private hands. They have been reluctant to let conditions deteriorate to the point where it has to be taken into public ownership. Things have not been easy.

Immediately after World War II small family firms dominated the industry. There were a large number of 'retailers' and 'bottled milk buyers' (BMBs) who bought processed and bottled milk from the processors and then distributed it through family-owned 'milk rounds'. There was a very small number of large commercial firms, principally the five who still dominate the London region. There was also a vigorous network of Co-operative Societies who were careful to define their catchment areas to avoid competition, and progressively pooled their processing requirements in regional plants.

The most obvious feature of the industry, given the unchanging product, is the changing ownership of the channels of distribution. This, in turn, leads to changing ownership of the plants which process the milk distributed. The commercial pressures are such that many firms, especially those family firms faced with estate duty complications, recognize that concentration is bound to continue to sweep the industry. Many small dairies decide to sell out while they are still viable. During the post-war period these small independents have been falling relentlessly into the hands of those majors who seek national coverage. Thus we need to distinguish changes in ownership from the other trends in demand, product type and processing technology which are also affecting the industry.

A processing and distributing dairy is two distinct operations. To remain viable, given the institutional control over the gross operating margins, both the processing plant and the distribution network must be more than averagely efficient. They must also be well matched in capacity, or have access to alternative sources of supply or demand with which they can balance their operations. The balance is dynamic, since the best way to stay ahead of 'the costings' is to expand throughput. As there is no shortage of milk, the capacity and throughput are controlled by (a) the cash available for new processing plant and (b) the volume which the distribution network can deliver. Every dairy wants to establish the volume demand before making investments in new plant. So dairymen say the way to the future is through getting greater gallonage, no simple matter when distribution patterns are stabilized and consumption is no longer increasing.

Expanding the business (Construct 2)

Barring changing consumption patterns, gallonage can be increased in three ways:

1 expanding the distribution system's catchment area;
2 buying up distribution channels used by other processors;
3 increasing penetration against competing distributors.

Not all firms have the option to expand their territory. The co-operative firms have informal but well respected arrangements about which society will supply which area. In practice there is a certain amount of poaching, but little outright competition. Overall the co-operative movement is encouraging concentration of both processing and distribution to achieve greater economies of scale. The London firms, though not part of a co-operative and in apparent direct competition, have arrived at informal territorial arrangements. As a result of these most areas are served by only two dairies, one independent and one co-operative. The very large firms, such as Express Dairies, have adjacent areas and their different regions have instructions not to encroach on each other's territories.

The area's retailers fall into three categories:

1 retailers with their own small-scale processing facilities, such as the smaller co-operative societies;
2 BMBs who buy in bulk from competing processing plants; and
3 those BMBs who are already supplied by one's own plant.

Within a fixed territory, gallonage can be increased by supplying to the first two categories The allowed 19 pence margin is split with 13 pence for distribution and 6 pence for processing. There is probably more opportunity for above average profits in the distribution business than in the processing. Thus capturing more business from the first two categories is especially attractive. It also opens up the opportunity for greater economies for scale in a larger centralized processing plant and diminishes some other processor's throughput.

A milk round, the series of drop off points which a particular milkman services, is an established pattern of distribution. Rounds are bought and sold as if they were tangible assets. Their value depends on the roundsman working the round, as well as on the total gallonage. Over the years a system of auditing has developed to establish value for transfer purposes. The preliminary negotiation is over the price per gallon. This will vary between £10 and £40. When there is agreement, the deal is done subject to audited sales. The round is transferred to the new owner before the final price is settled. The new owner and the vendor then operate the round together. The sales are audited one month after the new owner's roundsman has taken over. By this time all those customers who are disinclined to accept the new ownership, normally around 5 per cent of the total, will have disappeared from the round. The new owner can expect the remainder to stay.

Maintaining relations with local retailers (Construct 3)

The aggressive processor will try and get a head start in the market for milk rounds by maintaining friendly relations with all the BMBs in the planned catchment area. He will also try and get information about how well the BMB's business is going so as to establish the relative bargaining position, should a purchase opportunity arise.

Most of the BMBs are small family-owned businesses, often handed down through the family for many generations. When they come up for sale they do so for the customary reasons. Either they have not provided sufficient profit to enable the owner to re-equip, so they become less and less efficient, or the next generation decides not to come into the business, or because the owner wishes to cash out. Timing is often crucial and speed a great bargaining advantage. The negotiations are often more than normally delicate, since the vendor is generally of independent mind. If the expanding purchaser makes the first approach he will thereby raise the price. If the owner decides to sell and informally promises the round to some other dairy, he is not likely to break that promise.

Improving the rounds (Construct 4)

Apart from increasing the number of rounds, the other way of increasing gallonage is to improve the gallonage distributed on the rounds. The industry pays little attention to market share in a particular area. It attaches far greater importance to the structure of a round, by which it means its length and the number of drop points as well as the total gallonage. This determines the technology of the distribution system and the way the round can be developed.

The battery-powered float is now almost universal in urban areas, having almost entirely replaced the horse-drawn float. Although battery capacity is invariably limited, there are different sizes of float. The most generally used will carry between 40 and 80 cases or between 800 and 1,600 pint bottles. The amount of milk required at the drop points, be they households, offices, factories or schools, varies daily. The heaviest deliveries are required on Sunday. The float's range is affected by its load, so it will frequently leave the depot carrying less than 40 per cent of its nominal capacity. A balance needs to be struck between the round's length and total gallonage. Even lightly loaded, the round length cannot be more than eight miles. Given the float technology, a realistically optimum round is of four or less miles with the float initially 80 per cent loaded. The milk needs to be delivered in time to be taken in and put into the refrigerator or some other cool spot. This means most working households must be visited before 8 a.m., demanding an early start for a long round.

The Boards try to ensure all milk is delivered within 48 hours of milking. The actual time from farm to being bottled depends somewhat on the distances involved, so that London milk is more likely to be over-age than country milk. Generally the morning's milking will arrive at the processing plant the same day. It is stored in cold rooms overnight. The following day the plant processes the stored milk, beginning at around 3 a.m. It also processes any milk still arriving from the previous day. The processed and bottled milk is crated, loaded onto low-loaders and pallets and transported to the distribution depots. There it is again stored overnight in cold rooms.

The roundsmen's floats are loaded between 4 a.m. and 7 a.m., so that all the day's milk will be on the road by 8 a.m. In general, the milk being delivered left the farm about 40 hours previously. In some areas, where the bottles are loaded onto the floats at the processing plant rather than at the transhipment and storage depot, this will be reduced to 24 hours or less.

The length and gallonage of the average milk round operated out of the depot is a good measure of its financial viability and of the depot's penetration of the area around it. This figure will vary somewhat according to the type and density of the local population. But unlike services such as the telephone, where penetration varies widely according to socio-economic status, milk consumption is fairly constant across the entire spectrum. There is slightly higher consumption among poorer people.

Increasing the drop density (Construct 5)

Milk is an undifferentiated product whose quality is closely controlled. The norms for the timing and manner of delivery are widely shared. Hence it is extremely difficult to change an area's delivery patterns once they become established. The dairy can try to improve the quality of an established round by increasing the drop density, the total milk delivered on the round. This can be done in two ways. By increasing the number of customers in a particular area, or by increasing the amount of milk delivered to existing customers.

Over the years the dairies have explored many 'modern marketing' approaches in their attempts to increase their business, whether by taking trade away from the competing delivery service, or by creating new customers. A variety of free offers, special promotions, period discounts and other incentives have been used. Few of these were based on ideas and experiences coming from the milk trade. After many disappointments, the milk trade regards most of these as ineffectual and sometimes highly damaging. One reason is that they imply that the customer is buying milk from the dairy, the name being pushed in the promotion, rather than from the roundsman. In practice, the roundsman is the most important link in the channel from farm to household, and the point at which maximum product differentiation is likely to occur. The roundsman is especially ill-served by promotions inviting the competing dairy's customers to switch to his dairy, when similar benefits are not also offered to his own long-term customers. Nor are these promotions likely to be well received by customers such as housewives who are likely to be embarrassed meeting the spurned roundsman in the street. Switching dairies has different implications from those of changing one's allegiance to a store.

If, as I am suggesting, the average customer is more responsive to the relationship with the roundsman than to that with the dairy, then that redefines the dairy's most critical marketing problem. There is no possibility of managing the market through the product and its packaging, as is the case with most foodstuffs, especially those associated with brand names. The product can only be managed through the roundsmen.

6.5 Interpreting the Interviews, 2: Managing the Depot

Introduction

The roundsman's place in the distribution channel places special burdens on depot management, who are directly responsible for the roundsmen. There are problems because the roundsmen are seldom in the depot together except very early in the morning when preparing for the round. Few people are at their best at that hour. By the time the roundsmen start to arrive back from their rounds, generally from noon onwards, they are anxious to complete the day's business and go home. They are not at all pleased to stay on for a meeting about administrative or marketing matters.

The roundsmen are running small independent businesses, treating the depot and the dairy as a wholesaler who provides a comprehensive franchise; bottled milk, a float, a uniform, an accounting and billing service, etc. The roundsmen tend to be loners, happy to deal with the pleasures and risks of small scale entrepreneurship. They operate on their own for the greater part of the day, though sometimes with a school-age helper. They work remote from the depot, generally where the depot manager cannot check up on the way a roundsman is performing. The roundsmen also handle cash, presenting them and their helpers with great temptation, especially since they are not well paid. As Ditton's important study shows, a certain degree of 'fiddling' is institutionalized, though there are powerful informal norms which ensure that all parties operate within clearly understood boundaries (1977). The bottles are glass and so breakages occur, both full and empty. Such 'accidents' give roundsmen plenty of margin to falsify stock and receipts records. The depot manager's feedback is highly limited, comprising the roundsmen's own records and verbal reports, rumours from other roundsmen and possibly some customer complaints or commendations.

The depot manager's job is not easy and the pressures, including that of a very long day, call for an extremely able person with a profound understanding of the roundsmen's task. The good depot managers come from the ranks of the roundsmen. It does not follow, of course, that good roundsmen make good depot managers. In fact most good roundsmen do not wish to become managers.

The depot manager must achieve a delicate balance of economy and effectiveness in his relationships with the roundsmen. He must support the roundsman, appreciate his independence, listen to his ideas for maintaining and improving the service, and listen to his schemes for increasing gallonage, extending his round, etc. But at the same time he must demand sufficient personal organization to maintain accurate records of breakages, sales, cash collected, debts outstanding, etc. This is a hard management school. One consequence is that the industry is noted for the quality of its senior non-financial managers who are generally ex-roundsmen.

Since roundsmen are so crucial to the dairy's business, we might expect that some thought is given to their recruitment and training. This is seldom the case. In part this reflects the independence of the roundsman. In part it reflects the basic wage which compares poorly with that of a manual labourer. The dairy can also not afford to incur any additional expense, given the tight margin. In practice there is no shortage of people prepared to try this type of work. The roundsmen come from a general pool of unskilled labour. They are selected by the depot manager who must subsequently manage them. Many of the recruits do not work out well. Though the work is simple and meeting so many people makes it tolerably interesting, not all unskilled labourers have the necessary degree of self discipline to be able to get to work in the early hours and run such an independent cash business. Nor do many have the people skills. The ill-suited drift away quite quickly. Equally, of course, some apparently overly talented and highly qualified people grow to like the independence and unusual hours. The population of roundsmen therefore varies from the highly transient to the highly committed who have been doing the job for 20 years or more. The variety of abilities and motivations adds to the depot manager's difficulties. Having to hire and fire his own, while keeping his depot viable and his roundsmen's customers happy, adds further to his burdens.

While the dairy delegates much responsibility for the roundsmen, it is extremely cautious about those promoted to depot manager. It selects carefully and also trains. There is a certain amount of lip-service paid to these deliberations, but the pattern of promoting certain kinds of roundsmen to work as assistant depot managers was established long before management selection and training became popular.

Evaluating the depot (Construct 6)

Dairies evaluate their depot managers by results. This seems reasonable until we look more carefully at the depot manager's power and discretion, which is extremely limited. His authority and responsibility are ill-matched. He works to a budget prepared by the head office staff which is based on the depot's proven gallonage, the areas it covers, the character of the rounds, and so forth. The depot manager's principal task is to ensure the budget is met. He generally reports weekly against these budget figures. He often has to work hard, given his labour problems, to sustain sales and minimize pilferage, breakages, bad debts and complaints. But he is also likely to be given a target for finding new customers. This can add to the pressures and, at the extremes, lead him to encourage activities which bring the roundsmen and the dairy into disrepute.

The depot manager's job is therefore quite comprehensively structured. He cannot demonstrate entrepreneurial initiative because he has so little control over the depot overhead. The depot group consists of himself and his assistant, who takes responsibility for some of the seven-day week, a records clerk, a couple of labourers who load and unload crates, and a technician who is responsible for the cold-store, the float battery charging plant and for float maintenance. This depot staff cannot be cut back much. The overhead is also traditionally carried by the depot, which implies a minimum gallonage before a depot can become profitable.

There is also an upper bound to the amount of business that can be handled from a single depot. Increasing the number of rounds and their gallonage will spread the depot's overhead over a larger amount of revenue. But there comes a point at which the depot has more business than it can handle efficiently. Mistakes begin to get out of control, milk gets mis-stored and delivered over-age, cash goes missing, breakages and stock control run awry, and the depot manager's relationships with his roundsmen deteriorate. These difficulties can expose all of the depot's business to competition. For these reasons, the best measure of the depot manager's performance is the number of rounds he can control efficiently. The average manager is able to handle about 40 rounds. Exceptional managers can handle more, maybe up to 70 rounds.

Increasing total sales per customer (Construct 7)

Dairies have found it unwise to be too competitive about the supply of milk in established areas. However, there is an increasing awareness of the possibility of increasing sales per customer by delivering goods other than milk. Orange squash and chocolate drink are already widely distributed. Dairy products such as butter, cream and yoghurt are obvious possibilities. But there are snags. Such products bring the roundsman into competition with the local grocer who is also likely to be one of his major customers. Second, these other products are high value items and much more attractive to pilferers. The roundsman must leave the float every time he goes to a front or back door. When delivering to a block of flats, he is likely to be absent for some time. Consequently, high value items need to be put into a secure compartment on the float. This means modifying the float, taking up some of its capacity. The compartment is also quite difficult to engineer because it must be a cold compartment and be kept clean because of butter's special tendency to pick up ambient flavours. Similar problems arise at the depot. New types of food must be stored for considerable periods of time, the stock is perishable and the stock-in-trade is substantially increased. Items such as eggs, jams and cordials are also liable to pilferage and breakage.

An alternative approach is to capitalize on the float's carrying capacity and deliver heavy items such as potatoes, fruit and bread straight to the home. Again there is the problem of competing with the local grocery trade, especially if it also operates mobile stores. Dairies have explored a variety of such aggressive marketing ventures with mixed results. The goods that need to be carried are very much determined by the socio-economic and ethnic characteristics of the people being served, and by the extent and type of local competition. In general the depot manager is free to try and build up business this way.

Areas of population change (Construct 8)

Competitive activity within an already developed territory demands the depot manager's close attention. There is business to be gained and less likelihood of problems if the population is increasing. Conversely things are likely to be even more difficult if the population is declining. During the period of this research, there was widespread population movement as new estates opened up, older urban areas were cleared and redeveloped, etc. Curiously, dairymen call urban slum clearance 'sterilization'. In general most dairies have to deal with considerable instability in the territories they cover. Such change makes it possible to find new customers and gain ground over competitors.

The general tendency is for urban areas to be cleared and remain empty for many years. Rural areas experience little change until they are developed, particularly for commuters. Then they experience very rapid rises in population and socio-economic status. For this reason many dairies buy up rural BMBs and milk rounds, so building a 'delivery bank' in the same way that property companies build 'land banks'. Although there is a carrying cost, and the round will generally also run at a loss, it puts the dairy in a strong position to know when development is going to take place. This may not always work, depending on the type of people moving into the new development. Some managers believe that working class people will inevitably use the most convenient co-operative dairy because of the co-op movement's working class background. This would give the co-op a big advantage if the new development were occupied by people from an urban slum clearance. In practice the allegiance does not seem strong.

When a new estate is being opened up the local dairies are likely to keep a specially trained team in the area to make sure that every tenant is signed up immediately he or she moves in. Many dairies will offer a period of free delivery or some special promotion. Once the delivery pattern stabilizes, the trail-blazing team hands over to a regular roundsman. The depot manager will later rationalize the rounds to optimize their efficiency.

It may happen that a dairy finds itself an also-ran in the new territory. In such cases there is often some informal trading of customers between the rival dairies. Each exchanges so much business here, which cannot be profitably serviced, for so much there, which can. The roundsmen then effect the transfer with as much grace as possible. Most of the time a dairy probes in all adjacent areas to try and spot territories where the competitors are weak and can be pushed into abandoning them.

6.6 Summary

These first eight constructs reveal much of how the dairy manages the distribution side of its business. We see the pivotal place of the roundsman. We see something of the difficulties the depot manager, and thus the dairy management, has in managing the roundsmen and controlling the little businesses that they run. Dairies sometimes try to go around the roundsmen and influence their market directly, though there is much disagreement about the effectiveness of such campaigns. More often the dairies combine forces with the Boards to encourage milk consumption generally. The 'drinka pinta' promotion was a classic campaign and highly successful.

The dairies are often ambivalent about such campaigns because they benefit every supplier, including their competitors. They tend instead, to focus on the more tangible ways in which they can improve their competitive position.

6.7 Interpreting the Interviews, 3: Managing the Plant

Concentrating production (Construct 9)

Expanding gallonage, on its own, is no way to beat the costings. The increased throughput needs to be matched by plant investment that translates directly into greater economies of scale. The substantial economies of scale at the processing and storage side of the business must not be frittered away in the distribution side where economies of scale are much harder to obtain. Indeed, there is an ever present danger of dis-economies of scale in distribution for the technology is geared to the roundsman. The optimum depot is a matter of managerial capability, not technology, and much easier to get wrong.

Processing plant managements tend to focus on processing rather than on distribution, delegating the distribution side to their depot managers. The pattern of operation, variations in demand and the pattern of growth conspire to make it easier, less risky and more profitable to operate with excess plant capacity than be over-optimum with an older, smaller plant. This puts the larger, more technically aggressive dairies further ahead of their poorer, smaller competitors, so accelerating the industry's concentration. As plants reach their capacity, so there is a tendency to close them and further concentrate production in the pursuit of further economies. There is a strong incentive to invest aggressively. This, in turn, leads to increased pressure on the depot managers to find greater gallonage.

Plant vulnerability (Construct 10)

The successful pursuit of economies of scale is balanced by some rising dis-economies. Sometimes these are technical, since the newer plant may be less reliable, less readily serviced, etc. The more serious are to do with the larger plant's exposure to strikes and other types of labour disturbance. The newer technology is not significantly less labour intensive, indeed it is more complex and therefore requires more technicians than previously.

While unions have seldom achieved a great following among the roundsmen, perhaps another reflection of their independence, they are exceedingly powerful among the process workers at the plants. A large, new, technologically aggressive plant is a natural target for the union recruiters. The process workers understand the milk business very well. They know that interrupting supply for even a single day may cost the dairy a substantial number of customers. The dairy will also have to do something with the undelivered milk, an exceedingly fast-wasting asset. At the time of the research, recent labour difficulties had made dairy managements more sensitive to these problems. Like the motor manufacturers, many dairies have begun to look to 'double sourcing' their processing capacity as a method of insurance against union activity or catastrophic plant failures.

Managing the process plant (Construct 11)

The process plant technology is gauged by its line speed, the number of bottles which can be filled in each minute. Each plant will have a number of lines, which need not be all at the same speed. The older technology will present a fresh bottle to the filling line, fill it precisely with one pint of fresh milk, cap it, and deliver it to the automatic crating equipment 200 times every minute. The most advanced technology will run at 600 bottles a minute (bpm).

The lines operate intermittently, starting up at around 5 a.m., closing down for a thorough cleaning at around noon. This manner of operation, dictated by milk's short life, is more susceptible to other unanticipated stoppages than a line operating continuously with a non-perishable product. A plant with three 200 bpm lines will lose less output from stoppages than with a single 600 bpm line. Three lines will allow a more flexible manning schedule which is less vulnerable to part of the shift not turning up on time. Dairies feel much of the newer technology is over-engineered and that the designers pay insufficient attention to operational issues. The increasingly complex technology demands better qualified operators, and this puts additional pressure on the dairies, who must anyway find people willing to work unsocial hours.

6.8 Interpreting the Interviews, 4: Managing Customer Relations

Plant catchment area (Construct 12)

The exposure to labour problems affects the management's decisions about plant location as well as its choice of processing technology. Plant location cannot be determined solely by the pursuit of economies in production. There are also collection and distribution considerations. The more production is centralized, the longer these chains become. The management faces increased trip duration, transport cost, the possibility of an accident disrupting supply and the operation's exposure to labour problems among the dairy's highly unionized flat-bed truck drivers.

The optimum plant catchment area was reduced by 1973's sharp rise in oil costs, and the industry now regards a 40 mile radius as reasonably appropriate. This distance is also close enough to allow plants to back each other up in the event of disruption by labour or accident. This radius implies a certain minimum distribution density and, therefore, milk round structure. The total volume processed at the plant must be sufficient to support the overheads of the plant. This is easier once the volume is enough to warrant newer technology.

The plant managers of the larger firms report to area managers. These area managers control the plant capital spending. They also develop the plant catchment areas through the dairy's BMB purchases, competitive marketing manoeuvres and deals with adjacent suppliers. They generally supervise the plant managers with daily personal visits. The optimum size of an area is therefore limited by the number of plants which they can visit during a single day.

The corporate identity (Construct 13)

The industry's dependence on good relations with three groups of quite different workers, the roundsmen, the process workers and the distribution system drivers, present senior management with special labour challenges. This has created great sensitivity to labour problems.

The management style throughout the industry is based on the prevalence of ex-roundsmen among senior management. The roundsman's experience is of 'managing' a group of customers whom he does not employ. As every small businessman can attest, this produces a healthy respect for the customer, even though he or she may not always be right. Success at this level requires integrity, professional dependability and a talent for dealing with many types of people in an informal and personal manner. At their respective levels of depot manager, plant manager, area manager and senior manager, the industry manifests the same style. The managers tend to pursue what might now be called MBWA, management by being on the spot, walking around and talking to the workpeople. The depot manager must not allow himself to take on more roundsmen than he can manage with this informal style. The industry views an authoritarian style buttressed with bureaucratic controls as inappropriate to the management of roundsmen. Likewise the area manager must not spread himself too thin. The margins in the business are so tight that a high level of plant and depot efficiency must be maintained.

Very senior managements try to make frequent visits to both the processing plants and the depots. They attach a lot of importance to meeting the roundsmen and attending their social functions. The overall objective, given such a widely scattered organization made up of such disparate people, is to foster a strong sense of corporate identity, pride in the product and tradition of service. There is a commitment, a spirit of 'the milk must get through'.

6.9 Interpreting the Interviews, 5: Managing Change

Future sources of strain

The long-term trend towards tighter margins, rising labour costs, more expensive capital equipment and greater concentration, while all the time confronting static demand, is pushing the industry inexorably towards a crisis. This is likely to hit the distribution system first.

At the time of this research, the industry has been agonizing over dropping Sunday deliveries, so moving to a six-day week, for many years. The unions are not particularly in favour of this. The process workers and the drivers have flexible shift arrangements that they can adapt to suit their personal tastes. The seven-day week also suits many roundsmen who work a 'four and one'. This means 28 days on and seven off. The European experience is that the six-day week quickly leads to a five-day week with Saturday deliveries also being dropped. This produces a crisis in many homes because three days' consumption can be a large quantity of milk which they have difficulty storing. This drives them to buy weekend milk at the local store or supermarket. With two-sevenths of the trade no longer delivered to the door, and the dairy forced to equip itself to deliver in bulk to the stores, buying habits change and the milk round oriented distribution system collapses. Soon all milk is channelled through the stores. Restructuring of this order requires considerable capital and it also radically changes the dairies' labour problems. The industry feels these changes are inevitable and views them with great trepidation.

Somewhat different changes to the distribution system will come from packaging. There are many alternatives to bottles. Waxed paper tetrahedra are common, though increasingly replaced by the regular square packs common throughout North America. Tetrahedra are inexpensive, being formed from strip, and extremely efficient to pack and transport. Square packs, in comparison, are expensive and very liable to damage and leakage during transport. But the tetrahedral package is tricky to open without spilling and is generally regarded as not very 'user friendly'.

The bottle is still the users' favourite packaging. It allows visual inspection of the contents, is clean and substantial and, probably most important, is familiar. A bottle's life is measured as a 'trip rate', the number of trips it makes between the processing plant and the user before it needs to be replaced. The cost of packaging milk in bottles is lower than any alternative provided the trip rate is around four or more. In some urban areas, of course, trip rates can drop to 1.5 or even less as milk bottles are used for target practice, for draining sump oil, or are subjected to other abuses.

Many within the industry have been forecasting the disappearance of the bottle for years. Yet it remains. It is becoming clear that the packaging and the distribution system must change together. Bottles are less suited to sale in stores than the waxed paper packages. Not only are they less easy to store and heavier to handle, there is no easy method of getting the bottles returned. Thus store sales lead to single trip rates. Conversely, paper packages are less suited to home deliveries, especially if the milk has to stand outside the house for some hours.

The response to change (Construct 14)

These other threats cast a shadow of uncertainty across the industry. Most dairies respond anxiously, keeping their options open, expecting the consequences of EEC entry and the consequent changes in food costs to trigger radical change in their industry.

The more aggressive dairies see this as a time of opportunity. Faced with limited potential in the liquid milk business, they want to anticipate change. They consider, for instance, diversifying into the manufacture, distribution and retailing of other foods.

The EEC structure also presents opportunities. The industry has been ruled by bureaucracy for so long that understanding how bureaucracies function, and how they create business opportunities, is a key part of dairy senior management. For instance, EEC regulations require a minimum 3.5 per cent fat content in liquid milk. Much of the milk produced in the UK contains more than this. Aggressive dairies will now skim the milk down to 3.5 per cent and sell the resulting fat as cream, butter or some other dairy product.

Sometimes playing the regulations does not work so well. The dismantling of the Commonwealth preference system severely curtailed the supply of traditional British-style cheeses, such as Cheddar and Gloucester, which were previously made in Australia and New Zealand. In anticipation of a large unsatisfied demand many dairies were cajoled into building cheese-making plants. Unfortunately for them, many stores started importing continental cheeses, such as Brie and Camembert, and the demand for hard cheeses plummeted.

Given the risks and costs, substantial diversification is only possible for the larger firms. The threat of change therefore creates enormous pressures for economic concentration through acquisition and merger. The smaller firms can concentrate on production efficiency, so giving themselves some breathing space, but the age of the family dairy is clearly disappearing fast and, with it, the old form of organization and the recipe that I have sketched out here.

The modern dairy must be able to play in a larger capital intensive game which includes, for instance, the exploitation of EEC tariff anomalies. One such exists in the production and classification of casein, one of the industrial products of the dairy industry. Moving this from one country to another, and then reclassifying it for re-export back to where it came from, makes the operator of this scheme a lot of money.

6.10 Analysis

The constructs

The narrative above is a precis of the recorded research interviews transcribed in Spender (1986). Although the number of interviews is small, the level of homogeneity is much higher than was the case in the interviews in the foundry industry. There is little residual ambiguity and we have no need of cluster analysis. The constructs which presently make up the dairy industry recipe are as follows.

Construct 1   Pursuing greater gallonage.
Construct 2   Expanding the business.
Construct 3   Awareness of other retailers' positions.
Construct 4   Improving the rounds.
Construct 5   Increasing the drop density.
Construct 6   Evaluating the depot manager.
Construct 7   Increasing sales per customer.

Construct 8   Population shifts in the area.
Construct 9   Concentrating processing throughput.
Construct 10   Minimising the plant's vulnerability.
Construct 11   Managing the new technology.
Construct 12   Developing optimum plant catchment areas
Construct 13   Developing a sense of corporate identity and pride.
Construct 14   Responding to longer term changes.

It is clear that these constructs are about to be transformed as new
kinds of firms, more extensive geographically, more diverse in product,
with far greater resources and more aggressive managements, take
over the dairies' traditional activities.

The industry recipe

As in the case of the iron foundries, once we make its elements clear
the recipe seems quite obvious and unremarkable. We can say, quite
correctly, that it is a simple matter of understanding how the market
is segmented, how the business must relate to its market, the
reciprocal patterns of influence and obligation, how these are sustained
and protected from internal disorder and external competition. Once
trading relations are established and the inputs and outputs defined,
then management focuses on the financial and structural determinants
of organizational efficiency. Finally all of this needs to be rewritten
into a dynamic framework that can respond to the environmental
developments that force managements to reconstruct their industry.

But saying this is simple does not mean that it is easy to access
this understanding. The generalities above do little to clarify the
industry's managerial behaviour until the recipe's elements are
clarified. They must be understood in their own context and in the
way they interrelate and are synthesized into an operational
rationality. That we are able to ground these loose generalities in
such a down-to-earth and mundane activity as delivering milk should
not go unremarked. Although we find milk a familiar product, and
know something about its distribution, we should realize that running
a dairy demands quite different knowledge. It is highly specific
knowledge. To enter into the appropriate recipe is not a trivial
achievement and should not blind us to the recipe's subtlety and
highly contingent contextuality. Once we see the recipe we get a
clear sense of what the industry's managers do to sustain their firms
and their activities.

In the dairy industry some of the most crucial burdens are carried by the roundsmen. The roundsmen are very independent and run small businesses which are the foundation of the dairy's activities. They must provide high reliability and a quality service, know when to withdraw service when their bills are unpaid, keep up pressure on existing customers to buy more, encourage competitors' customers to transfer their allegiances, guard the cash and the floats and be smilingly cheerful after a 4 a.m. start.

At the next level the depot manager must establish good working relations with his roundsmen and sustain their efficiency. But he must also manage the boundaries of his territory, its internal structure and his dairy's relations with other local suppliers. He must ensure effective use of the depot's facilities, the storage areas and the floats, and of the processing plant's capabilities. He must also manage the local marketing efforts and competitive activity.

The plant manager must maintain the efficiency of the depot managers, ensuring minimal losses, wastage and breakages with correct forecasting of the daily requirement for milk and other highly perishable products. He must manage the plant operations to sustain the flow of quality bottled milk and minimize interruption. He must have backup plans in place for alternative supplies. He must develop the plant, ensuring adequate maintenance and movement towards greater economies of scale. He must balance these investment needs against the problems and costs of distribution and the difficulties the depot managers have in optimizing the product mix and offtake variability. He must negotiate with the depot managers and ensure his capital investment plans match their territory development plans.

At the most senior level, the dairy managements must bring all these activities into harmony. A corporate identity can be taken as evidence of their success. They must also reposition the dairy in the light of the changes coming to the industry. They must explore alternatives, whether they be to diversify into major food retailers, into dairy-based industrial products, into specialist dairy product manufacturers such as yoghurt producers, or other less obvious moves. They must develop a strategy which gives them a bridge into a future dominated by big, highly efficient firms.

We can see that the pace and pattern of technological development has a very important impact on the structure of the dairy's operations and on its thinking. Despite the importance of people, be they roundsmen, depot managers or more senior managers, the organization's structure and process is very much determined by the various technologies of the bottling lines, of bulk storage, of plant to depot delivery, of depot facilities and of the milk-float.

If we look at the dairy recipe's elements we see that Constructs 4, 5, 6, 9, 10, 11 and 12 are largely technologically defined. We sense that we could quite easily model and optimize a dairy if we had suitable information about the technologies employed. Constructs 3 and 8 are 'unmodifiable facts' of each dairy's environment. Constructs 1, 2, 7, 13 and 14 are completely under the control of the dairy's management, to handle as it thinks best. They focus primarily on marketing. While Construct 6 depends on managerial ability and the administrative machinery is clearly subtle, only Construct 13 refers specifically to structuring.

6.11 Conclusion

Part of the theory of managerial creativity that I am exploring in this research is that an organization is nothing other than a knowledge-base, a set of behaviour modifying concepts. In the case of the dairies I am saying that the knowledge-base's underlying structure is principally determined by the technologies employed. This contrasts somewhat with the foundry industry which, as we saw in those recipes, seems relatively more dependent on human judgement to interpret the environmental and technical situation, limit the options and focus the organization's activities. In the foundry recipe, Constructs 1, 2, 3, 6 and 7 are the 'facts' reflecting the firm's markets. But, as the cluster analysis made clear, there is sufficient heterogeneity in the industry's markets to allow managements a significant degree of strategic choice over the market characteristics they experience. The essence of the A-Group recipe is management's recognition that these 'facts' are not beyond its control. Only Construct 11, dealing with new process possibilities, seems predominantly technically determined, and even then management has considerable choice over which technology is to be brought into its foundry. Constructs 8, 9, 10, 12, 13, 14 and 15 are under management's control and all deal with organizational structure.

This brief comparison shows that although each recipe is a rationality and a 'world view' unto itself, there are some ways in which recipes can be compared.

7

The Forklift Truck Rental Industry

7.1 Introduction

This chapter deals with those firms which own fleets of forklift trucks and rent them out to users. The forklift truck is a piece of modern industrial materials handling equipment, increasingly used to replace those gangs of labourers who might previously have loaded railway wagons, moved bins of semi-finished goods, loaded paper rolls onto printing presses, and to perform a thousand and one typical heavy industrial jobs. These trucks are used because they are less expensive than labourers. Part of their cost is that of financing the considerable capital outlay. Unless the truck is used most of the time it becomes cheaper to rent it for the times it is needed rather than own it all the time. There are other benefits to hiring; the particular type of truck can be changed to suit the job on hand, there are no maintenance costs or complications, it will be replaced quickly in the event of breakdown, etc. But the basic *raison d'être* of the industry is its ability to be cost competitive with owning a forklift truck.

My analysis follows the same lines as that in Chapter 6. The recipe falls out fairly easily for there is a high degree of homogeneity among the interviews. The recipe which emerges is interesting, especially when we compare it with that of the dairy industry. The dairies are struggling with significant technological change in the face of stagnant demand, severely constrained by industry norms governing competitive activity. The forklift rental industry is technologically stable with explosive demand and tooth and claw competition. Their common thread is how each firm is limited by a shortage of suitable first and second line managers. These recipes therefore go some way to empirically testing and so proving Barnard's principal hypothesis; that 'leadership' is the critical limiting factor in most businesses.

7.2 The Industry Background

The industry is typical of many in the tertiary sector in that its existence is unnoticed except by those who have had direct dealings with renting forklift trucks. The micro-structure, subtlety and patterns of interdependency in the tertiary service sector are some of the wonders of our time. Few of us can go through the local yellow pages and not be surprised by what we find there. How many of us realize that there are firms who specialize in eradicating the fungi which live in aircraft fuel tanks, or those who specialize in marking auto spares so that pirated designs and fakes can be identified? The forklift truck rental business is comparatively mundane and unremarkable by comparison.

While the market for equipment rental comprises those who might otherwise buy, there have to be matching economic reasons for others to supply this market. Hirers will own and rent equipment only if they can contract the equipment out for a sufficient proportion of its life. They have to find ways of getting better utilization than their customers. They also have to recognize that they compete with the manufacturers who want to sell equipment outright.

Rental forms a significant part of the overall activity in the forklift truck industry. At the time of this research there are around 100,000 trucks in the UK worth around £180 million. Of these around 15 per cent are in the rental fleets. The rental sector of the industry is young. It is extremely aggressive, growing fast and able to produce high rates of return. With 40 per cent annual growth and 25 per cent ROI, a canny entrepreneur can make a great deal of money very fast.

This equipment rental industry has its roots in the hire of specialist construction plant such as cranes, earthmoving equipment, drilling rigs, etc. Most plant hire customers are in the construction business. They have intermittent loads, and the type of equipment they require varies during the course of a contract. This disinclines them to purchase all the equipment they need.

Before World War II most plant hire companies kept a small fleet of forklift trucks, more for the convenience of their customers than as a profit centre. Since the war, there has been a revolution in materials handling. This has been the consequence of a number of convergent trends. There have been developments in the legislation governing labouring work. Many cover the maximum weights that can be moved without lifting and moving equipment. There has been a great change in the relative costs of labour and capital. It is now worthwhile to substitute capital equipment for labour in many areas. There have also been technological changes. Forklift trucks are more efficient, more reliable and easier to operate. Labourers are better educated, able to read and learn about equipment. There are better communications, enabling a truck to be despatched around a large site to do work as needed.

Construction is now far from the most important user of forklift trucks. Changes have transformed the packaging and transportation of most consumer goods and foodstuffs. The public has become aware of this change as containers have begun to clog the roads and destroy medieval villages. Forklift trucks are an essential part of loading, moving, shipping and unloading containers. Pallets have become widespread. For instance, pre-packed palletted butter is often loaded into a refrigerated container by an electrically driven truck. Containers are lifted and stacked with specially designed forklift trucks such as straddle carriers.

The average forklift truck is in the handy middle range, able to lift around 3 tons up to 12 or so feet and move around with the manoeuvrability of rear wheel steering. Most truck manufacturers' ranges run from small pallet trucks, which lift a few hundred pounds, to heavyweights which can handle and stack a full container.

At first the post-war revolution and the accompanying boom in construction and manufacture seemed merely to increase the rental market for all types of plant. Most plant hire companies invested heavily, and in forklift trucks as well. Around 1965 most realized that the forklift side of their business was not doing well. Some disposed of their trucks, no longer deeming the service to their customers sufficiently worthwhile. Most separated the forklift business from the rest of the plant hire and put it under its own management. At the same time many of the truck manufacturers saw this period of confusion as an opportunity to get into the business themselves, integrating forward into a protected position. This gave them better insight into the market's developing needs and an opportunity to test new technical developments. The rental market cycles run counter to those of the outright sales market. As outright sales drop off, due perhaps to rising interest rates or general economic trends, so some business is transferred into the rental market.

The separation of the forklift and plant rental businesses was a period of great uncertainty as companies sought different ways of doing business. Some merely put a fence down the middle of the rental site, built another office and set up parallel operations. Others opened up new branches for forklift business only. Some rationalized their territories, quitting some areas and entering others. Underlying these changes, of course, was the search for a new industry recipe as the previous ill-fitting one was abandoned.

Thus the new industry recipe dates from 1965 and reflects many of the industry's concerns at that time. It pulls together the new conditions in the market-place, the new labour situation, the new truck technology and new financing and marketing techniques. By 1967 the industry had stabilized and the better organized companies were increasing their business at around 60 per cent per annum. This success interacted with and partly caused an explosion in demand. These developments were primarily local, corresponding to the second phase of Chandler's growth model. The truck rental companies are still in one business with roughly similar operations in several locations. The most aggressive are just beginning to push for full national coverage.

7.3 The Research Sample and Interviews

At the time of the research there were about 15 major forklift rental companies in the UK. While they had the lion's share of the total business, there were also hundreds of small local family operations. The majors had between 300 and 1,500 trucks, the local operators between five and 50. The situation is ripe for concentration, and we can surmise that the national business will eventually be dominated by eight or so majors. But the concentration has not yet begun. It will follow only when the majors, whose operations are growing faster than the locals, meet some barriers to their continued progress. In the meantime they are fully occupied with the problems generated by their own growth.

If Chandler's model is to be believed, the majors will go through a period of internal rationalization when they meet these barriers as they shift their focus from growth to competition with each other. Then they are likely to mop up the local businesses as part of their competition strategy, much as the dairy majors are mopping up the BMBs. This presumes an undifferentiated product. Alternatively, specialisms might develop in the market-place as the customers' needs become more specific and the truck technology becomes more complex. This would give the majors, and the locals, the opportunity to build quasi-monopolistic positions like the companies in the foundry business.

These problems lie in the future. All the companies in the sample were expanding as fast as they were able. Many were borrowing heavily against their equipment assets. All faced the temptation to 'over-trade', to do more business than they could adequately finance. They were also tempted to do too much low-profit business, and so get themselves into spectacular financial trouble as their hugely leveraged financial skyscrapers toppled. The firms visited were the survivors of those who crashed in the early seventies and most saw these particular risks quite clearly. This tempered their wild pursuit of growth.

Seven of the eight companies visited typified this cautious approach to a market all too ready to invite them to self-destruct. The eighth company (Case 31) is exceptional, but is moving towards this position quite rapidly. The companies visited are shown in Table 8. Five other firms were contacted, one refused to see me, the others proved too awkward or expensive to visit. Apart from Case 34, there is a high degree of homogeneity among these firms. The fact that some, like Case 32, are set up as subsidiaries of forklift truck manufacturers, and others, such as Case 30, operate only in forklift rental, does not seem to lead them to adopt different recipes.

Table 8   The forklift truck rental companies

Case number	Forklift truck rental company	Location
Case 27	Barlow-Myers	Maidenhead, Berks.
Case 28	Eddison Plant	Grantham, Lincs.
Case 29	Greenham Plant	Isleworth, Surrey
Case 30	Harvey Plant	Newton Abbott, Devon
Case 31	Hawkins Mechanical Handling	Staines, Middx
Case 32	Lancer Boss (Rentals)	Leighton Buzzard, Bucks.
Case 33	Lansing Bagnall (Rentals)	Basingstoke, Hants
Case 34	Springfield Mechanical Handling	Manchester, Lancs.

Case 28 - Eddison Plant

The companies' histories are typically varied. Eddison Plant was set up as a subsidiary of Aveling-Barford, one of the longest lived manufacturers of fine Victorian steam traction engines. In due course Aveling-Barford was bought by British Leyland and became its construction equipment division. As such it manufactured cranes, earthmoving equipment, etc. Eddison Plant now operates as an independent profit centre, part owned by British Traction. It has both plant and forklift truck hire divisions. It went through a period of substantial rationalization in the 1960s. It is now run by a youthful team which is well grounded in its industry.

Case 29 - Greenham Plant

Greenham Plant is a subsidiary of Taylor Woodrow, one of the UK's largest home and office builders. It began as an internal reorganization to bring all Taylor Woodrow's plant under one management team and so improve plant utilization. All plant purchase and maintenance was handled by this group, servicing internal demand. Eventually it began offering similar services to other customers outside the Taylor Woodrow organization. Eventually the forklift and plant hire operations were separated and they now operate independently.

Case 30 - Harvey Plant

Harvey Plant is a subsidiary of Lex, a highly successful UK conglomerate founded in the motor trade. Harvey is the largest UK forklift rental organization. It is also the largest crane hire operation. The group is still run by the same team that put Lex together and, at this stage, it is still intimately familiar with all the operations under its ownership.

Case 31 - Hawkins Mechanical Handling

The outlier in the sample is Hawkins Mechanical Handling. This markets the forklift trucks built by Ransome's. This major UK manufacturer opted to assign the exclusive marketing rights to an entrepreneur who then built up Hawkins on very thin financing. At the time of the research he was setting up branches and establishing sales, service and rental cover throughout the UK. He was under a tough deadline to complete this and so retain the contract.

Cases 32 and 33 - Lancer Boss and Lansing Bagnall

Lancer Boss and Lansing Bagnall are among the UK's four leading forklift truck manufacturers. Cases 32 and 33 are their rental divisions, set up to integrate forward into part of their market. They were in competition with the other rental companies who bought trucks from them for their rental fleets. Both operate with considerable autonomy in most matters. An exception concerns decisions about the size of the rental fleet. This is determined by the parent company as part of its production plan.

Case 34 - Springfield Mechanical Handling

Springfield is somewhat similar to Hawkins, holding exclusive UK marketing rights for the Italian Fiat forklift trucks.

7.4 Interpreting the Interviews, I: General Environment

The truck fleet's composition (Construct I)

The first steps towards a recipe focus on the static product-market definition of the industry's market-place. The next steps focus on the input-output flows and systems. The final constructs deal with the synthesis of the subsystems into the recipe's rationality, focused on the crucial strategic issues facing the industry.

The rental firm's basic resource is its truck fleet. In general, the fleet's composition is determined by the market the firm intends to serve. Case 32 (Lancer Boss) and Case 33 (Lansing Bagnall), are different in that their primary objective is to serve their manufacturing parents. They have to find customers for the trucks the parent decides they are to take. The rest of the companies are free to select the trucks which best serve their chosen product-markets.

There are some options. The truck fleet can be one of general purpose trucks, suitable for a wide range of jobs, or they can be specialized to a particular purpose such as foodstuffs cold-room work. The market for specialized equipment will be smaller than the market for generalized equipment. It may well be further diminished by users purchasing their own general purpose trucks and making their own specialized modifications. The more specialized the equipment, the smaller the rental market, but the greater the scarcity value.

The different manufacturing companies produce different kinds of trucks. The fleet operator must make a decision about which manufacturer to deal with. The greater his commitment to a particular supplier, the more likely there is to be a 'special relationship' with some reciprocity. The growth of the rental companies is often limited by the availability of trucks. The better the relationship with the supplier, the more chance of getting trucks when supplies are short. Most truck manufacturers rationalize as many components as they can across their product range. Buying the whole fleet from a single manufacturer minimizes the spare parts inventory and the maintenance overhead. If the fleet comprises trucks from many different manufacturers, the service personnel requires many more parts and has to be familiar with many more types of machine. Conversely, if all the fleet comes from a single supplier the operator exposes himself far more to strikes and other problems which prevent the manufacturer from properly supporting the fleet with technical assistance, spare parts, etc. This is especially true if the manufacturer is Italian, Japanese, German, etc., at the mercy of a long road, rail and shipping systems and an additional exposure to customs, agents and legal complications.

Range of services (Construct 2)

Whatever the composition of the fleet, there are options about the level of service accompanying the truck itself. Generally this includes complete servicing support. If the truck breaks down, customers typically expect it to be repaired or replaced within 24 hours. Service can be compulsory or optional. Some companies may own and service a large number of their own trucks and so be able to service the rented trucks. The level of service may be variable, depending on speed of service, the distance from the rental branch, the number of trucks rented and so forth. It may also be contingent on the renter's use of the rented truck.

The rental company's product is far more than the truck. It includes the service, the financial packaging and many other aspects. The product is a complex of attributes. As we move from the secondary manufacturing sector to the tertiary service sector the intangible attributes rise in relative significance.

Types of service (Construct 3)

The operator must determine what trucks to offer and what service to offer. He must also decide how to offer service. The technology of the forklift truck makes preventative maintenance (PM) financially sensible and operationally effective. The returns of PM diminish rapidly. No matter how extensive the PM, breakdowns will still occur. But it will cut down the number of breakdowns. PM has the advantage that it can be planned, while breakdowns are unanticipated. Thus most rental companies will insist on doing PM.

Having the PM engineer make regular calls at the customer's site has other benefits. The rental company gets regular sight of its equipment and where it is being used, which may be quite unlike the place to which it was delivered by the rental company. This enables the renter to keep a fairly close eye on whether his property is being abused. The presence of the PM engineer encourages a sense of responsibility among the customer's forklift drivers. The visits also ensure regular sales contact, a chance to see if other trucks are required, if the competitor's trucks are being evaluated, if another type of truck would serve better, and so forth.

When the truck breaks down, it can be serviced by the PM engineer who will break out of his regular schedule, probably at some other customer's site. This has the advantage that the PM engineer will be familiar with the machine and its particular history. But he may be difficult to find and he may have more than one emergency to attend to. Alternatively, the rental company may have a special group of fitters who do not work on maintenance and work only on emergency breakdowns. As the trucks become more complex, their components become more standardized and more readily repairable by anyone properly trained. In general the industry finds separate PM and breakdown teams work better. But having two groups work on the same equipment demands good communications between both of them and the branch.

The logistics for the service operation are very demanding. They are also sensitive to some advanced administrative and communications technologies, such as radio control in the service vans, and to computerized route and call planning algorithms. A good PM man, with radio control and a good stock of spares in his van, may be able to maintain a distributed group of between 100 and 150 trucks. A good emergency breakdown man, assuming good PM on the fleet, should be able to service around 30 trucks.

The optimal logistics depend on the type of truck, the quality of the manufacturer's support, the work it is used for, the quality of the drivers, the geographical locations of sites and branch, the roads in the area and so forth. Some trucks are better engineered than others, which may be reflected in their price and availability (Construct 1). Some applications are more severe than others. Tanneries are especially bad and expose the truck to savage corrosion. Aluminium smelters are bad because the airborne aluminium cannot be filtered out of the truck engine's air supply. It plates the engine interior, eventually destroying the moving parts. Different industries generate different attitudes towards forklift trucks. The women who tend to drive the trucks used in the frozen food industry are notoriously hard on their vehicles. Some drivers run 'grand prix' on construction sites and think nothing of turning the trucks over. Few engineering companies do their 'housekeeping' well, leaving much material outside, exposed to the weather. They tend to leave the forklifts outside as well.

7.5 Interpreting the Interviews, 2: Customers and Contracts

The customer list (Construct 4)

The fleet operator must make decisions about all of these issues as he develops a list of the customers he wants to do business with and on whose needs he must base his truck purchase and marketing decisions. He needs to be clear about how he is segmenting his market and how he intends to achieve a measure of control over it. Similarly, he may know that certain firms do not pay well. The rental business offers little recourse with bad debts. Customers may complain a great deal or be otherwise unnecessarily difficult to deal with. In the same way that foundries need to spend much thought and time on developing their customer portfolios, so the truck rental operator needs to be careful to end up with the kind of customer he really wants. This is especially important when the market is expanding rapidly and tempting the operator into over-trading, or otherwise doing more business than he can adequately handle.

The operator chooses his marketing and sales methods as he chooses the market segments he wishes to serve. It is clear that the bulk of the market opportunity arising since the end of World War II is the result of the changing fashions and economics of materials handling. The real costs of labour are rising compared to those of mechanical handling equipment. Those who understand this best are the stockroom and warehouse supervisors, the production managers, the despatch department personnel, etc. who are close to the action and understand the personal productivity which the equipment generates. The rental operator gets more attention calling on these people rather than on the company's senior managers. Selling at this level requires the salespeople to understand the operations as well as being able to get on with this type of customer. The plant hire business, where the rental decision is made at a more senior level, is therefore quite different. It is the differences in segment purchase behaviour rather than in the equipment technology that account for the difference between the construction plant and forklift equipment rental businesses and the resulting need to separate the activities. In fact many rental companies are finding that some of their most successful salespeople are women.

Structuring for local sales (Construct 5)

The warehouse, despatch department and production supervisors often have enough financial discretion to be able to rent a truck, but not to purchase one. Hence they will often look to a local supplier to bring a machine in on rent before proposing purchase to the senior management. Most rental sales are local to the site at which they will be used. Low level marketing, focusing on awareness and being available, is crucial. The yellow pages are a good example.

Even though the advertising may be national and handled centrally, the resulting sales leads are handled locally. This affects the structure of the organization, just as it did for the dairies. It also affects the distribution of trucks because the local branch must keep a number of trucks idle ready to service new enquiries. New customers will generally want something immediately, so there must be trucks available. One such short-term need can lead to a major contract.

Balancing contract types (Construct 6)

Most users begin with short-term or day by day 'casual' hire. This meets the need of the market segment driven by a once only materials or equipment delivery, such as a new machine tool or computer. It also addresses the firm that needs something because its own forklift truck has broken down. But it does not meet the need of those who want to subcontract the whole responsibility for managing the forklift trucks used in their works, nor those who simply want to subcontract the maintenance risks. Nor do short-term contracts meet the need of those who see better uses for their capital.

The operator must decide whether to offer longer-term contracts and, if so, how they are to be constructed. These contracts are negotiated with the customer's senior officers, who may be less enthusiastic about the technology than the department level management who have recommended using trucks. The contracts involve more money and deeper commitments and will be tough to come to terms on. The customer is not in any immediate hurry and can afford to risk there being no deal. He also has time to negotiate with the operator's competitors. The customer may also bargain hard for fringe benefits, such as the promise of a full time maintenance man on site, or a lower rate if he commits to use the truck for only 40 hours per week. The operator must be extremely confident of his margins, and his ability to control those margins over the length of the contract, before he can dare to commit himself. For these reasons the long-term or 'contract' business is quite unlike the casual business.

The advantage of contract business is that the utilization of the operator's fleet is very high. Indeed, he can make it 100 per cent if he buys the trucks specially for this customer and ensures that they are completely paid for during the length of the contract.

The advantage of casual business is that it is much more profitable. Indeed, if the sale is to departmental management who can renew a weekly contract which can be covered in the budget, but who do not have the authority to commit the company to a long-term contract, the sale may turn out to be a long-term contract at short-term rates. Sometimes a truck hired for an afternoon becomes a permanent fixture. Even though the customer realizes that it is an inefficient way to do business, switching contracts takes time and he may want to retain the option to send the truck back at a moment's notice. The disadvantages of casual business are that it presupposes lower utilization of the fleet and it offers greater exposure to truck abuse by the customers.

While contract hire competes nationally with equipment leasing, casual business is local. Contract hire is likely to be handled by head office. Casual hire is local, a vital marketing tool spearheading the development of the local branch. It is something that everyone in the branch, from receptionist and the branch manager to the PM engineer, can help to sell (Construct 5).

7.6 First Summary

These six constructs do much to define the rental fleet operator's product and product-market posture. They also carry implications for the way the operations are organized, especially those at the local branch. This must be able to maintain the local fleet as well as sell the chosen package of services (Constructs 1, 2 and 3) to the chosen customers (Constructs 4 and 6). The branch is the local sales centre (Construct 5). Telephone leads must be followed promptly and professionally. The branch must also administer the business in its territory, ensure that payments are made, services charged for, trucks taken out on time and so forth. The maintenance facilities are important because trucks often need rebuilding between contracts. Trucks that are pulled out after proving irreparable on site must also be fixed. Idle trucks must be properly stored.

7.7 Interpreting the Interviews, 3: Managing the Branch

The branch operation (Construct 7)

As with the dairies, the local branch requires a minimum level of investment before it can operate at all, implying a certain level of business before it will be profitable. Assuming around half the fleet is on contract hire, with the remainder available for casual hire, the average branch needs around 50 trucks before it can break even. This level fluctuates according to the type of truck, the cost of money, the cost of the branch site, the pressure on contract terms and so forth.

There is also an upper bound to the branch's size. Once the branch is handling around 150 trucks, and trying to find local casual business for 75 trucks, the branch management problems become severe. The engineering maintenance problem requires a full-time engineering manager, even if some of the load can be taken by the four service engineers and three breakdown specialists which the branch now needs. The branch manager is no longer able to keep tabs on the local market and its changing patterns. The actual upper limit depends on the manager's ability, but it also depends on the casual/ contract ratio, the state of the local market, local competition, the geographical dispersion of the fleet and so forth. Between 120 and 200 trucks is likely to strike a good balance between overhead recovery and branch efficiency.

Geography has a powerful impact on the maintenance problems since visiting the trucks becomes more time consuming as distances increase. Travel time is a crucial variable when designing the logistical system supporting the fleet. The geography is more a function of travel time than simple distance, good road access significantly expanding the size of the territory which can be managed efficiently. The industry regard a radius of 40 miles around the branch as reasonable. In heavily urbanized areas with poor access and traffic jams, this can drop to ten miles.

As we shall see, this carries implications for the structure of the overall firm. The relatively small size of the optimum branch's catchment area means that the business can best grow by opening up new branches which then operate relatively isolated from one another. This corresponds to Chandler's model of regional development and produces a requirement for a central or head office to manage both new branch expansion and inter-branch affairs.

Fleet utilization (Construct 8)

I have shown that the branch can be evaluated by the number of trucks managed, the casual/contract ratio, the service efficiency, and the territory covered. The financial viability of the branch is a function of the marketing, financing and service cost per unit of rental revenue. Monitoring these costs is difficult because of the steepness of the profitability curve as turnover passes through the break-even level. Truck financing and servicing costs comprise the greater part of the firm's expenses. Because the business is so highly leveraged, losses mount rapidly as turnover drops. This can be better contained if the number of trucks can be balanced to turnover. In practice this cannot be done with the speed and finesse necessary to use turnover as a control, so fleet utilization becomes the most important variable.

Under normal circumstances fleet utilization must be around 85 per cent. Since probably 5 per cent of the fleet will be moving between contracts or under repair at the branch depot, this leaves little to play with. Thus utilization is monitored with great frequency. Most of the industry believes in balancing the firm's fleet between branches. It will generally prove impossible to achieve adequate utilization unless the branches can share their fleets. This means having further capital equipment, such as low-loaders which can carry one or two trucks to an adjoining branch.

Service costs (Construct 9)

Provided utilization is adequate, the next most sensitive measure of branch performance will be average cost per truck. Utilization measures the efficiency of the sales side of the operation. Maintenance costs measure the efficiency of the service and support side, the area where the profits can be eaten up. Branch management can lose control here because of managerial inefficiency or its inability to operate with too large a fleet or territory. Since the patterns of repair, replacement and PM are likely to vary quite widely, most firms use a rolling average measure.

The technology of maintenance is labour intensive. Given a steady rise in wages, service managers need ingenuity and relevant technology to contain costs. This is a slower process and less likely to lead to competitive disadvantage than a sudden loss of fleet utilization. But it is also difficult to reduce these costs quickly.

The branch managers have control problems which are somewhat similar to those of the dairy depot managers. For the most part the fleet maintenance people operate out of sight away from the depot. They can easily take time off. Planning and measuring performance against that plan becomes important. Statistical records are essential to detect irregularities in the PM programme. Taken together, the fleet utilization and the service cost per truck measures provide a good short-term view of the branch's health.

Siting the next depot (Construct 10)

As I have shown, the limited size of the optimal branch forces the firm to grow in two dimensions. First the branch grows from its initial establishment to optimum size, with around 200 trucks in its fleet. Then the firm opens an additional branch. This needs to be managed by head office.

The operator needs to be sure that a new branch has a good chance of profitability before setting this process in motion. The prospective area must have enough demand for the branch to establish, in due course, a fleet sufficient for it to become profitable. The optimal catchment area must be determined, the customers meeting the firm's criteria listed, their total demand potential calculated, the effect of competition thought through and so forth. This is classic market research. The use of forklift trucks is spreading to new industries and applications. They are used on farms, for food production, in market gardens, in fish docks, sawmills and so forth. Despite these trends, few rural areas will have the use density sufficient to sustain a 200-truck fleet within a 40 mile radius.

The industry sees the country as an archipelago of potentially viable urban areas. These areas vary in density, customer type, application, truck type and so forth. The high density areas also tend to be areas where the applications are tougher; heavy industry, ports and railheads. Thus the attractiveness of high density needs to be cautioned by estimating the likely maintenance costs. With really severe applications, truck life is shortened and the contracts need to be specific to ensure adequate recovery before the truck is scrapped. High density is also usually associated with heavy traffic, poor roads and inefficient maintenance support.

The most attractive areas are the new industrial estates. These have modern warehousing, light industry, a cadre of machine respecting workmen, and the roads and communications are good. The oil boom created an excellent area around Aberdeen. The increase in cross-Channel food traffic led to new port facilities in Dorset and Hampshire.

Most firms offer a general kind of service with mid-size trucks for typical applications. The product is undifferentiated and there is strong competition. Areas with high potential attract most competition. It also fosters the growth of local small-scale operators whose businesses are often spin-offs from some other activities and operate under different financial constraints. With competition come price wars. The bigger companies especially make a commitment to an area and are prepared to buy market share with the intent of later capitalizing on a quasi-monopolistic position. This often fails.

Another way to open up, as in the dairy industry, is to buy up the local operators. This has another advantage. Given exploding demand, albeit concentrated in specific areas and applications, the limits to corporate growth are not those of demand or finance. There are input limitations for the supply of trucks is sometimes limited (Construct 1). But the primary limitations are administrative. The optimum size of the branch is a reflection of the limitations of the branch manager, given a particular and generally shared set of technologies for moving trucks in and out of customers' sites, for getting repairmen to trucks in the field, for doing PM to control the frequency of breakdown and so forth. But the limited supply of adequately able branch managers is a direct constraint on the rate at which new branches can be opened.

7.8 Second Summary

At several points we have seen the necessity for headquarters control, whether it be in managing the flow of trucks between adjacent branches (Construct 8), or the surveying of new urban centres (Construct 10), or in doing strong purchase deals with truck suppliers (Construct 1). In fact there is little that can be delegated to the branch apart from opening up the market (Constructs 5 and 6) and running the branch efficiently (Constructs 7, 8 and 9). Committing to a new territory, funding a new branch, finding a new branch manager, opening the branch up or buying up a local operator, dealing with the competition and responding to a price war; these are things that must be co-ordinated across the organization.

7.9 Interpreting the Interviews, 4: Central Management

Central management of organizational growth (Construct 11)

Acquisition seems attractive because it can result in the firm buying management as well as trucks, market share and local knowledge. But it is difficult to buy experienced managers who will operate the same policies and strategies as have been chosen by head office. The local operator is more likely to continue with business as usual, being less highly motivated and readier to spend the new parent's money than he was his own.

An alternative way of opening up a new branch, without either starting one afresh or buying up an existing business, is to spin it off from a neighbouring branch. The existing branch is deliberately extended beyond its normal optimum so as to build up a population of trucks and service cover in the prospective new branch's area. When that population begins to approach the company's accepted break-even level, the territory can be separated and the new branch set up. This technique is particularly useful when the new manager is inexperienced, for he can be closely overseen by the manager of the established adjacent branch for he has considerable knowledge of the new branch's territory. This is feasible only when the distance between the branches is modest, no greater than that which lets the senior manager visit the new branch and return to his office within the same day. If this is not possible the inconvenience of a visit radically changes the relationship between the branches, changing the control mechanism from purely personal guidance into a formal administrative link. The senior manager then controls through data not personality. Only experienced managers can be put into new areas that are so isolated from other experienced field managers.

Capital management (Construct 12)

Head office handles the financing and sets the types of contract which the branches may offer. These change as the price of money changes. Prior to 1973 many rental companies offered three- or even five- year contracts. The rates were such that the trucks would be paid off within 18 months, leaving the remainder of the income stream to cover the cost of the service, the administration and the profit. After 1973 the cost of inflation increased dramatically and the loss of option to increase the revenue proved extremely costly. Most companies decreased the contract period to two years or less.

As the contract period shortens, its net present value drops sharply. This radically alters the firm's capital management scheme. Equipment rental companies are naturally extremely hungry for capital. They turn investors' capital into a revenue stream. The rental operators cannot continue to buy equipment and expand at the rate which allows them to maintain or improve their position in the industry unless they raise fresh capital. The risks of investing in this business are high and investors expect high returns. This capital is therefore relatively expensive.

The business works because the original high-cost investment produces assets (contracts) which are of lower risk and can therefore be turned into capital at a lower cost. The contracts must be of adequate quality, that is legally sound and with companies with secure businesses and good ratings. These contracts can be factored, assigned or sold for cash, or used as collateral for lower cost loans. One way or another, they must be turned into a fresh supply of trucks and new branches. The rental operation is an arbitrage operating between different levels of commercial risk. The original high-cost capital base is hugely leveraged by this additional low-cost capital. The dangers of over-trading are high because the rental operation can spend very fast, and it takes time to turn the resulting contracts back into money. Unless the cash flows are well matched the operation falls apart in the middle, with the rental operator breaching the service contract and so making further sale of his contracts unlikely. As the company's rate of expansion accelerates, so the time the average contract has run diminishes and the overall financial quality of the business drops. The fleet, as a whole, moves further and further from the point at which it breaks even.

A slightly different financing scheme has an investment house owning all the trucks which are then leased in bulk to the rental operator. He puts them out on an individual, shorter term, fuller service and significantly higher cost lease to his customer, the gross on the rate difference covering all his costs and leaving his operating profit. Some truck manufacturers are also interested in financing bulk purchases of their own trucks.

There is a vast range of possible financing schemes but the principles remain the same. The rental operator is either a 'local', expanding out of retained profits, or a 'national', using the exploding need for forklift trucks to build a high velocity money machine. My analysis applies only to the nationals.

Opening up procedures (Construct 13)

The financial risks of expansion are considerable and the management of the finances increasingly complex, expensive and liable to error and oversight. But the risks of over-caution are equally grave. Within each catchment area, the branch must strive to achieve quick market dominance, keeping the other operators below their break-even levels or pushing them into unsustainable losses. The entry barriers, which are initially negligible, are raised by this mutual warring. The company must know how to time its moves, when to get in, how hard to push, when to make peace and settle for its share, when to get out and how to best dispose of its share.

Inevitably, whether the new branch is established by acquiring a local operator, spinning out of a neighbouring branch or starting out afresh, the initial period is one of losses. The speed with which the branch can move into break-even and then profit is crucial to the headquarters people trying to manage the cash flow. This becomes especially urgent when the new branch's losses are made on trucks which could be put out profitably in other established branches.

The rate of new branch growth depends on headquarters making good quality trucks available, along with local and national advertising to generate awareness. As the economy booms and the demand for labour rises, so the demand for trucks rises too. This seems the best time to open a new branch. But the truck manufacturers are now likely to be getting better prices from end users and so will push the rental fleet operators for better prices and for deposits for places in the production queue. Just when the operators need trucks most, they are most expensive and least available. It is not easy to know the best time to open a new branch. The business is somewhat sensitive to trade cycles, since when business is down customers are less tempted to use labour saving equipment. At the same time some customers will put off the capital decision and rent rather than buy.

The new branch's progress depends most on the efforts of the branch manager and the local sales team. They must determine which customers to target on the basis of what their trucks are really going to be used for. Much of the business which they will find easiest to pick up will be undesirable; poor payers, damaging applications, unserviceable locations and so forth. The new service arrangements will take time to shake down. No branch would ever get through this initial period if headquarters was unable to support it.

At the same time, headquarters must know when to pull out. Generally the industry allows new branches about 12 months to reach break-even. During this year, the branch is a heavy burden on the company. The extent and duration of the loss will depend on the conditions in the area. If the potential is great, the firm may decide to soldier on for longer. The opposition, be it local operators or a national competitor, will be equally determined. The combination of effort may well increase the overall size of the market as more sales people tell more potential customers of the advantages of using or renting forklift trucks. As overall growth accelerates the company will have more and more of these early stage branches, until it eventually begins to close on complete national coverage.

As I have already mentioned the scarcity of branch managers is what limits the growth of most firms. Branch management is the junction where the technical considerations of truck selection and maintenance, the financial considerations of capital availability, branch expenditure and product pricing, the marketing considerations of customer selection, sales management and competition come together with the administrative considerations of managing the branch's sales and service activities and reporting to headquarters. It makes a full plate. Anyone able to do this job well attracts a lot of attention in the industry and is regularly approached by competitors. There is a great deal of poaching.

The long-term strategy (Construct 14)

I mentioned above that the branch by branch growth cannot continue once the company achieves national coverage. The branch growth plan presumes a supply of territories waiting to be opened up. The long-term strategy needs to look beyond this point. Plans for this change in the growth strategy, which drives the financing, the employment, the administration and the competitive strategies, must be laid well in advance. If the Chandler model applies, we will see a period of great internal rationalization among those firms who have achieved national coverage. They will increase local market share by buying up or pushing out the local operators. Then they will begin to compete for national market share.

7.10 Analysis

Although the number of companies in the sample is quite small, they represent over half of the business in the UK and can be taken as representative of the general pattern. With the exception of Case 31, whose financial and marketing approach is unlike that of the remainder of the sample, there is remarkable homogeneity in the issues which came up in the interviews.

The constructs

The constructs which have been brought out are as follows.

Construct 1	The fleet's equipment.
Construct 2	The range of services offered.
Construct 3	The type of service offered.
Construct 4	Selecting customers and applications.
Construct 5	Structuring for local sales.
Construct 6	The casual/contract ratio.
Construct 7	Branch management.
Construct 8	Fleet utilization.
Construct 9	Service costs.
Construct 10	Siting the next depot.
Construct 11	Central management of organizational growth.
Construct 12	Capital management.
Construct 13	Opening up procedures.
Construct 14	The long-term plan for recipe change.

These constructs give us a sense of what the rental fleet operator has to do to get things under control. The picture is not complete and there will be other problems, but it creates the right context for understanding what the specific companies are doing. We see what the rental product really is and how it must be packaged. We see the strategies that competitors are able to adopt. We see the delicacy of the timing of expenditure and revenue, and the extreme risks of getting it wrong. We see the pivotal place of branch managers.

The industry recipe

In this industry, even more sharply than in the dairy and foundry industries, it is possible to sense the recipe's finite life. This recipe originated in the 1960s and cannot last much longer. As soon as the industry majors achieve national coverage, this recipe will become obsolete. It could also be made instantly irrelevant by a change in the tax structure which cuts off the supply of new capital.

We see again the relationship between the truck's technology, the technology for administering the service people, the technology for bringing service facilities to truck work sites and the technology for transporting trucks between branches. These various technologies are all determined beyond the organization's boundary, so the organization's designers and strategists have to find ways of fitting them together into a viable co-operative operation. Their answers will be quite different if, for instance, the service crews travel by helicopter, or if the trucks could be diagnosed by being put on-line to a central computer which could then order parts and schedule a service call.

In this industry there is also a very specific form of financing. This too might be deemed a technology, a science of investor and customer behaviour, and legal and tax structuring. This technology might now be called 'asset securitization'. The equipment rental industry is arguably more dependent on this technology than on any other, though ranking the constructs does little to clarify a recipe. It directly addresses the opportunity created because investors' expectations differ from those of the customers. The customers would rather pay high rates on a rented truck than a lower rate on a purchased truck, because of the added flexibility and lower risk of the rental contract. Furthermore there is a division of labour. The rental company specializes in arranging to supply trucks with the kind of financial and operational risk packaging that the customers find attractive. The customers specialize in applying their investment to improving productivity in their own operations.

This financial technology can be applied in many other markets which meet the same criteria. Construction plant hire is an example. The history of the forklift truck business suggests that financial technology was the central technology transferred from the plant hire business. Seeing that the two products must be sold differently came later. The need to know how to service the trucks is also clearly subordinate.

The subsequent separation of the industries highlights the difference between a technology and a recipe. While the financial technology is identical, as it is in the leasing of railway wagons, computers and many other forms of production equipment, the recipe for running any one of these businesses is quite specific. The recipe must synthesize all the relevant technologies into a coherent rationality which captures the 'correspondence rules' relevant to that industry's context of activity.

7.11 Conclusions

The purpose of the research reported in this book is to test a framework of ideas. I will look at some of the implications in the next and final chapter. But it is necessary to understand the place of the empirical results in this more general framework.

A research project is not a haphazard gathering of facts in the hope of finding something worth remarking on. Research begins and ends with ideas. There are some initial ideas – hypotheses – and some final ideas – conclusions. The purpose of an empirical test is to see whether this set of ideas holds together when confronted with reality. The empirical results have no meaning when separated from the initial hypotheses. The results I have explored here are to do with whether business executives use 'recipes', which is to ask whether businesses imitate each other when confronted with uncertain situations. The interviews and the constructs may tell us something about how to run a company in one or another of these industries, but that is peripheral to the main endeavour. The results test whether the hypotheses and the conclusions hold together.

The structure of the research is straightforward. Uncertainty produces either creativity or imitation. If we wish to research imitation, then we must hypothesize what is imitated, how and why. Trademarks and registered brand names protect against imitation in naming and packaging products, for that is clearly a temptation. The 'why' is brand recognition, which costs money to generate. The trademark law is there to protect the originating company's investment in intellectual property. Once the product is in the market place imitation is easy. It is almost certainly quicker and cheaper for competitors to imitate than to start afresh.

There are clear perceptions of how cars, computers, and washing machines should look if they are to appeal to the public, and there are many classic cases, such as the *Edsel*, of the risks of ignoring the norms of product fashion. Behavioural norms, a recognized aspect of any culture, are another type of imitation. Indeed, imitation is so widespread it is scarcely worth remarking on. In this research I may be pushing the notion a bit further by hypothesizing that businessmen imitate each other in the way they think, or more specifically, in the way they make creative judgements. The empirical question is not really whether businessmen imitate each other and how. It is more concerned with whom they imitate. In the same way that it is probably a mistake to make a computer look like a washing machine, so it may be a mistake for an engineering company to imitate a bank.

We can readily observe people imitating each other within an organization. It produces what we recognize as the organization's culture and style. My research tries to focus on broader patterns of imitation, specifically at the 'industry' level. This does not get us very far, for the term 'industry' is exceptionally vague and, as I will explain in the next chapter, has been partially displaced by a new term, the 'strategic group' (Hunt 1972). The most important conclusion that I could draw is that imitation is predictable between companies in the same industry or strategic group. But I cannot come to that conclusion yet. The methods adopted here are simply too open to interviewer and analyst bias, misunderstanding, small samples, misclassification and so forth to allow that. I might say that a set of ideas has been outlined and there is some supporting evidence which might warrant a stronger, more rigorous test. Ultimately the best research outcome is that other researchers are then able to ask tougher, more critical and more illuminating questions and be more efficient in their empirical work.

In the final chapter I touch on some other work being done in this general area. But the major thrust of this book remains speculative. The final chapter is an attempt to think through some of the implications of a pattern of ideas which may eventually be borne out by subsequent research.

8

Managerial Creativity

8.1 Introduction

In this chapter I summarize my theory of industry recipes and managerial creativity and consider some of its implications.

In Chapter 1 I argued that managers need both knowledge and skills. The dichotomy is weak, for skills are a type of knowledge. But the dichotomy is substantial enough for us to see that managers need the skill to create knowledge where suitable knowledge is not available to them. My theory proposes managers as knowledge creators as well as knowledge users. In uncertain situations the ideas they create are the essence of what allows their firms to move forward in a controllable way.

I argue that organizational behaviour is managed, at the most fundamental level, through the ideas adopted by the people in the organization. Management, as I define it, is the creation, selection and communication of these ideas. Eventually these ideas are so completely integrated into the organizational system that they take on new meanings unfamiliar to those 'outside' the organization. Insiders, the employees and maybe those others who do business with them, are socialized into what I have called the organization's rationality. This defines the organization as, in essence, a body of knowledge about the organization's circumstances, resources, causal mechanisms, objectives, attitudes, policies and so forth. I might also call this a 'knowledge-base' or 'universe of practical discourse'.

The organization becomes manifest in its activity; it has no separate existence or substance. Its assets, such as buildings, plant, products and profits, are matched by liabilities, all the result of the organization's past behaviour. Although important, especially to the owners, they are not managed directly. They are no more than vehicles for management's ideas and so incidental measures for their successes and failures.

Not all of what managers do can be usefully distinguished from
the functional productive activity of the managed. Parts of a manager's
work are purely functional–to act, communicate and observe on the
organization's behalf. Managers can act as the organization's sensors,
picking up information, and as its communications links, transmitting
that information. Even when making decisions, managers can act as
passive functionaries, implementing others' ideas much as dignitaries
sign documents or operators mind numerically controlled machine
tools.

My focus is on the active aspects of management, in particular on
the manager's creative intellectual activity. Following Locke and
many other writers I widely separate thinking into two parts. One
part is decision–making, the logical processing of what are taken as
facts. The conclusions are contained in these facts, the thinking is
the analysis process that extracts them. The other part of thinking
is creative, the application of human judgement in response to
uncertainty. Judgement creates facts from uncertain data. I define
strategy as the intellectual response to the uncertainties present in
the managers' ideas and data about the organization. The organization's goals, purposes and other policies are often chosen by outsiders
who have power over the organization. The strategy articulates the
rationality the managers develop to implement these. Managers
cannot work out the behavioural implications of the policy choices
without a strategy. These choices are logically prior to the organization
and have no meaning for managers until the strategy has been
created. Even when the organization has been in existence for some
time and policies change, the meaning of the changes is determined
by the strategy developed to implement the new policies.

This knowledge-oriented definition of the organization leads me to
argue, following Barnard, that uncertainty resolution is the essence
of corporate leadership. As Simon notes, our knowledge of any
situation is inevitably uncertain. Uncertainty forces managers beyond
decision-making, creating an extra-logical task with which they must
deal. Following Thompson, therefore, I argue that as the executives'
judgements extinguish these uncertainties, they create a bounded
context of certainty. This certainty is artificial, for the managers
merely judge things to be facts in ways that they cannot justify. They
do not know these things, they are matters of opinion. In theory
subordinates operate within this protected context and, relieved of
the burdens of intellectual leadership, become purely logical decision-
makers. Here I suggest 'ideal types', Weberian analytic stereotypes,

and must admit that all real managers, indeed all real employees, make logical decisions and also use their judgement. But for the purposes of this analysis I assume these subordinates are decision-makers and functionaries, sufficiently well directed and trained to achieve pure logicality within the organization's constructed rationality.

There are many reasons why we should pay more attention to the judgemental or extra-logical parts of managerial work. Some of these reasons are to do with leadership, an important and much researched yet still puzzling feature of organizational behaviour. In this book I define leadership in a way that is particularly significant for knowledge based social systems. Other reasons for investigating organizational leadership are to do with scientific enquiry. Organizations are the most complex, important and yet limiting of human artefacts. Despite an enormous literature and prodigous research we are still in desperate need of adequate theories of management, leadership and strategy. We cannot hope to apply the powerful methods of positivistic science to these topics if our prior notions and categories are grossly inappropriate. We will not then be able to anticipate and so measure the informative aspects of managerial behaviour. We will misunderstand what we see and assign what seems non-logical to some residual category of which we implicitly disapprove.

Yet further reasons are ethical. Ignoring the extra-logical we conspire by default to sustain the myth that managers can be purely objective and avoid 'value judgements'. We will help conceal the moral content of management's activity and so avoid saying that the exercise of judgement, most obviously where it affects others' lives, entails moral responsibilities. The result of a purely logical decision may seem independent of the decider, but when we exercise our judgement we clearly make ourselves manifest in the world. We cannot allow ourselves to think that we need not bear the responsibility for our judgements.

The concept of judgement breaks up the causal model linking the data about the manager's situation to his conclusions. I define uncertainty as a condition of information deficiency in which the data by themselves neither contain nor determine a conclusion. A manager who draws a conclusion can only do so by adding something of himself to the data available. This addition, which may be some simple unrelated data which the manager judges relevant, cannot be justified logically. I suggest that the burdens and risks of exercising judgement cause managers to cast around for guidance. I hypothesize that they draw their primary support from other managers operating in the same industry.

There is no simple imitation involved here. These managers do not seek support that is substantive, detailed or prescriptive, a specific formula which tells them precisely what to do. They know well enough that other firms are in different circumstances and may well be pursuing different policies. I hypothesize that the imitation is at an extremely intellectual level, a sharing of those judgements which give organizational data their meaning. In this way the managers adopt a way of looking at their situations that is widely shared within their industry. I call this pattern of judgements the industry's 'recipe'. I argue that the recipe is an unintended consequence of managers' need to communicate, because of their uncertainties, by word and example within the industry. The recipe develops as a context and experience bound synthesis of the knowledge the industry considers managers need to have in order to acquire an adequate conceptual grasp of their firms.

There is some danger of vicious circularity here, for an industry tends to be defined by the participating managers' perceptions and so becomes the set of those who have adopted similar recipes. The circularity is strong when the industry recipe is mature and unchallenged, weaker when the industry is going through a transition from one recipe to another.

The empirical work presented in Chapters 5, 6 and 7 provides some tentative support for this set of ideas. In this final chapter I discuss the dynamics of recipe formation and the recipe's application while managers are making the firm's strategy. I then look at some of the implications for management teaching. In conclusion, I suggest some relationships between this research and that of others interested in managers' perceptions and their impact on managerial behaviour.

8.2 The Recipe's Structure and Content

In Chapter 3 I categorize uncertainties in four ways. Uncertainties are the result of informational defects due to:

1 incompleteness;
2 indeterminacy;
3 irrelevance;
4 incommensurability.

Classical management theory ignores uncertainty. Although classical theory is criticized as too prescriptive, the criticism turns out to be irrelevant. In practice, as Simon points out, the uncertainties are invariably sufficient to prevent managers from following the classicists' prescriptions. Different uncertainties give rise to different managerial responses. Following Barnard, I argue that incommensurability is the defect which most damages the classicists' analysis of organizational thinking. Dealing with it demands executive leadership, the creative response which I call strategy-making.

I argue that, despite the criticisms, classical theorising remains central to management training and thought. It has not been significantly extended by mathematical treatments of risk. Of the various types of uncertainty, we are in greatest need of an effective treatment of incommensurability. My analysis of classical theory illustrates some of the incommensurabilities which lie between the ideas which today's managers are taught to bring to their analysis. I note particularly the incommensurability between, on the one hand, the methods of setting up and controlling the transformation of material resources into finished goods and, on the other, the methods of controlling the people who perform these tasks.

To some extent the classicists formalize the ideas underlying these methods into 'technologies', which we label the technologies of production and of administration. In Adam Smith and Taylor we find what are ultimately unsuccessful attempts to bring these technologies onto a common footing. In Weber we see formalizations of the ideas of work structure and employee control that are commonplace for today's managers. We also see that the two technologies differ because the presuppositions or axioms which underlie them are incommensurate.

As we go through the empirical data of the recipes it is clear that there are other ideas which belong to other equally incommensurate technologies. These are brought out in Barnard's work and apply to the methods of setting up and controlling the relations between the organization and its environment, that is its customers and sources of finance, materials and labour. We can see there are technologies of selling, distribution, financing, purchasing and recruitment. I have not explored the extent to which these other technologies of business have been formalized. Nor have I isolated the axioms on which such ideas depend.

The recipe is made up from elemental judgements which are identified through construct analysis. These judgements indicate how, in the somewhat generalized view of the industry, the various technologies are to be applied to the organization's situation. I hypothesize, following Kelly, that some 15 elemental judgements make up a rationality or view of the situation which can then be used as the basis for corporate strategy-making. It is a conceptual compromise which is sufficiently rich to capture most of the organization's experience and sufficiently realistic to prove acceptable for a considerable period of time. Yet it is also sufficiently simple to be communicated around the organization and be used as a basis for everyday action.

The recipe is not a prescription, formula, or even a comprehensive picture, so we must not expect great consistency between its elements. Indeed, inconsistency is crucial to the recipe's ability to change and so capture the industry's 'learning'. Inconsistency is also the source of the recipe's flexibility. Each firm has its specific circumstances so no formula can be usefully applied to all. The strategist takes the recipe's general prescriptions and attaches them to the specifics of the firm. He cannot escape the consequences of his firm's particular circumstances. Nevertheless, the recipe will be of some help in his search for an appropriate response to the uncertainties which he faces. The recipe is useful simply because it offers partial and somewhat ambiguous guidance which can then be adapted to the firm's particular situation. The recipe is an industry level concept and cannot be applied to the firm without creative amendment.

8.3 Applying the Recipe

The firm's strategy is one of a family of statements of the rationality underlying the organization's managed behaviour. An effective strategy must embrace the entirety of the situation. It must deal with the middle level issues, the integration of production and administration. It must also deal with the upper level issues, the integration of the firm into the socio-economic environment, and the lower level issues, the integration of the individuals into their work-roles. The organization must be designed in terms of specific models of society and the individuals within it.

The societal model appears, for instance, in the way the strategist believes the market is segmented and stabilized. While there is competition in all of the industries I examined, the strategies revealed attempt to limit each firm's exposure by exploiting particular environmental characteristics or market imperfections. These characteristics are perceived features of the environment and are central to the strategist's societal model. The result is multi-faceted and complex and in each recipe we see features balanced off against each other.

In the dairy industry, for instance, the market is segmented into territories, for the product is undifferentiated and its price is fixed. This implies complete exposure to any competitor who wishes to walk into the dairy's territory. In practice, the balance of features determines the size of the depot's territory. The processes of meeting demand and satisfying customers raise entry barriers and secure the territory against competition from outsiders. But without balancing dis-economies of scale, the territory would expand continuously. Similarly, the dairy's ability to open new depots and territories is balanced off against the processes of negotiating directly with competitors when new territories are being opened up and indirectly through the 'costings'.

In the forklift rental industry the market is segmented by the variety of user needs and the product supplied is highly differentiated. There is, for instance, an opportunity to go for a low risk, low maintenance, low profit market or for a high risk, high maintenance market which may allow abnormal profits. The company that tries to do both will achieve neither, so there is a balance between competitors as each focuses its strategy on different market imperfections.

The foundrymen's market is segmented in terms of each individual customer. The objective is to strike up and sustain a 'special relationship' with each customer, which then secures that business against competition. This task is so severe that having to deal with 'the market' rather than with specific customers is a sure sign that the foundry is in dire straits.

In these three industries we see quite different notions of segmentation. In each we can usefully talk about market segmentation as an abstraction, but without the recipe to guide us to the specific basis of segmentation, we cannot develop strategy.

The recipes similarly guide us to appropriate models of the individuals the firm must employ. The decision to participate is a function of the societal context–whether there is a tradition of work, whether there is alternative employment. Each industry needs to segment the available labour force. The dairy industry distinguishes the transients and long-servers. It also distinguishes long-service roundsmen from depot managers. The foundry industry makes crucial distinctions between the skilled and semi-skilled moulders, and technological management. There are many ways to categorize employees but the recipe guides them to the distinctions of strategic significance.

While the recipe offers guidance, the firm's circumstances may prevent it acting in the way the recipe implies. The recipe suggests a pattern of appropriate resources as well as a way of looking at the world. It suggests a firm of a particular size and structure, with particular technological and administrative capabilities. The firm attempting to adopt the recipe may be quite unlike this 'ideal type' firm. It may have to compromise in ways that are wholly beyond the recipe's advice. The dairy, for instance, may not have any experienced roundsmen. The strategist must then find some other way of bringing the various parts of his strategy together. He might instruct the depot managers to accompany the roundsmen as a method of training. The rate of territory development will then be limited by the depot manager's training ability. Alternatively he might decide to train the roundsmen at headquarters, so relieving the depot managers. In the case of the forklift depot, there might be no adequate location from which to service a new area, so keeping an adjoining branch well over its optimal size. The firm might decide to split the branch and have two branch managers in one location in order to bring the task within the scope of one person. These are illustrations of the tension between the individual firm's capabilities and circumstances and the recipe's implications. These tensions are an important source of change in an industry as strategists struggle to develop innovative solutions to new problems.

The recipe also carries implications about the corporate policies which the industry regards as appropriate. The tensions between the firm and the recipe in matters of policy are even greater than those in the resource area. In the foundry industry we see that tied foundries adopted policies which others in the industry saw as damaging their market. We also see that the product-market and investor oriented analyses miss much of the picture. The 'special relationship' and the pattern of reciprocal obligations do not emerge until we are deeper into the recipe. Only then do we get this clear image of the recipe's implicitly approved policy.

The struggle over policy is exceptionally demanding. Since the recipe is mere guidance, the strategist is forced to make a personal judgement about the relevance of the recipe to his firm's situation. Since he is also, at this point, trying to enact policies which logically

MANAGERIAL CREATIVITY 193

precede the strategy, he will be particularly sensitive to the recipe implying that the policies are unreasonable in the light of the industry's experience. If he rejects the recipe, he then assumes the whole of the uncertainty resolution task. If he accepts the recipe he may well find himself laying out strategies directed towards policies which the firm did not choose. This tension reaches crisis point when the industry seems to be intent on self-destruction, when the industry recipe is losing its potential as a guide to performance and survival.

The strategy results from four inputs:

1 the policies chosen;
2 the recipe adopted;
3 the firm's resources and obligations;
4 the strategist's creative abilities.

Good strategies are effective, they implement the chosen policies. They are also efficient, they make good use of available resources and do not demand unavailable resources. Good strategies are also robust, able to withstand the shocks of unanticipated uncertainties. They are also resilient and can be readily rebuilt in the light of changed circumstances. They have more potential along each of these four dimensions. In general we can assume that the potential of the strategy is not derived directly from the potential implicit in the recipe. The strategy's potential will be compromised if the firm's resources do not match the recipe's resource implications. Equally, the strategy will be compromised if the firm's policies do not match the recipe's policy implications.

8.4 The Dynamics of Recipe Change

A recipe is a shared set of ideas. Yet these ideas reflect what managers think about their own companies rather than about their industry. Change occurs because of what happens to companies, not what happens to the industry. As different firms develop different strategies and experience different results, messages are broadcast back to others in the industry about what works and what fails. Sometimes those others are influenced and their ideas change. Then the recipe itself begins to change, though it is a mistake to think of the recipe as existing apart from the executives whom it influences and who influence it. But, in practice, analysts and other newcomers to the industry can pick up the recipe directly without being concerned about the individual corporate events and experiences on which it is based. The recipe is institutionalized, it finds its way into the language, dress, customs and rituals of an industry, it begins to take on an existence of its own. As a sociological phenomenon it makes sense to think of the recipe changing without requiring any analysis of the individual experiences at the level of the firm.

The recipe is not a closed formula. It is a rationality which remains open and somewhat ambiguous. The strategies it spawns can be highly varied, both because of the adopting firms' different policies and circumstances, and the different interpretations that strategists can reasonably put on the recipe. These are variations within a relatively unchanged recipe. Strategies can change without a recipe change. Thus a dairy can begin to sell groceries without changing much else because this variation is implicit within the current recipe.

The recipe is a partially closed knowledge-base, with some sense of identity but still open to other rationalities. In Barnard's terms it is an open system or organism, its separate and distinctive rationality struggling to survive in a largely indifferent environment. It must interact with that environment. As society changes, so the recipe must change if it is to remain viable.

The essence of the recipe is more in the way its elements come together and synthesize into a coherent rationality than in the particular elements themselves. We might see changes over time as the emphasis of the recipe changes. In the dairy business we might see a shift in emphasis from bottling and process efficiency to a more imaginative use of industrial by-products and a broader dairy product line. This kind of change is developmental and is likely to be common when the industry is young, still finding its way.

A recipe changes in more radical ways when its elements change. We might see this as a transition, the abandonment of one recipe and the adoption of another. There is the same sense of discontinuity between two identifiable rationalities as there is between two cultures. There is a clear gap between the A-group and B-group in the foundry industry. While the A and A' strategies seem like variations, the A-group and B-group take radically different views on the world. Yet the fact that an organization can cross the gap, as Case 5 did, shows that firms can switch recipes in a transitional way. We can reasonably expect a fair percentage of foundries to choose to adopt a variation of the A-group recipe as the squeeze on the B-group gets tighter. In this way the industry itself can experience a transition from the B-group approach to the A-group.

It seems paradoxical that the foundry business, which most observers would take to be mature, is going through a major transitional change of recipe while the forklift truck industry recipe seems stable, despite the novelty and vitality of the industry. Thus the recipe gives us a different way of thinking about industry maturity. One measure of maturity is the rate of technological change. The problem here is that the true impact of a technology must be measured on the organizational system as a whole, not on some detached scale of technical innovativeness. Another measure of industry maturity is profit, the supposition being that in a young industry abnormal profits are obtainable, while in a mature industry these have been competed away. The problem here is that profit is a gross measure and so exposed to intervening variables that it is difficult to know what determines it in any particular firm. It is even less tenable to assume that profit is determined in the same way across a sample of businesses whose specific circumstances are different. It seems more reasonable to speculate about the potential for profit being determined by technology, maturity and so forth and allow that this potential may or may not be realized because of quite different circumstances, such as poor management.

A recipe is a set of ideas that has a certain potential under the specific circumstances which are the recipe's implicit expectations. We can expect this potential to vary through time, though there is no particular reason to expect it to follow a life-cycle. While technologies are likely to become obsolete they are no more than implementations of the ideas which comprise the recipe. Recipes must lose their potential when the models of society and individual they assume become irrelevant to the context in which the industry's firms are operating. The consequences for firms finding themselves in this situation are generally catastrophic. They become anachronisms and find updating themselves extremely dangerous (Grinyer & Spender 1979b).

When recipes change, they do so because some firm or firms adopt a new rationality which then spreads across the rest of the industry. Research in technical innovation shows that while 'early adopters' are important agents in the process of change, they may not be its originators. The technical and product changes which have major impact often originate outside the industry. But there is an important difference between some technical innovation which seems to trigger change, and the managerial creativity which actually incorporates that change into a new organizational rationality and process. The innovation seems more like a catalyst which leads to a comprehensive re-ordering of the industry's way of doing business. The essential prerequisite of change is management's ability to take up the innovation and fit it into its organization's activities. I have not researched the ways in which such innovations spread out across an industry.

In the most abstract sense, recipes must adapt or be replaced as industry's total social, technological, economic and cultural context develops–in short, as society changes. The opportunity to do business, as Adam Smith notes, is a function of social differentiation and specialization. People of one specialization exchange their production with others of different specialization. This tells us something about how markets are built as producer specializations and consumer needs proliferate. Smith also applies this proposition in the reverse direction and tells us something obvious about the stuff from which businesses must be built. Management's raw material is the specializations that exist in the firm's socio-economic context. In particular, Smith argues that industry is the coming together of capital, land and labour, and that these inputs indicate the most fundamental of social categories. Society, he asserts, is itself organized around these specializations. The undertaker's task is to synthesize these incommensurate specialisms into co-operative and harmonious systems of production. There has been a massive proliferation of specializations and needs since Smith's time. We can see thousands of unrelated productive specializations and millions of differing consumer needs. But the managerial task remains the same. The raw material that has to be forged into a business is a subset of the specialisms that comprise the society in which the business is embedded. As the society changes, or rather as the relevant specialisms and needs change, so the managerial task changes.

8.5 Strategic Diagnosis

When we diagnose a company's performance we compare it against two types of target. One is internal to the company, the other is external. The internal target is the chosen objective that the strategy was formulated to achieve. The external one is what seems to be reasonable to expect of the company. We can expect a company to be profitable, and argue quite logically that it must be profitable in the long run if it is to survive. These performance criteria are far from satisfactory. They suffer from two kinds of defect. First, they tend to be useful only after the event, for conducting 'post-mortems'. They would be more useful if they could offer some sense of performance before it became clear that the targets were missed. Second, the targets tend to be either vague or arbitrary and hence unrealistic. Sometimes they are both. The range of 'reasonable' short-run performance is so wide as to provide no effective reference. The internally chosen target is often quite arbitrary, a mere statement of intent inadequately related to what can be achieved. It is sometimes a mere communication revealing more about management's style of motivation and control than about where the business will go.

These points map onto the three level model with which I began this text. The 'external' reference is comparing the firm, at the middle level, with the economic society at the upper level and with individual expectations at the lower level. The internal reference is circular, addressing the rationality within the middle level. When we introduce the recipe, a new level between the firm and its socio-economic background, we introduce a new basis for comparison. We can see the recipe as a set of operationally meaningful standards against which the firm's rationality and performance can be measured. These standards can also be used to assess the strategy well before it is played out into corporate performance.

In this text, following Thompson, I propose a two step management process. First, the uncertainties are resolved with policy and strategy choices. Second comes implementation, as the various chosen technologies of administration, production, distribution and so forth are applied.

We can surmise that corporate performance is a function of both the potential of the strategy created and the quality of its implementation. When performance falls below planned expectation, one of management's most enduring problems is to find out where things began to go wrong. It is extremely difficult to work back from a single end point, such as poor market share, through the myriad possible links to a single cause. The problem of diagnosing failure to achieve the planned objectives is exacerbated by the division of labour which generally occurs between those responsible for making the policy and strategy choices, and those responsible for their implementation. Inasmuch as poor performance has a cause, it can lie with either step of the managerial process. Yet the greater political power of the strategists will generally lead to the first criticisms being levelled at the implementers. This is a clear dysfunction of the division of managerial labour, and is difficult to control without some external reference point.

With the aid of hindsight, it is obvious that corporate failure often comes not so much from failing to do something properly, as from trying to do the wrong thing. This is a comment about the strategy. The right strategy must reflect, in part, the constraints that the firm is under, its particular policies, resources and obligations. The strategy must make sense in terms of the firm's circumstances. The recipe may prove inappropriate as a guide to the firm's strategy if its presuppositions are incompatible with the firm's circumstances.

Irrespective of the recipe's policy and resource injunctions, a strategy is better when it can be pursued under environmental conditions that differ from those which the strategist assumed. This is a measure of its robustness. It is also better when it is flexible and can be readily redirected towards new objectives or is otherwise responsive to internally generated changes. This is a measure of its resilience. Robustness and resilience are internal measures of a strategy's quality in the same way that logicality and consistency are internal measures of a decision's quality. But no strategy can be at the same time highly robust, resilient and efficient, since the robustness and resilience both imply some 'slack' or redundancy. Thus a strategy cannot be evaluated with these measures alone. Nor can it be clearly evaluated in terms of the outcome. There must be some other external sense of the strategy's reasonableness.

This is where the recipe provides a reference; it is external to the firm yet guides firms to behave in ways that the industry regards as reasonable. It is also detached from the ultimate outcome. It is a rationality indicating how it is reasonable to think. It carries no message about how strategy should be implemented.

Diagnosing poor performance can begin with checking the implementation. Were the planned technologies of administration, production, distribution, etc. applied? Were the planned resources available and used? If the failure remains unexplained, it is time to look at the strategy and ask whether it was sufficiently robust, resilient, efficient and reasonable. If the failure is still unexplained, then it is time to look at the recipe and ask whether it is an appropriate starting point, given the firm's circumstances.

8.6 Planning and Partial Control

The classicists' inability to deal with uncertainty fosters several myths about managerial work. Even though they are hopelessly inconsistent with managers' experience, these myths persist. The myth most central to this book is that which says that since organizations have information adequate to the decisions that must be taken, managers can be wholly objective. As soon as we recognize that their information is inadequate and uncertain, we extend the managers' task beyond the purely logical decision-making into the creative application of their judgement. A second related myth is that since managers know everything relevant about the organization they can control it completely. This myth has generated excessive expectations of corporate planning, which currently has a rather poor reputation among business people. This is unfortunate since planning is central to control. Planning establishes the reference against which performance is measured. Business is impossible without planning.

The challenge is to balance the effort put into planning against its benefit in terms of the degree of control made possible. If the business is not exposed to any uncertainties it is wholly predictable and controllable. The plan becomes a complete model of the business. If the business is completely at the mercy of unforecastable events or other sources of uncertainty, the plan can never be an effective model of the firm or an adequate basis for control. This does not mean, of course, that the planning activity is worthless as a framework for allocating resources and thinking through the causal links that are understood. We can contrast the efficacy of planning a satellite rendezvous with the activity of chartists on the stock-exchange. A satellite flight takes place within an almost completely known environment, so the plan can be extremely precise. The moment of rendezvous can be predicted within seconds. The stock chartist operates in an almost completely uncertain environment. Ultimately he develops a complete jargon of 'false bottoms', 'shoulders' and 'double tops', none of which do much to protect him against market declines.

The recipe is also a set of heuristics. It suggests the type of planning appropriate, and the balance of effort and expectation that others find workable. It focuses attention on which of the firm's many activities should be planned. It carries messages about how to deal with the uncertainties and unintended consequences that arise as the plan is applied.

8.7 Management Style

The two step model I use in this analysis, and the accompanying implication of a complete division of labour between the senior executives, who resolve uncertainty, and the rest of the employees, who act without having to apply their judgement, is grossly unrealistic. As Simon points out, real administration is impossibly burdensome unless employees at all levels apply their judgement. The problem that Simon then addresses is how to influence that judgement so that it is convergent with the firm's policies. I have not addressed this problem directly. There is some overlap between the idea of a strategy as the manifestation of a rationality or a culture, and the idea of controlling employees by manipulating the organizational culture.

The common typologies of management style—authoritative versus participative, input oriented versus output oriented, formal versus informal, document oriented versus face-to-face, etc.—all presuppose certainty in the nature of the information with which subordinates must deal.

As soon as we treat uncertainty as a significant issue for management's attention, then we can see that the manner of responding to uncertainty is a key attribute of management style. Anyone who has been through a period of professional apprenticeship must recognize the extremely sharp distinction between, on the one hand, watching one's mentor doing the job and, on the other, actually doing the job under the mentor's critical supervision. In the first case the burden of uncertainty is being carried by the mentor. In the second case the burden is being borne by the apprentice. We can see, therefore, that the way superiors choose to resolve the uncertainties which impact their area of responsibility is a powerful indicator of their managerial style. Similarly, they show themselves in the way they select the uncertainties which they pass down for resolution by their subordinates.

8.8 Management Teaching

Fayol remarks that there can be no teaching without theory (1949:14). This is true, and it makes a very important point about the continuing need for management theorizing, even if that work seems of little relevance to today's practising managers. We might hope to develop theories for the next generation. However, it may be more important to note the corollary to Fayol's point, that we only teach what we can theorize about. Management teaching is still dominated by the work of the classical theorists discussed in Chapter 2. There are pockets of interest in some of the critiques outlined in Chapter 3. So we can find political sociology, dialectical philosophy, the psychology of creativity and game theory taught from time to time, but seldom as the core of an understanding of management. Even when Barnard's work is discussed it is generally as one of the 'great books'. Overall, we cannot deny that there is little effective treatment of uncertainty or of managers' responses to it in most mainstream management courses. Nor is it seen as necessary.

What is taught are, for the most part, the bodies of knowledge that I have called the 'technologies' of business. These are suitably abstract; they can be written into texts, learned and examined. They suit the current technology of teaching. They match the recipe which most management teaching organizations adopt. This should not lead us to think that they are the most suitable to the managerial task nor the most valuable to the students.

Leavitt separates managerial activities into three categories: implementation, analysis and 'pathfinding' (1986). These categories match the multistep model proposed in this text. Implementation is done by subordinates, it is the domain of action according to plans prepared during the analysis phase. Pathfinding activities resolve uncertainty. Leavitt argues that management education is relatively strong on implementation, very strong on analysis and woefully weak on the pathfinding processes. As I write there are no generally accepted, academically respected or adequately teachable theories of pathfinding activity. Leavitt sees this as occasioning a deep crisis in management education, with implications spreading far beyond the academic world into business generally and to the US economy in particular. He sees the apparent fall in ethical standards in business as intimately tied up with the absence of pathfinding teaching in US business schools.

Courses on organization theory teach aspects of the technology of administration. They deal with role design, communication, organizational structure, performance measurement and so forth. These are the substantive aspects of administration discussed in a somewhat general and abstract way. What students pick up is applicable to many industries and may even apply beyond the bounds of a particular culture. We might argue that the idea of the span of control, for instance, is grounded in a human being's limited capacity. The object of all this teaching is to help managers identify the actual substantive administrative issues present in the firm and to indicate ways in which administrative solutions can help to implement the chosen policies. Similarly, we teach the technologies of production, financing, distribution, marketing, purchasing and so forth. We treat these abstractions as if they refer to self evident facts, and it is this that gives our education its predominantly analytic character.

Learning by doing, as during an apprenticeship as a deputy manager, teaches students skills as well as knowledge. It helps students judge the applicability of ideas. It will also teach something about how to make the transition between abstraction and practice. But there is no theory to guide either teacher or student.

Focusing on uncertainty allows us to separate theorizing about management into two categories. The first deals with knowledge, the 'substantive' issues that are taken as the relevant facts. The second deals with the 'judgemental' issues, the ways in which the typical uncertainties are resolved. Clearly we imply a relationship between judgement and skills with knowledge. Ignoring uncertainty, current business teaching deals best with the substantive issues. The shortfall is in teaching about judgement. Laboratory studies, such as those of Kahneman, Slovic and Tversky (1982), are important explorations of the boundaries between the purely logical and the judgemental aspects of human behaviour. But they do not provide much immediate illumination for managers.

Judgement is often taught as a philosophical, epistemological or psychological notion. It is not obvious that this kind of abstraction helps managers understand why they need judgement. Nor does it help them develop skills in applying their judgement to the problems they must solve. Nor will it help them perceive and evaluate the application of judgement in others.

The theory of executive judgement proposed in this book asserts that managerial judgement is inevitably and intimately bound up with particular contexts of activity and experience. We say that the structure of our knowledge of these contexts is uncertain and that managers perforce use their judgement to resolve these uncertainties before they can act in a purposive, rational way. We assert again that management is both purposive and rational. This behaviour is not that implied by Simon's 'total rationality'. Nor is it the same as logicality. It is ordered, predictable and therefore knowable behaviour. But it is contained and analysed within a specific limited and contextualized rationality that is itself the product of creative managerial effort.

The close relationship we assert between judgement and context gives us different ways of investigating and teaching judgement's application. We can explore the structure of the knowledge we have about a particular context. Inasmuch as we find uncertainties or unintegrated information, we can illustrate judgement as the process of information integration which precedes rational decision-making in that context. A pilot landing in a gusty wind is presented with a large amount of information which cannot be readily integrated. He judges the landing, integrating the look of the strip, the attitude of the plane, the sound of the engines, his airspeed instrument, the feel of the controls, the attitude of the windsock and so forth. His judgement is tightly bound to that particular context. It does not help him to drive a car. Indeed, there are aircraft types he will not be able to fly. Yet he applies judgement rather than simply drawing logical conclusions from the data presented.

An automatic landing system (ALS) does not handle the same information. A substantial number of additional sensors are required, different kinds of information are generated, and the whole system requires extensive adjustment as field, atmosphere, weather and aircraft specific constants are entered. These constants are the judgements which contextualize the system. They are entered by technicians, and make judgements by the pilot less necessary. Hence, the ALS does not solve the same problem as the pilot solves. The additional information makes the ALS problem different from the pilot's problem. We are deceived by the fact that both pilot and ALS land the aircraft.

An alternative approach to analysing judgement is to search the boundaries of the context. A body of knowledge is grounded on a set of distinctions. These are revealed at the boundaries or 'limiting conditions' of the knowledge-base. In practice we question whether the knowledge-base is applicable to the context of experience. We test whether the judgements apply. We decide whether the case is like or unlike the ones on which our judgement is based. The pilot will learn about his judgement as he explores which aircraft types he can fly and which he cannot. We learn about the texture of the ALS's knowledge as we explore its operating envelope.

Case studies are a method of teaching related to a context. Instead of dealing with experience, the students are given reports and summaries of experience. The case can be open-ended, in which event the students review the data and then exercise and develop their judgement as they explore and evaluate alternative decisions. This gives them a good feel for the difference between logical decisions, teasing out the implications of adequately integrated data, and the exercise of judgement. The case can be historical, in which event the students review the data and then critique the judgement of those whose decisions are also presented in the case. This helps them recognize the exercise of judgement by others.

Case studies, however, are not always what they seem to be. The historical case study must be contrasted with the case study as an exemplar of a particular theoretical point. The first presents the data in an inadequately structured form which demands the exercise of judgement. The second presents data that is integrated and consistent, which demands the exercise of the student's analytic and logical decision-making skills. In the first case the student's conclusions make him manifest, and we can expect every student to take an idiosyncratic and personal approach. In the second case the conclusions are in the data, the student's judgement should make no difference and every student should arrive at the same conclusion. In the second case the data drives the conclusion, in the first the student drives the conclusion. As Donham relates, the historical case study was carried over into the Harvard Business School, and thence into management education all over the world, from Langdell's work at the Harvard Law School (1922: 8). In the absence of a general theory of law, the case study is regarded as an appropriate way of presenting data which is unintegrated, for which the theoretical structure remains unknown. Because it is easier to teach analysis than it is to teach judgement, many contemporary cases are written as exemplars of analytic points which the teacher wishes to contextualize. This use of cases has nothing whatsoever to do with what Donham has in mind.

The student's judgement can be exercised even more directly with simulations. These are increasingly easy to set up on personal computers, and many business games, such as Business Advantage and MarkStrat, are now available commercially. But the background model presents problems similar to that above with the two types of case. The model can 'know' the correct answer that the student is trying to find, or the system can be used in a 'what if' mode to present the results of the student's judgements. The most common business games are of the first type. The model is static, in which circumstance the student's real challenge is to decode the game's model. In others the model is dynamic and under the influence of exogenous variables such as 'economic recession'. There is some element of incompleteness, for further case information can be requested and provided. In MarkStrat the model is more complex. An element of indeterminacy is introduced by having the model change according to the other players' inputs. The model is also dynamic, simulating the impact of external events.

These models are able to simulate only the first two types of uncertainty, incompleteness and indeterminacy. Completely different techniques are necessary if the system is to test the student's response to incommensurability which, I assert, is the most prevalent and demanding type of uncertainty that business people face. This kind of problem can be created in expert systems. These are more familiar to pilots, as flight simulators, or military commanders, as battle simulators. The internal structure of an expert system is one that allows for all four types of uncertainty.

A less sophisticated but adequately powerful type of non-computer-ized simulation is the 'Critical Incident Exercise' (Spender 1983). This involves role-playing simulations using 'in basket' techniques, presenting the students with memoranda, computer printouts, corre-spondence, notes of telephone calls, etc.–that is all the information that an executive is likely to have available about a situation that becomes the focus of the 'critical incident'. A very narrow context is identified, but the information supplied is intentionally fragmentary and, in part, contradictory. The exercise begins with the incident which demands management action. The student begins to grasp the situation by absorbing the data. But at the same time he begins to see that the answer is not in the data. At their most powerful the data supplied balance so perfectly that a good, well substantiated argument can be raised against every imaginable managerial response. The case becomes a complete double bind.

Many students find this situation extremely uncomfortable, and the teacher must manage this stage of the exercise very carefully. This is the point, of course, at which the student is being forced out of the familiar analytic mode into the judgemental mode. After coming to terms with this, the students begin to bring themselves, their own attitudes and experience, into play. They abandon their 'objective' standpoint and are drawn into the exercise. They begin to see that they can choose alternative futures and so get a sense of how they judge things. Instead of, as in the familiar analytic exercises, there being one action which solves the problem, they see that in this situation each possible action gives rise to further problems. They get a sense of alternatives. Their judgement becomes manifest as the particular set or sequence of problems they choose to create for themselves. Their strategies are good when they create second and third order problems which are easier to deal with than the initial problem. The better students begin to construct robust and resilient plans whose details can be filled in as the situation develops.

The difficulty with critical incident exercises, as with the more demanding simulations, is that if the student has nothing to base his judgements on the exercise becomes unbearably frustrating. The teacher needs to be sensitive to the possibility that:

1 the student is not able to make a judgement; or
2 the student may not wish to make a judgement.

This poses deeper questions about the type of student in the programme and his motivation. For many students, courses are a relatively risk-free place to spend their time. They are only called on to analyse. Out in the 'real world' they are forced to use their judgement and are much more exposed. Many students come into business education intending to move into highly paid staff jobs, expressly avoiding the judgemental burdens which line managers must bear. The teacher who forces his students to expose their judgement, when their expectation is to learn about analysis, takes a considerable risk, and must exercise his own judgement.

8.9 Strategic Group Research

This book explores a system of ideas which, taken singly, can be found in much other work on management and strategic analysis. The idea of a contextually limited theory of the firm emerges clearly in the work on strategic grouping (Hunt 1972; Hatten 1975; Hatten et al. 1976). This has led to the large body of research summarized in McGee and Thomas (1986). Strategic grouping is also a component of Porter's popular work (1980, 1985).

The idea of strategic groups is quite different from that of industry recipes. There is no concern with or treatment of uncertainty. There is no two step model of the managerial process. The presumption is that corporate performance is a direct function of industry structure and competitive behaviour. There is no suggestion that the process of developing measures of structure and behaviour and the process of creating a strategy reflecting these facts are different. They are both aspects of the same rational model which is straightforwardly positivistic and hopefully predictive. The work on strategic groups is important primarily because it is a critique of the prevailing notions of industry definition. It allows us to say that an industry defined as homogeneous by, say, having a single SIC code, is actually heterogeneous and made up of significantly different parts.

Hunt defines a strategic group within an industry as a group of firms that is highly symmetric with respect to cost structure, degree of cost differentiation, degree of vertical integration, the degree of product diversification, formal organization, control systems, management rewards and punishments, and personal views and preferences for various possible outcomes. While these measures imply that Hunt is searching for a rich and complex multidimensional space in which to locate the firms, his research findings and the methodological problems such richness generates actually lead to considerable simplification. Hunt finds that the various firms in his sample of 'white goods' manufacturers, firms that make washing machines, refrigerators, freezers, etc., could best be located within a three dimensional space. The three dimensions are: the extent of vertical integration, the degree of product diversification and the degree of product differentiation. The firms cluster in this space. In Hunt's sample there are four strategic groups located in different parts of this space.

The methodology is wholly positivistic. These grouping measures are an essential part of a predictive model of corporate performance, which is now determined by the performance of the strategic group of which the firm is a member. Porter proposes a model which can predict the performance of the strategic group based on five external 'forces': the threat of new entrants into the group, the bargaining power of those who buy from the group, the threat of substitute products, the bargaining power of suppliers to the group and the rivalry among the group's existing firms (1980). Later research has sought to modify this model by introducing measures of the individual firm's 'competencies' which then mediate the determining effect of group performance. The amended model is that corporate performance is a function of both group performance and the firm's competencies. It is not clear that these measures have yet been successfully operationalized. Such empirical work as has been presented indicates that performance variations within the groups are not significantly smaller than performance variations between groups.

This literature tends to obscure the fact that the whole strategic group research endeavour is couched within the industrial economics tradition. It is largely derived from an idiosyncratic and overly positivistic reading of Bain's important and influential work. The categories and measures suggested are all those which the earlier IO economists sought, unsuccessfully, to operationalize. While Porter's books have reawakened interest in IO economics it is not clear that managerial understanding has been much advanced.

These remarks are not criticisms of the potential that industrial economics has to clarify notions of inter-firm imitation, industry membership, inter-industry technology transfer, etc. Indeed, industrial economists such as Scherer (1980) are exerting a powerful and practical influence on some of the more abstractly quantitative economic research that has lately influenced strategy research. The remarks are criticisms of our expectations of this kind of work. Ignoring uncertainty, many current researchers are seeking theories which again take managements out of the picture, save as readers of those exogenous variables which alone determine performance. It is not clear how such theories could ever be associated with the work of business historians or could ever account for or even illuminate the evident changes which industries go through.

Notwithstanding these criticisms, there should obviously be some convergence between the research into strategic groups and that on recipes. They are not, however, alternatives. As I have noted in Chapter 4, the relationship between positivist and phenomenological methodologies is one of complementaries rather than alternatives (Spender 1979). The strategic group programme takes its categories from industrial economics and then proposes a predictive model. Industrial economics, depending as it does on the soundness of the notion of 'an industry', sought measures which would predict behaviour without requiring detailed knowledge of a firm's resources, inner workings or thoughts. The resulting measures, which form the substance of the idea of 'industry structure', are validated by relating them to corporate performance. IO economists are not concerned with managerial problems, behaviour or thought. The relationship between industry structure and performance is by no means the only use IO economists wish to make of these measures. Bain, for instance, is more concerned with competition, cartels and with the general task of providing a theoretical foundation to anti-trust legislation. The recipe programme, in contrast, is about the determination of the categories managers use to aid their control of the firm.

It is worth noting that Hatten's starting point is the work of Griesedieck (1952) and other brewing industry analysts who, being journalists and historians, have not been trained out of their natural phenomenological tendencies. From these analyses Hatten draws up a set of 16 variables which he validates in personal interviews with executives in the US brewing industry (personal communication, 1977). He scores each of the 13 firms in his sample and uses cluster analysis to arrange them into five groups. Each has a characteristic view of the brewing industry, and a characteristic strategy which is laid out in narrative form disclosing how its elements fit together.

8.10 Contingency Theory

With the notion of recipe in mind, we can think about contingency theory in a rather different way from that suggested in Chapter 2. Instead of looking for universal relationships between strategy and structure, or environmental turbulence and management style, we might see contingency theory as capturing some managerial judgements about how firms should be organized to best cope with certain environmental conditions. In both Chandler's work and that of Burns and Stalker, the boundaries of the context in which these judgements are to apply are left unspecified. Nor are they an issue in the theoretical analysis. Nor are they addressed within the research which followed.

Chandler's analysis can be seen as capturing judgements about the application of the theory of administration. These perceptions were shared among a small group of firms whose executives were in communication, in some cases the same people were actually involved in the different firms (Chandler & Salsbury, 1971). Possibly the proposed strategy/structure relationship was a common part of what were widely different recipes, involving as they did all the other 'technologies' which were not shared across Chandler's research sample. The difference here is again that between the positivistic and phenomenological methodologies. Chandler is a historian, intimately concerned with the detail of memoranda, personal communications, the individuals involved, etc. While the recipe approach might capture a judgement about the appropriateness of certain strategy/structure relationships in forming a view of the firm and what its management needs to do, the programmes which Chandler's book spawned are increasingly positivistic as researchers seek a causal relationship determining corporate performance.

Chandler is not so concerned with corporate performance as he is with the nature, development and communication of managerial ideas. There is a sense in which this is connected with performance, for if the ideas are hopelessly inappropriate, then the implication is that the firm will crash or crumble, if not in terms of short-term profitability then at least in the long run. But the relationship between the major ideas of those of Chandler or of Burns and Stalker, and performance as measure in the short term are extremely complex. The ability of firms to maintain their financial performance in spite of appalling strategic leadership is amazing (Grinyer & Spender 1979b). Hence the strategic diagnostics presented in Section 8.5 are suggested as ways of thinking rather than as causal models.

Positivistic contingency theory is put onto a somewhat richer footing by the work of Miller (1979) and Miller and Friesen (1978), working under Mintzberg at McGill. They explore a contingency model with 30 independent variables of which six are environmental, 12 are structural and 12 focus on the firm's strategy-making process. Again the dependent variable is the firm's success or failure. The data for 81 companies is taken from articles in *Fortune* and from the Harvard case studies. The data is factor analysed and displays six successful and four unsuccessful 'archetypes' or patterns of strategic response.

8.11 Phenomenological Work

Mitroff (1971, 1973) and others (Mason 1969; Mason & Mitroff 1973; Mitroff & Emshoff 1979) work in a more phenomenological tradition based on the teachings of the American philosopher Wes Churchman (1971). The essence of this approach is to develop the antithesis of any plan as a test for conceptual integrity. It also provides a method for searching for alternatives.

No discussion of the application of phenomenological methods to organizational analysis can ignore the vast output of Karl Weick, whose influence has spread wide through his impact on the ASQ. His appreciation of the problematic nature of perception goes back to his apprenticeship as a social psychologist and his work on research team productivity with Pepinsky. He is probably best known for his work on the social construction of reality, extending Garfinkel's earlier analyses. Weick also extends Tolman's concept of cognitive mapping, adding Maruyama's causal mapping. One result is the classic analysis of the perceptions of the Utrecht Jazz Orchestra (Bougon et al. 1977). However, it seems the notion of cause maps, also built into Jay Forrester's Dynamo programming language, hinders rather than helps our understanding of managerial creativity. If the cause map were complete, then it would be as prescriptive as any theory, for it would be merely a pictorial representation of a theory typically too complex to express as a comprehensive set of hypotheses. Axelrod (1976) and Eden et al. (1979) apply similar analyses.

The conjunction and balancing of positive feedback and negative feedback loops does something to recapture the recipe's sense of ambiguity, part of an attempt to capture some 'multiple causality' phenomena which stand apart from such two-dimensional ordering schemes. In the same way field theory phenomena escape analysis in circuit terms. It seems that expert systems and, maybe, neural nets are more powerful methodologies for capturing such phenomena.

Benson's work on the limitations of rational decision-making in organizations draws him inevitably towards the phenomenological methods and so into a critique of organization theory (1977a). He argues that 'an adequate approach to organizational analysis must deal with:

(a) the social production of organizational reality, including the reality-constructing activity of the organization scientist,
(b) the political bases of organizational realities, including the ties of theorists to power structures,
(c) the connection of organizations to the larger set of structural arrangements in the society, and
(d) the continuously emergent character of organizational patterns.' (1977b: 14)

Aspects of this sociological work on the development of shared meanings come out in the work of Weick (1969), Hedberg et al. (1976) and Mintzberg et al. (1976). Turner offers a particularly rich analysis of industrial subcultures (1971).

212 MANAGERIAL CREATIVITY

A similar line of research is also being pursued at SIAR in Stockholm (Rhenman 1968, 1973; Rhenman et al. 1970; Zander 1969). This focuses on empirical generalizations about the ways in which managers perceive things and is much concerned with managerial creativity and learning. The school philosophy is presented in Normann (1976, 1977) and Dahlman and Ray (1977). The position is that managerial rationality is local rather than universal, but local to the firm rather than to the industry. Each firm has its unique 'business idea'. Most of the data is anecdotal, the by-product of SIAR's consultancy work rather than of carefully structured research. Nevertheless, the programme deliberately seeks the actor's view of the situation and of the means-ends relationships judged relevant (Normann 1976: 354). The results are wholly consistent with the notions of managerial rationality and industry recipes advanced in this book.

Unfortunately the 'business idea' is never operationalized. Normann writes: 'the word idea may be misleading on two counts; first our term 'business idea' refers not only to conditions in the world of ideas but also to definite concrete conditions in the material world. Secondly, the circumstances which we wish to describe have, in most cases, a very complex character and this is something the word idea barely even suggests' (1976: 46). It is really not clear whether the idea is at the level of the firm or of the industry, nor whether these differ. Gardborn and Rhenman note that the business idea develops experientially, thereby embracing the pattern of judgement developed (1976: 12). Similarly, Dahlman and Ray stress the historical pattern of development and note that 'almost every industry carries its own myths about how to do business, and that it is just these myths which have hindered other business ideas from developing' (1977: 26).

8.12 Other Research Directions

In considering any research into managerial thought or behaviour, the acid test is whether there is any treatment of uncertainty. As I argue in Chapter 3, progress in this will immediately impact the enormous body of managerial thought and practice which derives from the classical theorists. Thus future research in this area is likely to focus on the types of uncertainty that managers face and on their mechanisms for dealing with them. It is not necessary that managerial creativity, or the kind of imitation researched here, be the only mechanism. We can imagine an increasing interest in expert systems and other information systems which imitate by encapsulating the wisdom and knowledge-base of 'expert' practitioners. Expert systems can support managements who face uncertainty or even, under some circumstances, deal with uncertainty without management's involvement.

Our categories of uncertainty are based on the assertion that the behavioural responses differ in each category. This is clearly suspect and needs much more research. But the significance of Kahneman, Slovic and Tversky's work is the relationship explored between information deficiencies and behaviour. Behaviour is the key to categorizing uncertainty. Kelly's interest is in the way perception and behaviour are linked, how certain ways of gathering and processing information interfere with normal behaviour and eventually disable a person completely. We can go back to Kelly's model of constructive thinking and suggest the recipe is a measure of the industry managers' mean ability to handle uncertainty. If the recipe were more complex, it would go beyond the amount of uncertainty and ambiguity which the average industry manager could tolerate. We can speculate that industries grow, and shrink, so as to bring the total uncertainty faced to some tolerable level.

Managers have mechanisms other than industry recipes for coping with uncertainty. Firms operating in highly uncertain environments often seek to establish inter-organizational agreements and cartels of various types to reduce uncertainty as distinct from increasing profits. The recipe implies another way of researching the optimum size of the firm. While the various technologies of business are all capable of yielding economies of scale, the growth of uncertainty is clearly a dis-economy. There comes a point where further growth will still yield economies, but the firm cannot manage any more uncertainty without rebuilding its uncertainty processing mechanisms. This may be the essence of the 'rationalizations' that Chandler observed between shifts in structure. Balancing internal resources with outside resources, the make or buy decision can be put in a new framework. Once the recipe is clear, its sensitivity to size can be explored element by element. Problems of corporate style and culture, especially as they affect mergers and acquisitions, can be re-cast in terms of handling uncertainty. Whether conglomerates can employ largely financial technologies to manage a variety of operating companies can be addressed in terms of where and how the relevant uncertainties are addressed.

These remarks are not intended to present the recipe as a solution to these many research questions. Quite the opposite. As the work of Huff (1982) and an expanding group of researchers working with her shows, the recipe is a very limited concept. It is merely one method of addressing the larger question of uncertainty. It is uncertainty that affects every research topic.

0.13 Conclusion

This book presents a theory of managerial creativity as the response to the uncertainties which inevitably face managers at all levels. It proposes four distinct types of managerial activity.

1 Choosing policies.
2 Making strategy.
3 Choosing technologies to implement strategy.
4 Supervizing operations.

The first two involve choice and are primarily uncertainty resolving. Policies are chosen in the context of the rationalities that exist outside the firm. Societal norms and laws delimit what the firm can decide to do. Policies are also constrained by what competitors permit, and by what the owners wish to do. The image here is consistent with the four-fold (want to do, might do, can do, ought to do) typology underlying Learned et al.'s classic text (1965). Strategy, however, requires the chosen policies to be brought together through the synthesis or construction of a rationality which becomes the essence of the firm. The resulting rationality is still chosen but is clearly separate from and distinctively different from the rationalities in which the policy choices were made. The resulting internal bases for choice are so different that outsiders are frequently shocked when they are exposed to a corporation's rationality.

This book deals with managers' behaviour as they face the daunting task of creating an organization's rationality. I hypothesize that they often turn for advice to a body of judgement which is shared by those socialized into the industry. I call this the industry recipe. If this hypothesis is correct it should be revealed in the way various managers at different firms talk about their problems. The research reported is tentative and employs interpretive rather than positivistic methods. Nevertheless, there is limited support for the underlying ideas. The implications of this way of thinking are profound. If shared patterns of belief are common amongst those we believe to be competitors we must ask why. It is clear that such beliefs may work in the same way that myths do for all of human society, to address the uncertainty of life, death, the hereafter and those other awesome concomitants of being alive and conscious.

Bibliography and References

Aaker, D. (1971) *Multivariate Analysis in Marketing*, Delmont, Calif, Wadsworth

Alchian, A. (1965) 'The basis of some recent advances in the theory of management' *Journal of Industrial Economics* vol. 14: 30–41

Alford, B. (1976) 'The Chandler thesis – some general observations' in Hannah (ed.) (1976): 52–70

Andersen, T., Ansoff, H. I., Norton, F. E., & Weston J. F. (1959) 'Planning for diversification through merger' *California Management Review* vol. 1 no. 4.

Andrews, K. (1971) *The Concept of Corporate Strategy*, Homewood, Illinois: Irwin

Ansoff, H. I. (1957) 'Strategies for Diversification' *Harvard Business Review* vol. 35: 113–21

Ansoff, H. I. (1958) 'A model for diversification' *Management Science* vol. 4 no. 4: 392–414

Ansoff, H. I. (1965) *Corporate Strategy*, New York: McGraw-Hill

Argyle, M. (1975) *Bodily Communication*, London: Methuen

Argyris, C. (1962) *Social Science Approaches to Business Behavior*, Homewood, Illinois: Irwin

Aron, R. (1970) *Main Currents of Sociological Thought*, London: Penguin

Ashton, T. (1963) *Iron and Steel in the Industrial Revolution*, Manchester: Manchester U. P.

Assael, H. (1968) 'The political role of trade associations' *Journal of Marketing* vol. 32: 21–8

Axelrod, R. (ed.) (1976) *Structure of Decision*, Princeton, NJ: Princeton U. P.

Ayer, A. (1946) *Language, Truth and Logic*, London: Gollancz

Bailey, F. (1969) *Stratagems and Spoils*, Oxford: Blackwell

Barnard, C. (1948) *Organization and Management*, Cambridge, Mass: Harvard U. P.
Barnard, C. (1968) *The Functions of the Executive*, Cambridge, Mass: Harvard U. P.
Bass, F. (1974) 'Profit and the A/S ratio' *Journal of Advertising Research* vol. 14: 9–19
Beattie, J. (1966) *Other Cultures*, London: Routledge & Kegan Paul
Becker, H., Geer, B., Hughes, E., & Strauss, A. (1961) *Boys in White*, Chicago: University of Chicago Press
Beer, S. (1972) *The Brain of the Firm*, London: Allen Lane
Bendix, R. (1963) *Work and Authority in Industry*, New York: Harper & Row
Benedict, R. (1959) *Pattern of Culture*, Boston, Mass: Houghton Mifflin
Bennion, E. (1956) 'Capital Budgeting and Game Theory' *Harvard Business Review* vol. 34: 115–23
Bennis, W., Benne, K., & Chin, R. (1970) *The Planning of Change*, New York: Holt, Rinehart & Winston
Benson, J. (1977a) 'Innovation and Crisis in Organizational Analysis' *Sociological Quarterly* vol. 18: 3–16
Benson, J. (1977b) 'Organizations: A dialectical view' *Administrative Science Quarterly* vol. 22: 1–21
Berg, N. (1965) 'Strategic planning in conglomerate companies' *Harvard Business Review* vol. 43: 79–92
Berg, N. (1973) 'Corporate role in diversified companies' in Taylor & Macmillan (eds) (1973): 298
Berger, P., & Luckman, T. (1971) *The Social Construction of Reality*, London: Penguin
Bernal, J. (1971) *Science in History*, Cambridge, Mass: M.I.T. Press
Bierman, H., Fouraker, L., & Jaedicke, R. (1961) *Quantitative Analysis for Business Decisions*, Homewood, Illinois: Irwin
Blau, P. (1965) 'The comparative study of organisation' *Industrial & Labour Relations Review*, vol. 18: 323–38
Blau, J., & McKinley, W. (1979) 'Idea, complexity and innovation' *Administrative Science Quarterly* vol. 24 no. 2: 200–19
Blau, P., & Scott, W. (1963) *Formal Organisations*, London: Routledge & Kegan Paul
Bohannan, P., & Glazer, M. (eds) (1973) *High Points in Anthropology*, New York: Knopf
Bouchet, J.-L. (1976) 'Diversification: The composition of the top management team' *EGOS Working Paper*, December
Bougon, M., Weick, K., & Binkhorst, D. (1977) 'Cognition in

Organizations' *Administrative Science Quarterly* vol. 22 no. 4: 606–39

Bowey, A. (1976) *The Sociology of Organisations*, London: Hodder & Stoughton

Bramson, L. (1961) *The Political Context of Sociology*, Princeton, NJ: Princeton U. P.

Braverman, H. (1974) *Labour and Monopoly Capital*, New York: Monthly Review of Books

Budd, R., Thorp R., & Donohew, L. (1967) *Content Analysis of Communications*, New York: Macmillan

Burns, T., & Stalker, G. (1961) *The Management of Innovation*, London: Tavistock

Chandler, A. (1962) *Strategy and Structure*, Cambridge, Mass. M.I.T. Press

Chandler, A., & Redlich, F. (1961) 'Recent developments in American business administration' *Business History Review*, vol. 35 no. 1: 1–27

Chandler, A. & Salsbury, S. (1971). *Pierre S. Du Pont and the Making of the Modern Corporation*, New York: Harper & Row

Channon, D. (1973) *The Strategy and Structure of British Enterprise*, London: Macmillan

Checkland, S. (1964) *The Rise of Industrial Society in England*, London: Longman

Child, J. (1964) 'Quaker employees and industrial relations' *Sociological Review* vol. 12 no. 3: 293–315

Child, J. (1968) 'British management thought as a case study within the sociology of knowledge' *Sociological Review* vol. 16 no. 2: 217–39

Child, J. (1969) *The British Enterprise in Modern Industrial Society*, London: Collier-Macmillan

Child, J. (1970) 'More myths of management organisation?' *Journal of Management Studies* vol. 7 no. 4: 376–90

Child, J. (1972) 'Organisation structure, environment and performance' *Sociology* vol. 6: 1–21

Child, J. (1973a) *Man and Organisation: The Search for Explanation and Social Relevance*, London: Allen & Unwin

Child, J. (1973b) 'Predicting and understanding organisational structure' *Administrative Science Quarterly* vol. 18 no. 2: 168

Christensen, R., Berg, N., & Salter, M. (1976) *Policy Formulation and Administration*, Homewood, Illinois: Irwin

Church, A. (1912) 'Practical principles of rational management' *Engineering Magazine* vol. 44: 487

Church, A., & Alford, L. (1912) 'The principles of management' *American Machinist*, vol. 36 no. 22: 857–61

Churchman, W. (1971) *The Design of Enquiring Systems*, New York: Basic Books

Cicourel, A. (1964) *Method and Measurement in Sociology*, New York: Free Press

Cicourel, A. (1968) *The Social Organization of Social Justice*, New York: Wiley

Cicourel, A., & Kitsuse, J. (1963) *The Educational Decision-Makers*, Indianapolis, Ind: Bobbs-Merril

Clarkson, G., & Meltzer, A. (1960) 'Portfolio selection: A heuristic approach' *Journal of Finance* vol. 15 no. 4: 465–80

Clarkson, G., & Simon, H. (1960) 'Simulation of individual and group behavior' *American Economic Review* vol. 50: 920–32

Clausewitz, K. (1968) *War, Politics and Power*, Chicago: Regnery & Co.

Coase, R. (1937) 'The nature of the firm' *Economica* vol. 4: 386–405

Cohen, P. (1968) *Modern Sociological Theory*, London: Heinemann

Cole, A. (1969) *Numerical Taxonomy*, London: Academic Press

Cooper & Lybrand Assoc. (1978) *Report on the Investment Attitudes: Research Report No. 1*, London: H.M.S.O.

Coopersmith, S. (1962) *Personality Research*, Copenhagen: Munksgaard

Copeland, M. (1939) 'The job of an executive' *Harvard Business Review* vol. 18: 148–60

Cunnison, S. (1966) *Wages and Work Allocation*, London: Tavistock

Cyert, R., & March, J. (1963) *A Behavioral Theory of the Firm*, Englewood Cliffs, NJ: Prentice-Hall

Dahlman, C., & Ray, J.-O. (1977) *Business Opportunity Studies*, Stockholm: SIAR

Dalton, M. (1959) *Men who Manage*, New York: Wiley

Dean, J., & Whyte, W. (1958) 'How do you know if the informant is telling the truth?' *Human Organization* vol. 17 no. 2: 34–8

Diesing, P. (1972) *Patterns of Discovery in the Social Sciences*, London: Routledge & Kegan Paul

Ditton, J. (1977) *Part-time Crime*, London: Macmillan

Donham, W. (1922) 'Essential groundwork for a broad executive theory' *Harvard Business Review* vol. 1 no. 1: 1–10

Dowling, J., & Pfeffer, J. (1975) 'Organizational Legitimacy' *Pacific Sociological Review* vol. 18 no. 1: 122–36

Drucker, P. (1954) *The Practice of Management*, New York: Harper & Row

Duncan, H. (1962) *Communication and Social Order*, Totowa, NJ: Bedminster Press

Duncan, R. (1972) 'Characteristics of organizational environments' *Administrative Science Quarterly* vol. 17 no. 3: 313

Durkheim, E. (1964) *The Division of Labor in Society*, New York: Free Press

Dutton, H. P. (1927) *The Business and its Organization*, Chicago: A. W. Shaw Co.

Eden, C., Jones, S., & Sims, D (1979) *Thinking in Organisations*, London: Macmillan

Ekeh, P. (1974) *Social Exchange Theory*, London: Heinemann

Emery, F. (1969) *Systems Thinking*, London: Penguin

Etzioni, A. (1971) *Comparative Analysis of Complex Organizations*, New York: Free Press

Evans Pritchard, E. (1951) *Social Anthropology*, London: Cohen & West

Everitt, B. (1974) *Cluster Analysis*, London. Heinemann

FITC (1974) *Patterns of Employment in the Foundry Industry*, London: FITC

F.U.K.M.M.B. (1974) *United Kingdom: Dairy Facts and Figures*, London: Federation of Milk Marketing Boards

Fayol, H. (1949) *General and Industrial Management*, London: Pitman

Fiedler, F. (1967) *A Theory of Leadership Effectiveness*, New York: McGraw-Hill

Filmer, P., Phillipson, M., Silverman, D., & Walsh, D. (1972) *New Directions in Sociological Theory*, London: Collier-Macmillan

Florence, P. (1961) *The Logic of British and American Industry*, London: Routledge & Kegan Paul

Fouraker, L., & Stopford, J. (1968) 'Organizational structure and multinational strategy' *Administrative Science Quarterly* vol. 13: 64

Fox, A. (1971) *A Sociology of Work in Industry*, London: Collier-Macmillan

Franko, L. (1974) 'The move towards a multidivisional structure' *Administrative Science Quarterly* vol. 19: 493

Frijda, N., & Jahoda, M. (1966) 'On the scope and methods of cross-cultural research' *International Journal of Psychology* vol 1: 110–27

Fruhan, W. (1972) *The Fight for Competitive Advantage*, Cambridge, Mass: Harvard U. P.

Fulmer, R., & Rue, L. (1973) *The Practice and Profitability of Long-Range Planning*, Oxford, Ohio: Planning Executives Institute

Galtung, J. (1967) *Theory and Methods in Social Research*, London: Allen & Unwin

Gardborn, T., & Rhenman, E. (1976) *Construction Consultancy: Strategies for International Growth*, Stockholm: SIAR

Gasking, D. (1955) 'Causation and Recipes' *Mind* 479–87

Georges, R. (1968) *Studies on Mythology*, Homewood, Illinois: Irwin

Gibbs, J. (1972) *Sociological Theory Construction*, Hinsdale, Illinois: Drysdale Press

Giddens, A. (1976) *New Rules of Sociological Method*, London: Hutchinson

Gidlow, B. (1972) 'Ethnomethodology – a new name for old practices' *British Journal of Sociology* vol. 23: 395–405

Gifford, W., Bobbitt, H., & Slocum, J. (1979) 'Message characteristics and perceptions of uncertainty' *Academy of Management Journal* vol. 22 no. 3: 458–81

Giglioni, P. (1972) *Language and Social Context*, London: Penguin

Gilmore, F. (1970) *Formulation and Advocacy of Business Policy*, Ithaca, NY: Cornell U. P.

Gilmore, F., & Brandenburg, R. (1962) 'Anatomy of corporate planning' *Harvard Business Review* vol. 40: 61–9

Glaser, B., & Strauss, A (1967) *The Discovery of Grounded Theory*, Chicago: Aldine Press

Glueck, W. (1976) *Business Policy*, New York: McGraw-Hill

Goffman, E. (1956) *The Presentation of Self in Everyday Life*, Edinburgh: Edinburgh U. P.

Goldthorpe, J., & Lockwood, D. (1963) 'Affluence and the British class structure' *Sociological Review* vol. 11 no. 2: 133–63

Goodenough, W. (1966) 'Cultural anthropology and linguistics' in Hymes (ed.) (1966): 36

Gordon, R. (1975) *Interviewing: Strategy, Tactics and Techniques*, Homewood, Illinois: Irwin

Gordon, R. (1976) 'Rigour and relevance in a changing institutional setting' *American Economic Review* vol. 66 no. 1: 1

Green, P., & Tull, D. (1975) *Research for Marketing Decisions*, Englewood Cliffs, NJ: Prentice-Hall

Green, P., Frank, T., & Robinson, J. (1967) 'Cluster analysis in test-market selection' *Management Science* vol. 13 no. 8: B–387

Griesedieck, A. (1952) *The Falstaff Story*, St. Louis, Minn: Falstaff Corp

Grinyer, P. (1973) 'Some dangerous axioms of corporate planning' *Journal of Business Policy* vol. 3 no. 1: 3

Grinyer, P., & Norburn, D. (1974) 'Strategic planning in 21 UK companies' *Long-Range Planning*, August: 80–8

Grinyer, P., & Spender, J.-C. (1979a) 'Recipes, crises and adaptation in mature businesses' *International Studies of Management & Organisation* vol. 9: 113

Grinyer, P., & Spender, J.-C. (1979b) *Turnaround: The Fall and Rise of the Newton Chambers Group*, London: Associated Business Press

Grinyer, P., & Yasai-Ardekani, A. (1978) 'Dimensions of organisational structure' *City University Working Paper* no. 8

Hannah, L. (ed.) (1976) *Management Strategy and Business Development*, London: Macmillan

Hatten, K. (1975) 'Strategy, profits and beer' *Harvard Business School Working Paper 76–27*

Hatten, K. (1977) 'Business Policy Research the quantitative way' circa 1977' *Business Policy Conference Paper*, Pittsburgh, Pa

Hatten, K., & Schendel, D. (1976) 'Heterogeneity within an industry' *Harvard Business School Working Paper 76–27*

Hatten, K., Schendel, D., & Cooper, A. (1978) 'A strategic model of the US brewing industry' *Harvard Business School Working Paper 76–24*

Hedberg, B., Nystrom, P., & Starbuck, W. (1976) 'Camping on seesaws' *Administrative Science Quarterly* vol. 21: 41

Hempel, C. (1966) *The Philosophy of Natural Science*, Englewood Cliffs, NJ: Prentice-Hall

Henderson, L. J. (1970) *On the Social System*, Chicago: University of Chicago Press

Hicks, H., & Gullett, C. (1975) *Organizations: Theory and Behavior*, New York: McGraw-Hill

Hicks, J. (1969) *A Theory of Economic History*, Oxford: Oxford U. P.

Hirsch, P. (1975) 'Organizational effectiveness and the institutional environment' *Administrative Science Quarterly* vol. 20: 327–44

Hitchens, D. (1977) *Business Efficiency in Ironfounding*, Stonehouse, Glos: Technicopy

Hoagland, J. (1955) 'Management before Frederick Taylor' *Proceedings of the Academy of Management*, December: 15–24

Hofer, C. (1975) 'Towards a contingency theory of business strategy' *Academy of Management Journal* vol. 18 no. 4: 784

Hollis, M. (1967) 'The limits of irrationality' *Archives Européenne de Sociologie* vol. 7: 265–71

Horton, R. (1967) 'African traditional thought and western science' *Africa* vol. 27 no. 1: 50–71 and no. 2: 155–87

Horton, R., & Finnegan, R. (1973) *Modes of Thought*, London: Faber

Hudson, K. (1975) *Exploring our Industrial Past*, London: Hodder & Stoughton

Huff, A. S. (1982) 'Industry Influences on Strategy Reformulation' *Strategic Management Journal* vol. 3: 119–31

Hunt, M. S. (1972) *Competition in the Major Home Appliance Industry 1960–1970*, DBA Dissertation Harvard University

Hyman, R. (1972) *Strikes*, London: Fontana

Hymes, B. (ed) (1966) *Language in Culture and Society*, New York: Harper & Row

Jarvie, I. (1967) *The Revolution in Anthropology*, London: Routledge & Kegan Paul

Kahn, R., & Cannell, C. (1957) *The Dynamics of Interviewing*, New York: Wiley

Kahneman, D., Slovic, P., & Tversky, A. (1982) *Judgement under Uncertainty*, New York: Cambridge U. P.

Kakar, S. (1970) *Frederick Taylor: A Study in Personality and Innovation*, Cambridge, Mass: M.I.T. Press

Kaplan, A. (1964) *The Conduct of Inquiry*, San Francisco, Calif: Chandler Publishing

Katona, G., & Morgan, J. (1952) 'The quantitative study of the factors affecting business decisions' *Quarterly Journal of Economics* vol. 1: 67–90

Kelly, G. (1955) *The Psychology of Personal Constructs*, New York: Norton

Kelly, G. (1962) 'Abstraction of human processes' in Coopersmith (1962): 220

Kelly, G. (1963) *The Theory of Personal Constructs*, New York: Norton

Kelly, G. (1970) 'The expert as historical actor' in Bennis et al. (1970): 14

Keynes, J. (1954) *The General Theory of Employment, Interest and Money*, London: Macmillan

Khandwalla, P. (1977) *Design of Organizations*, New York: Harcourt, Brace & Jovanovich

Klapp, O. (1975) 'Opening and closing of open systems' *Behavioural Science* vol. 20: 251–7

Knight, F. H. (1965) *Risk, Uncertainty and Profit*, New York: Harper & Row

Kolakowski, L. (1972) *Positivist Philosophy*, London: Penguin

Krupp, S. (1961) *Pattern in Organizational Analysis*, New York: Holt, Rinehart & Winston

Kuehn, A., & Hamburger, M. (1963) 'A heuristic program for locating warehouses' *Management Science* vol. 9: 43–66

224 BIBLIOGRAPHY AND REFERENCES

Kuhn, T. (1970) *The Structure of Scientific Revolutions*, Chicago: University of Chicago Press

Lakatos, I., & Musgrave, A. (1970) *Criticism and the Growth of Knowledge*, Cambridge: Cambridge U. P.

Lauer, Q. (1965) *Phenomenology: Its Genesis and Prospect*, New York: Harper & Row

Lawrence, P., & Lorsch, J. (1967) *Organization and Environment*, Cambridge, Mass: Harvard U. P.

Lawrence, P., & Lorsch, J. (1969) *Developing Organizations*, Belmont, Calif: Addison-Wesley

Lazarsfeld, P., & Rosenberg, M. (1955) *The Language of Social Research*, New York: Free Press

Learned, E., Christensen, R., Andrews, K., & Guth, W. (1965) *Business Policy: Text and Cases*, Homewood, Illinois: Irwin

Leavitt, H. (1966) *Corporate Pathfinders*, Homewood, Illinois: Irwin

Leibenstein, H. (1960) *Economic Theory and Organizational Analysis*, New York: Harper & Row

Lewin, K. (1935) *A Dynamic Theory of Personality*, New York: McGraw-Hill

Lewin, K. (1936) *Principles of Topological Psychology*, New York: McGraw-Hill

Lindblom, C. (1959) 'The science of muddling through' *Public Administration Review* vol. 19: 79–88

Lindblom, C. (1968) *The Policy-Making Process*, Englewood Cliffs, NJ: Prentice-Hall

Lindzey, G., & Aronson, E. (1968) *The Handbook of Social Psychology*, Reading, Mass: Addison-Wesley

Litterer, J. (1961a) 'Alexander Hamilton Church and the development of modern management' *Business History Review* vol. 35: 211–25

Litterer, J. (1961b) 'Systematic management: the search for order and integration' *Business History Review* vol. 35 no. 4: 461–76

Litterer, J. (1963) 'Systematic management: design for organisational recoupling' *Business History Review* vol. 37 no. 4: 369–91

Locke, J. (1928) *Selections*, New York: Scribners

Lockwood, D. (1966) 'Sources of variation in working-class images of society' *Sociological Review* vol. 14 no. 3: 249–67

Lofland, J. (1971) *Analyzing Social Settings*, Belmont, Calif: Wadsworth

Lukes, S. (1967) 'Some problems about rationality' *Archives Européenne de Sociologie* vol. 8: 247–64

Lupton, T. (1963) *On the Shopfloor*, London: Pergamon

Lupton, T. (1971) *Management and the Social Sciences*, London: Penguin

MacRae, D. (1969) *Spencer's 'The Man versus the State'*, London: Penguin
MacRae, D. (1974) *Weber*, London: Fontana
March, J., & Simon, H. (1958) *Organizations*, New York: Wiley
Markham, J. (1973) *Conglomerate Enterprise and Public Policy*, Cambridge, Mass: Harvard Business School
Maslow, A. (1954) *Motivation and Personality*, New York: Harper Bros
Mason, R. (1969) 'A dialectical approach to strategic planning' *Management Science* vol. 15 no. 8: B403–B414
Mason, R., & Mitroff, I. (1973) 'A program for research on management information systems' *Management Science* vol. 19 no. 5: 475–07
Masterman, M. (1970) 'The nature of paradigm' in Lakatos & Musgrave (1970): 59–90
Maus, H. (1971) *A Short History of Sociology*, London: Routledge & Kegan Paul
McCall, G., & Simmons, J. (1969) *Issues in Participant Observation*, Reading, Mass: Addison-Wesley
McGee, J., & Thomas, H. (1986) 'Strategic groups: Theory, research and taxonomy' *Strategic Management Journal* vol. 7: 141–60
McGuire, J. (1964) *Theories of Business Behavior*, Englewood Cliffs, NJ: Prentice-Hall
McNichols, T. (1977) *Policy-Making and Executive Action*, New York: McGraw-Hill
Meltzer, B., Petras, P., & Reynolds, G. (1975) *Symbolic Interactionism*, London: Routledge & Kegan Paul
Merton, R., Fiske, B., & Kendall, P. (1956) *The Focused Interview*, New York: Free Press
Merton, R., & Kendall, P. (1946) 'The focused interview' *American Journal of Sociology* vol. 51 no. 6: 541–57
Meyer, J., & Rowan, B. (1977) 'Institutionalized Organizations' *American Journal of Sociology* vol. 83 no. 2: 340–63
Miller, D. (1977) 'The role of multivariate Q-techniques in the study of organizations' *McGill University Working Paper*
Miller, D. (1979) 'Strategy, structure and environment' *Journal of Management Studies* vol. 16 no. 3: 294–316
Miller, D., & Friesen, P. (1978) 'Archetypes of organization transition' *McGill University Working Paper*
Miller, D., & Starr, M. (1960) *Executive Decision and Operations Research*, Englewood Cliffs, NJ: Prentice-Hall
Mintzberg, H. (1967) 'The science of strategy-making' *Industrial*

Management Review vol. 8 no. 2: 71–91

Mintzberg, H. (1972) 'Research on strategy-making' *Proceedings of the Academy of Management*: 90–4

Mintzberg, H. (1973) *The Nature of Managerial Work*, New York: Harper & Row

Mintzberg, H. (1976) 'Patterns in strategy formation' *McGill University Working Paper*

Mintzberg, H., Raisinghani, D., & Théorêt, A. (1976) 'The structure of unstructured decision processes' *Administrative Science Quarterly* vol. 21: 246–75

Mitroff, I. (1971) 'A communications model of dialectical inquiring systems' *Management Science* vol. 17 no. 10. D–634

Mitroff, I. (1973) 'Systems, inquiry and the meanings of falsification' *Philosophy of Science* vol. 40: 255–76

Mitroff, I., & Emshoff, J. (1979) 'On strategic assumption-making' *Academy of Management Review* vol. 4 no. 1: 1–12

Montanari, J. (1979) 'Strategic choice: A theoretical analysis' *Journal of Management Studies* vol. 16 no. 2: 202–21

Mueller, E., & Morgan, J. (1962) 'Location decisions of manufacturers' *American Economic Review* vol. 52: 204–17

NEDO (1974) *Industrial Review to 1977: Iron and Steel Castings*, London: NEDO

Nagel, E. (1963) 'On the method of Verstehen as the sole method of philosophy' in Natanson (1963): 262

Natanson, M. (1963) *Philosophy of the Social Sciences*, New York: Random House

Newbould, G. (1970) *Management and Merger Activity*, Liverpool: Guthstead

Newell, A., Shaw, J., & Simon, H. (1958) 'Elements of a theory of human problem-solving' *Psychological Review* vol. 65 no. 3: 151–66

Newell, A., & Simon, H. (1972) *Human Problem Solving*, Englewood Cliffs, NJ: Prentice-Hall

Newman, W., & Logan, J. (1976) *Strategy, Policy and Central Management*, Cincinnati, Ohio: Southwestern

Nicholls, J. (1978) 'Business policy research: A brief review' *University of Bath Working Paper in Industrial Economics* no. 6

Nichols, T. (1969) *Ownership, Control and Ideology*, London: Allen & Unwin

Normann, R. (1976) *Management and Statesmanship*, Stockholm: SIAR

Normann, R. (1977) *Management for Growth*, New York: Wiley

Olson, S. (1976) *Ideas and Data: The Process and Practice of Social*

Research, Homewood, Illinois: Irwin

Oppenheim, A. (1968) *Questionnaire Design and Attitude Measurement*, London: Heinemann

Paine, F., & Naumes, W. (1974) *Strategy and Policy Formation* Philadelphia, Pa: W. B. Saunders

Parsons, T. (1970) *The Social System*, London: Routledge & Kegan Paul

Pavan, R. (1972) *The Strategy and Structure of Italian Enterprise*, DBA Thesis, Harvard Business School

Perrow, C. (1970) *Organisational Analysis: A Sociological View*, London: Tavistock

Perrow, C. (1984) *Normal Accidents: Living with High Risk Technologies*, New York: Basic Books

Perry, N. (1979) 'Recovery and retrieval in organisational analysis' *Sociology* vol. 13 no. 2: 259–73

Pettigrew, A. (1972) 'Information control as a power source' *Sociology* vol. 6 no. 2: 187–204

Pettigrew, A. (1973) *The Politics of Organisational Decision-making*, London: Tavistock

Phillips, B. (1976) *Social Research: Strategy and Tactics*, New York: Macmillan

Phillipson, M. (1972) 'Phenomenological philosophy and sociology' in Filmer et al. (1972): 119–64

Pivcevic, E. (1972) 'Can there be a phenomenological sociology?' *Sociology* vol. 6: 335–49

Pollard, S. (1968) *The Genesis of Modern Management*, London: Penguin

Pollard, S., & Salt, J. (1971) *Robert Owen: Prophet of the Poor*, London: Macmillan

Popper, K. (1968) *The Logic of Scientific Discovery*, London: Hutchinson

Popper, K. (1969) *Conjectures and Refutations*, London: Routledge & Kegan Paul

Popper, K. (1972) *Objective Knowledge*, London: Oxford U. P.

Porter, M. (1980) *Competitive Strategy*, New York: Macmillan

Porter, M. (1985) *Competitive Advantage*, New York: Macmillan

Pugh, D., Hickson, D., Hinings, C., MacDonald, K., Turner, C., & Lupton, T. (1963) 'A conceptual scheme for organizational analysis' *Administrative Science Quarterly* vol. 8: 289–315

Pugh, D., Hickson, D., Hinings, C., & Turner, C. (1968) 'The context of organizational structure' *Administrative Science Quarterly* vol. 14 no. 1: 91–114

Raiffa, H. (1982) *The Art & Science of Negotiation*, Boston: Harvard U. P.

Raison, T. (1969) *The Founding Fathers of Sociology*, London: Penguin

Redlich, F. (1949) 'The business leader in theory and reality' *American Journal of Economics and Sociology* vol. 8: 223

Rhenman, E. (1968) *Industrial Democracy and Industrial Management*, London: Tavistock

Rhenman, E. (1973) *Organization Theory for Long-Range Planning*, New York: Wiley

Rhenman, E., Strömberg, L., & Westerlund, G. (1970) *Conflict and Co operation in Business Organizations*, New York: Wiley

Rice, S. (1931) *Methods in Social Science*, Chicago: University of Chicago Press

Robinson, E. (1958) *The Structure of Competitive Industry*, Cambridge: Cambridge U. P.

Roy, D. (1952) 'Quota restriction and gold-bricking in a machine shop' *American Journal of Sociology* vol. 57

Rue, L., & Fulmer, R. (1973) 'Is long-range planning profitable?' *Academy of Management Proceedings*, August

Rumelt, R. (1974) *Strategy, Structure and Economic Performance*, Cambridge, Mass: Harvard Business School

Rumelt, R. (1977) 'Strategy evaluation; The state of the art' *Business Policy Conference Paper*, Pittsburgh, Pa

Rummel, J., & Ballaine, W. (1963) *Research Methodology in Business*, New York: Harper & Row

Salaman, G. (1979) *Work Organisations: Resistance and Control*, London: Longman

Salter, M. (1970) 'Stages of corporate development' *Journal of Business Policy*, August: 23–37

Sasieni, M., Yaspan, A., & Friedman, L. (1959) *Operations Research: Methods and Problems*, New York: Wiley

Schegloff, E. (1971) 'Notes on conversational practice' in Sudnow (1971)

Schendel, D., & Hofer, C. (eds) (1979) *Strategic Management: A New View*, Boston, Mass: Little, Brown

Scherer, F.M. (1980) *Industrial Market Structure and Economic Performance*, Chicago: Rand-McNally

Schutz, A. (1944) 'The stranger: An essay in social psychology' *American Journal of Sociology* vol. 49: 499–507

Schutz, A. (1967) *Collected Papers: 1. The Problem of Social Reality*, Amsterdam: Martinus Nijhoff

Schutz, A. (1970a) *On Phenomenology and Social Relations*, Chicago: University of Chicago Press

Schutz, A. (1970b) *Reflections on the Problem of Relevance*, New Haven, Conn: Yale U. P.

Schutz, A. (1972) *The Phenomenology of the Social World*, London: Heinemann

Schwartz, M., & Schwartz, C. (1955) 'The problems in participant observation' *American Journal of Sociology* vol. 60: 343–54

Scott, B. (1963) *An Open-System Model of Organization*, DBA Thesis, Harvard Business School

Scott, W. (1959) 'The early record of a modern administrative dilemma' *Journal of the Academy of Management*, August: 97–110

Scott, W. (1961) 'Organization theory! An overview and an appraisal' *Journal of the Academy of Management*, April: 7

Seckler, D. (1975) *Thorstein Veblen and the Institutionalists*, London: Macmillan

Selltiz, C. (1965) *Research Methods in Social Relations*, London: Methuen

Shackle, G. (1961) *Decision, Order and Time in Human Affairs*, Cambridge: Cambridge U. P.

Shepard, R., Romney, N., & Nerlove, P. (1972) *Multidimensional Scaling*, New York: Seminar Press

Shirley, R., Peters, F., & El-Ansary, A. (1976) *Strategy and Policy Formulation*, New York: Wiley

Shortell, S. (1977) 'The role of environment in a configurational theory of organisations' *Human Relations* vol. 30 no. 3: 275–302

Shubik, M. (1954) 'Information, risk, ignorance and indeterminacy' *Quarterly Journal of Economics* vol. 4: 629

Shubik, M. (1956) 'The uses of game theory in management science' *Management Science* vol. 2: 40–54

Shubik, M. (1960) 'Games Decisions and Industrial Organisation' *Management Science* vol. 6

Simon, H. (1952a) 'A comparison of organization theories' *Review of Economic Studies* vol. 20 no. 1: 40

Simon, H. (1952b) 'Comments on the theory of organizations' *American Political Science Review* vol. 46 no. 4: 1130

Simon, H. (1956) 'Rational choice and the structure of the environment' *Psychological Review* vol. 63 no. 2: 129–38

Simon, H. (1957) *Administrative Behavior* 2nd edn, New York: Macmillan

Simon, H. (1959) 'Theories of decision-making in economics and behavioral science' *American Economic Review* vol. 49 no. 3

Simon, H. (1960) *The New Science of Management Decision*, New York: Harper & Row

Simon, H. (1962) 'New developments in the theory of the firm' *American Economic Review* vol. 52: 1–27

Smith, A. (1970) *The Wealth of Nations*, London: Penguin

Sokal, R., & Sneath, P. (1963) *The Principles of Numerical Taxonomy*, San Francisco, Calif: Freeman & Co

Spencer, H. (1904) *Autobiography*, London

Spender, J.-C. (1976) 'Programmes of research into business strategy' *ATM Policy Group Meeting Paper*, April, City University, London

Spender, J.-C. (1979) 'Theory-building and theory-testing in strategic management' In Schendel & Hofer (eds) (1979): 394–404

Spender, J.-C. (1983a) 'Crisis casework for policy courses' *Organisational Behaviour Teaching Review* vol. 8 no. 4: 35–9

Spender, J.-C. (1983b) 'Recipes and the business policy problem' in Lamb R. (ed.) *Advances in Strategic Management* vol. 2, Greenwich, Conn: JAI Press

Spender, J.-C. (1986) *Strategy-Making in Business* Ann Arbor, Mich: University Microfilm Int.

Staudt, T. (1954) 'Program for product diversification' *Harvard Business Review* vol. 32 no. 6: 121–31

Steiner, G. (1969) *Top Management Planning*, New York: Macmillan

Steiner, G., & Miner, J. (1977) *Management Policy and Strategy*, New York: Macmillan

Sudnow, D. (1971) *Studies in Social Interaction*, New York: Free Press

Tarski, A. (1965) *Introduction to Logic*, New York: Oxford U. P.

Tausky, C. (1970) *Work Organizations: Major Theoretical Perspectives*, Itasca, Illinois: E. Peacock Publishers

Taylor, B., & Macmillan, K. (eds) (1973) *Business Policy: Teaching and Research*, Bradford: Bradford U. P.

Taylor, F. W. (1967) *The Principles of Scientific Management*, New York: Harper & Row

Taylor, M. (1971) *Closures among Ironfounders*, London: Ironfoundries Association

Thanheiser, H. (1972) *Strategy and Structure of German Industrial Enterprise*, DBA Thesis, Harvard Business School

Thompson, J. (1967) *Organizations in Action*, New York: McGraw-Hill

Tilles, S. (1966) 'Strategies for allocating funds' *Harvard Business Review* vol. 44 no. 1: 72

Toennies, F. (1971) *On Sociology: Pure, Applied and Empirical*, Chicago: University of Chicago Press

Tosi, H., & Carroll, S. (1976) *Management: Contingencies, Structure and Process*, Chicago: St. Clair Press

Triffin, R. (1962) *Monopolistic Competition and General Equilibrium Theory* Cambridge, Mass: Harvard U. P.

Trist, E., & Bamforth, K. (1951) 'Some social and psychological consequences of the longwall method' *Human Relations* vol. 4 no. 1: 3–38

Turner, B. A. (1971) *Exploring the Industrial Sub-Culture*, London: Macmillan

Vidich, A., & Bensman, J. (1954) 'The validity of field data' *Human Organization* vol. 13 no. 1: 20–7

Walsh, D. (1972) 'An analysis of traditional sociology' in Filmer et al. (1972): 15–76

Weber, M. (1969) *The Theory of Social and Economic Organization*, New York: Free Press

Weick, K. (1968) 'Systematic observation methods' in Lindzey & Aronson (1968): 357

Weick, K. (1969) *The Social Psychology of Organizing*, Belmont, Calif: Addison-Wesley

Weick, K. (1977) 'Organizational design: Organizations as self-designing systems' *Organizational Dynamics* vol. 6 no. 2: 31–46

Winch, P. (1964) 'Understanding a primitive society' *American Philosophical Quarterly* vol. 1 no. 4: 307

Wishart, D. (1969) *Clustan 1A User's Manual*, Edinburgh: St. Andrews University Computing Laboratory

Wood, D. (1972) 'Decision systems approach to financial strategy' *Journal of Business Finance* vol. 4 no. 1

Wood, S. (1979) 'A re-appraisal of the contingency approach to organisation' *Journal of Management Studies*, vol. 16 no. 3: 334–54

Woodward, J. (1965) *Industrial Organisation: Theory and Practice*, Oxford: Oxford U. P.

Wrege, C., & Lattanzio, B. (1977) 'Pioneers in personnel' *Rutgers University Working Paper*, October

Wren, D. (1979) *The Evolution of Management Thought*, New York: Wiley

Wrigley, L. (1970) *Divisional Autonomy and Diversification*, DBA Thesis, Harvard Business School

Zander, A. (1969) 'Manager, group and company' *SIAR Working Paper 23–55*

Zeitlin, I. (1973) *Rethinking Sociology*, New York: Appleton-Century-Crofts

Zeitlin, I. (1974) 'Corporate ownership and control' *American Journal of Sociology* vol. 79 no. 5: 1073–119

Index

233